Twayne's United States Authors Series

Sylvia E. Bowman, *Editor*

INDIANA UNIVERSITY

Tennessee Williams

TENNESSEE WILLIAMS

by SIGNI LENEA FALK
Coe College

 10

Twayne Publishers, Inc.   ::   New York

To
TOPPY AND JEWELL

Preface

TENNESSEE WILLIAMS has become one of the best known literary figures on the American scene and also one of the most controversial. The arguments tend to fall into two categories, moral and aesthetic. Some critics deplore his preoccupation with sex and violence and others defend his daring to probe the dark areas of human desire and compulsion which have not been treated by other contemporary dramatists. Some critics, interested in theater as an art, welcome him as an original talent, an artist capable of giving objective form to highly subjective experience. Other critics, while recognizing his compassion for frustrated and sensitive persons trapped in a highly competitive, commercial world, question whether he has not sacrificed his talent for popular success.

Since much of the criticism is either excoriation or eulogy, this study attempts to give a detached, objective analysis of individual plays in order to discover how the dramatist has given form to a central idea, how he has developed the characters and the situation, and where he has placed the emphasis. *Tennessee Williams* is the result of careful study of the imaginative writing from the early fugitive poems, short stories, and short plays to the last Broadway production late in 1960; of the articles and introductions written by the dramatist; and of interviews recording his opinions about his craft as related to the theater. This book also attempts to give a generous and unbiased sampling of generally available critical comment on individual plays as well as on the range and development of the dramatist in order to suggest the startling differences in evaluation made by recognized authorities on contemporary drama.

Since the early writing of Williams has provided a source for later work, and since much of it is a record of personal experience, a rather extensive discussion has been given to the early poems, stories, and short plays. Some attempt is made to call attention to the interrelationship of the whole canon, but any student of Tennessee Williams knows that such a study can hardly be exhaustive, because the echoes and the repetitions are frequent. The early writing has formed a basis of much of the later work, but also the observations and opinions recorded *about* writing, particularly as it relates to the stage, give some clue to the way he has handled his material.

Because certain character types keep reappearing, the book has been organized as a series of discussions of plays in which a certain type plays a major role, as, for instance, the southern gentlewoman, the woman uninhibited by outworn mores, the frustrated poet-vagabond, and the decadent artist. The analysis of individual works, from the early trial pieces to the later full-scale productions, gives some indication of the progress of Tennessee Williams and of the development of his technique. The analysis also attempts, indirectly, to relate the dramatist to the increasing group of writers who have created the Southern Renaissance.

SIGNI FALK

Coe College
Cedar Rapids, Iowa
August 1961

Acknowledgments

To *The Catholic World* for permission to quote from the reviews by Euphemia Van Rensselaer Wyatt which appeared May, 1945, and May, 1953.

To *The Christian Century* for the review by Tom F. Driver which appeared January 29, 1958. "Quoted by permission of the author."

To Dodd, Mead and Company for permission to quote from Louis Kronenberger, *The Best Plays of 1958-1959*.

To Farrar, Straus and Cudahy, Inc., for permission to quote from Mary McCarthy, *Sights and Spectacles*.

To Samuel French, Inc., for permission to quote from *You Touched Me!* by Tennessee Williams and Donald Windham.

"Copyright, 1942, 1947, by Tennessee Williams,
Donald Windham, and Freda Lawrence
All Rights Reserved
Reprinted by permission of the authors
and Samuel French, Inc."

To The *New York Herald Tribune,* for permission to quote from Walter Kerr's review which appeared on March 25, 1955.

To Holt, Rinehart and Winston, Inc., for permission to quote from John Gassner, *Theatre at the Crossroads*.

To Alfred A. Knopf, Inc., for permission to quote from the reviews by the late George Jean Nathan which appeared in *The Theatre Book of the Year* 1947-1948; 1948-1949; 1950-1951.

To *Life* for permission to quote from the article by Lincoln Barnett which appeared February 16, 1948.

To The *Manchester Guardian Weekly* (Air Edition) for permission to quote from the article by W. J. Weatherby, "Lonely in Uptown New York," which appeared July 23, 1959.

To *The Nation* for permission to quote from reviews by Joseph Wood Krutch which appeared April 14, 1945; October 6, 1945; December 20, 1947; October 23, 1948; and from the review by Robert Hatch which appeared April 9, 1955; and for the reviews by Harold Clurman which appeared April 4, 1953; March 28, 1959; December 3, 1960.

To *Newsweek* for permission to quote from reviews which appeared April 1, 1957 and March 23, 1959.

To The *New York Times* for permission to quote from articles and reviews which appeared as follows:

Tennessee Williams, "On the Streetcar Named Success," November 30, 1947.

R. C. Lewis, "A Playwright Named Tennessee," December 7, 1947.

Brooks Atkinson, " 'Streetcar' Tragedy," December 14, 1947.

Tennessee Williams, "Questions Without Answers," October 3, 1948.

Brooks Atkinson, "Camino Real," March 29, 1953.

Brooks Atkinson, "Williams' 'Tin Roof,' " April 3, 1955.

Dudley Fitts, "Talking in Verse," The *New York Times* Book Review, July 8, 1956.

Brooks Atkinson, "Theatre: Early Williams," November 22, 1956.

Brooks Atkinson, "Garden District," January 19, 1958.

Tennessee Williams, "Williams' Wells of Violence," March 8, 1959.

Sam Zolotov, "Williams' Drama Attracts Throng," March 12, 1959.

Arthur Gelb, "Williams Booed at Film Preview," December 8, 1959.

Tennessee Williams, "Reflections on a Revival of a Controversial Fantasy," May 15, 1960.

Howard Taubman, "Hospital Ward," November 20, 1960.

———— "New Kazan Movie Put on Blacklist," November 28, 1956.

To *The New Republic* for permission to quote from the review by Stark Young which appeared April 16, 1945;

from the reviews of Harold Clurman which appeared October 25, 1948 and February 19, 1951; and from the review by Eric Bentley which appeared April 11, 1955.

To *Poetry* and to the authors, John Woods and Donald Justice, for permission to quote from reviews which appeared July 1957 and March 1959.

To *The Reporter* for permission to quote from reviews by Marya Mannes which appeared May 19, 1955 and April 16, 1959.

To *Time* for permission to quote from reviews which appeared May 2, 1955; April 9, 1945; April 4, 1955; March 23, 1959; November 21, 1960.

Contents

Chronology

Biographical data assembled in this section was gathered from various newspaper and periodical sources. Since reports vary and dates are not always the same, there may be minor errors in facts recorded about the earlier years. The record of productions outside of those in New York is obviously incomplete, but the information, as recorded, is given to suggest the great popular success of Tennessee Williams.

1914   March 26—Thomas Lanier Williams born in Columbus, Mississippi, where maternal grandfather was an Episcopal rector; father a traveling salesman for shoe company; childhood illnesses gave Tennessee extra time for books.

1926   Family moved to St. Louis when Williams about
or   twelve; urban ugliness made former life seem afflu-
1927   ent; harsh effect on boy and slightly crippled sister; apparent development of certain neuroses in Williams.

1930   First published story in *Weird Tales.*

1931- University of Missouri for three years where he joined
1934   a fraternity, flunked ROTC, picked up small prizes for prose and poetry, and discovered alcohol as a good cure for shyness. Alla Nazimova's performance in *Ghosts* inspired him to want to write plays.

1934- Depression separated him from the University of Mis-
1936   souri for a two-year stretch with a shoe company; commercial life developed in him a hypochondria; after dreary days in the warehouse he wrote most of the night, a routine which possibly contributed to a nervous breakdown. Year's rest at Memphis where grandfather had retired.

1936   Washington University, St. Louis, financed by grandmother; won first prize in a one-act play contest sponsored by the Webster Groves Little Theater; first work with Mummers, where Willard Holland, director, asked for a play on anti-militarism to supplement *Bury the Dead. Cairo, Shanghai, Bombay!* (farce) produced in Memphis.

1937 *Candles in the Sun* and *Fugitive Kind* (not to be confused with later film script) produced by St. Louis Mummers; withdrew from Washington University.

1938 State University of Iowa; *Spring Storm,* third long play, written for Professor E. C. Mabie's seminar in playwrighting: awarded a B. A. degree.

1939 "Field of Blue Children" published in *Story,* the first under his literary name; various explanations for the pseudonym, Tennessee Williams: nickname because of southern accent; feeling that given name sounded formidable; fear that early writing had compromised his own; gesture to ancestors who fought Indians in Tennessee.

1938- Became an itinerant writer, wandering from Chicago
1940 where he tried to locate work with WPA; to St. Louis where he rewrote the old play of violence and horror, *Fugitive Kind,* into *Not About Nightingales;* to New Orleans where he was a waiter in the French Quarter; to California, where, among other things, he worked on a pigeon ranch; to Los Angeles, and continued tramp life. Visited Frieda Lawrence in Taos, New Mexico, and expressed hope of writing a play about Lawrence's life.

    Group Theater Prize of $100 for one-act plays, *American Blues,* submitted with four long plays; return to St. Louis, and with financial help from grandmother, finished *Battle of Angels* "in the attic."

1940 Audrey Wood, literary agent and a valuable associate, secured for Williams, on basis of plays formerly submitted, a Rockefeller Fellowship of $1000. In February entered advanced playwrighting seminar at New School, New York City, with John Gassner and Theresa Hepburn; rewrote *Battle of Angels,* which was accepted by the Theatre Guild and produced in Boston in the fall; a fiasco; play withdrawn. Classified 4F by draft board because of a heart condition; submitted to first of four operations for cataract on left eye.

    Moony's Kid Don't Cry, from the collection, *American Blues,* included in *The Best One-Act Plays of 1940,* ed., Margaret Mayorga.

1940- Thin years; received partial renewal of Rockefeller
1942   grant; lived and wrote in New Orleans; doubled as
       waiter-entertainer—with eye patch after another eye
       operation—in Greenwich Village; worked as night ele-
       vator operator in New York Hotel; theater usher at
       $17 a week.

1942   MGM contract for six months at $250 a week, secured
       by Audrey Wood, to write a script for Lana Turner,
       then for Margaret O'Brien: when scripts rejected,
       turned to work on *The Glass Menagerie*, a manuscript
       submitted to and refused by MGM.

1943   Citation from National Institute of Arts and Letters.

1944   American Academy of Arts and Letters Award and
       $1000. Represented in *Five American Poets*, 1944,
       Third Series, New Directions.

1944   December 26—*The Glass Menagerie* opened in Chi-
       cago; enthusiastically received.

1945   March 31—*The Glass Menagerie* opened in New York
       City for 561 performances, closed August 3, 1946;
       won New York Critics Circle Award, 1944-1945, on
       the first ballot; won fourth annual award of Catholic
       Monthly, *Sign;* won Sidney Howard Memorial Award
       of $1500 given by Playwrights Company; published
       by Random House, 1945. After three months of "pop-
       ularity" and a fourth eye operation, Williams went to
       Chapala (residence variously stated) where he wrote
       The Poker Night, which was later incorporated into
       A Streetcar Named Desire.
           Battle of Angels, numbers one and two of *Pharos,*
       Murray, Utah, 1945; New Directions, 1945.

1945   September 25—*You Touched Me!* opened in New York
       for 100 performances.

1946   *Twenty-Seven Wagons Full of Cotton and Other Plays,*
       New Directions.

1946- *Stairs to the Roof*, theme used again in *Camino Real,*
1947   produced at Pasadena Community Playhouse—written
       about 1941.

Portrait of a Madonna, The Last of My Solid Gold Watches, and *Moony's Kid Don't Cry* produced by Actor's Laboratory Theater, Southern California.

1947 December 3—*A Streetcar Named Desire* opened in New York City for 855 performances, closed December 17, 1949; won for Williams a second New York Critics Circle Award, 1947-1948; won Pulitzer Prize, 1947-1948; published by New Directions, 1947.

1947 *You Touched Me!* published by Samuel French.

1948 *One Arm and Other Stories,* a limited edition of 1500 copies, New Directions, second edition, 1954.

1948 October 6—*Summer and Smoke* opened in New York City for 100 performances, closed January 1, 1949; first produced by Margo Jones, Dallas, 1947; published, New Directions, 1948.

1948 *American Blues: Five Short Plays,* Dramatists Play Service. First visit to Rome and Paris.

1950 *Roman Spring of Mrs. Stone,* New Directions.

1951 February 3—*The Rose Tattoo* opened in New York City for 306 performances, closed October 27, 1951; first tried out in Chicago; published, New Directions.

1951 *I Rise in Flame, Cried the Phoenix,* one-act play about D. H. Lawrence, published in two limited editions by New Directions, acting edition by Dramatists Play Service; produced off Broadway, 1958-59 season.

1952 Won election to National Institute of Arts and Letters.

1953 March 19—*Camino Real* opened in New York City for sixty performances, closed May 9, 1953; published, New Directions, 1953.

1953 *Twenty-Seven Wagons Full of Cotton.* Third edition. Augmented by two new plays, *Talk to Me Like the Rain and Let Me Listen,* and *Something Unspoken,* New Directions.

1954 *Hard Candy,* limited edition, New Directions; trade edition, 1959.

1955 March 24—*Cat on a Hot Tin Roof* opened in New York for seventy-nine performances. Won New York Drama

Critics Circle Award 1954-55 (Williams' third); won Pulitzer Prize, 1954-55 (Williams' second); published, New Directions, 1955.

1955 April 19—*Twenty-Seven Wagons Full of Cotton* produced in New York as part of *All in One.*

1956 December 18—*Baby Doll,* the film, opened in New York; published by New Directions, 1956.

1956 *Four Plays,* London: Secker and Warburg (*The Glass Menagerie, A Streetcar Named Desire, Summer and Smoke, Camino Real*). *In the Winter of Cities,* New Directions.

1957 March 21—*Orpheus Descending* opened in New York City for sixty-eight performances; published, with *Battle of Angels,* New Directions, 1958.

1957-
1958 *Summer and Smoke,* off-Broadway production.

1958 January 7—*Garden District* (*Something Unspoken* and *Suddenly Last Summer*) opened off Broadway at playwright's request; *Suddenly Last Summer,* New Directions, 1958.
April 16—*Moony's Kid Don't Cry, The Last of the Solid Gold Watches, This Property is Condemned* (all written before 1944) produced on Kraft Television Theatre.

1959 March 10—*Sweet Bird of Youth* opened in New York City for ninety-five performances; published, New Directions, 1959.

1959 April 15—*Portrait of a Madonna* produced as part of *Triple Play,* New York.

1959 *Garden District,* London: Secker and Warburg. Playwright's first trip to Far East.

1959-
1960 *The Purification,* off-Broadway production.

1960 *Three Players of a Summer Game,* London: Secker and Warburg.

1960 November 10—*Period of Adjustment* opened in N. Y., closed March 4, 1961; published, New Directions, 1960.

CHAPTER 1

The Southern Renaissance
and Tennessee Williams

O NE OF THE MOST SIGNIFICANT phenomena in
American culture has been the emergence in the middle decades of the twentieth century of a rich and varied
literature about the South. Writers from this area have distinguished themselves in poetry, fiction, and drama; in jour-
nalism of a high order; in the academic fields of criticism
and editing; and in a line of textbooks that has changed the
pattern of the teaching of literature. Southern writers have
exerted an influence on the American literary scene comparable only to that of the great New England writers of the
nineteenth century.

Teacher-critic-scholars like Randall Stewart partly explain
the Southern Renaissance by saying that the South has been
less affected than other areas by the cultural and industrial
changes which have tended to break down regional patterns.
Other critic-scholars write of the southern myth as being
either undisturbed by modern influences or destroyed by
them; but, in either instance, it has been a rich source of
material for the writer. A kind of regional loyalty to tradition; a nostalgia for a pattern of aristocratic, non-urban life
that was rich in promises; an awareness of distinctive character, mores, and beliefs peculiar to the southern areas—all
have provided inexhaustible resources.

A considerable part of this literary flowering began among
writers from Kentucky and Tennessee at Vanderbilt University in Nashville with John Crowe Ransom and a group
of his students—men like Allen Tate, David Davidson, Mer-
rill Moore, and Robert Penn Warren—and with *The Fugitive,*

a little magazine of verse published between 1922-25. In 1930 these fugitives and other southerners—among them John Gould Fletcher and Stark Young—published a collection of essays entitled *I'll Take My Stand*, a "manifesto of American Southern agrarianism." They proposed the idea that the South, with its type of old-fashioned agrarianism, might counter the materialism and cultural barbarism of the North which was threatening to destroy what was best in the southern tradition.

This group later became particularly concerned with the predicament of the poet in a society threatened to be torn apart by an industrial code of values imposed by the North. These men, poets themselves, became the vanguard of the new intellectuals, the perceptive readers of difficult and obscure poetry and fiction. They became the academic founders of the recently exclusive "New Criticism." Their influence was extended through a series of textbooks, written and edited by Robert Penn Warren and by a brilliant colleague, Cleanth Brooks; and their convictions determined the editorial policy of certain influential academic periodicals. This group developed not only critics and editors but writers. Robert Penn Warren's novel, *All the King's Men* (1946), has almost achieved the stature of a classic. The fiction and the poetry of such writers as Katherine Anne Porter, Caroline Gordon, and Randall Jarrell have added to the stature of this coterie.

While the university group was making its influence felt among the intellectuals, a Baltimore newspaperman was blasting the "booboisie" out of its doldrums. H. L. Mencken, an energetic apologist in the 1920's for the culture and gracious living of the old South, became editor of the *American Mercury*. The tremendous influence of this little magazine, which often encouraged southern writers and was under the editorship of a southerner who believed in the shock treatment, paved the way for other writers who also found industrial Protestant America falling short of the dream.

The Fugitives were a group of friends who began their work in a university center. Two of the most widely read of contemporary southern writers stand apart from any group: Thomas Wolfe and William Faulkner. Thomas Wolfe burnt out his tremendous vitality in thirty-eight years (1900-1938).

He recorded his own life in Asheville, North Carolina, in his first autobiographical novel, *Look Homeward Angel* (1929). In this and later novels he described in an avalanche of words the genius: a man of gigantic appetite and capacity for experience; a man marked from birth as different from other children, misunderstood, lonely, and shocked by the vulgarities of ordinary people. Thomas Wolfe, an uninhibited, romantic, talented writer who placed his faith in inspiration, who often exploded in wordy and adjectival violence, and who continually needed the patient pruning of a sympathetic editor, is a far cry from the disciplined intellectuals of *The Fugitive*.

The greatest figure of the Southern Renaissance is, of course, William Faulkner, the 1950 Nobel Prize winner, whose life has been spent almost entirely in Oxford, Mississippi. This town and the surrounding country—under the fictional name, Yoknapatawpha County—have provided theme and material for his many novels and stories which refer not merely to this limited territory, nor even to the entire South, but to the tragic condition of modern man. Faulkner's fiction encompasses a rich and complex overlay of several civilizations; they range from the life of the Indian to that of the Negro slave; to the disruption of southern culture after the Civil War; to the cheap and corrupt materialism of a later industrial society; to the fragmented, external twentieth-century life in which all religious and moral codes have become mechanical rituals.

Thomas Wolfe wrote of himself—and of the South only as it touched him. But William Faulkner has created, largely from his own imagination, a wide range of characters, both white and Negro, from southern aristocrats to the contemptible Snopes, who are the materialists largely responsible for the decay and sterility of the South. His work ranges from simple narrative to involved allegory. His early writing was realistic; but this form later gave way to a complex symbolism, to an extensive and rich lyricism, and to rather complicated stylistic devices. Faulkner is a writer of seemingly inexhaustible imagination and energy, but his work continues to grow out of a close observation of life and people. The same characters may reappear; but each story, by a shift in emphasis—as if another phase were being developed—is very different. On the burning issues of intolerance and segregation Faulkner offers no special or political remedy; but in his treatment of Negro and white, in which the Negro often stands superior to the decadent society of which he is part, Faulkner places the value where it should be: on the individual.

There are a number of other writers who have contributed in varying degrees to the Southern Renaissance. James Branch Cabell, a Virginia writer ahead of his time, published *Jurgen* in 1919, a mythological fantasy that has often been compared to the satire of Rabelais and Swift. Another Virginian, Ellen Glasgow, neither a southern patriot nor a novelist interested in the abnormal, nevertheless portrayed honestly a decadent society. But Erskine Caldwell, also writing from the eastern seaboard, makes Ellen Glasgow seem like a proper Victorian. Best known for *Tobacco Road* (1932) and *God's Little Acre* (1933), he described rural Georgians, both white and Negro, and made of them almost subhuman characters. His sensationalism, almost to the point of pornography, has brought both financial rewards and an international reputation to him at the expense of a distorted view of American life. The same decade also brought Margaret Mitchell's respectable and very successful novel of the Civil War, *Gone with the Wind* (1936).

Carson McCullers, who writes of Georgia mill towns and backroads areas always in terms of human loneliness and desire, creates her own special world of tragedy and violence, of the lost and the abnormal. She has a habit of reworking her material, of returning to the same situations and characters as if she were continually explaining to herself the significance of the myth. She seems to be interested in contrasts, in colors and in images, in the simple and the vaguely significant, in the realistic and the symbolic, and in the individual in a hostile environment. Perhaps her early musical training has made her more conscious of structural patterns—the playing of one motif against another, the building of tensions as the story gradually unfolds. Like Faulkner, she has an unusual capacity for creating characters, with a particular sensitivity for the delicate.

Another gifted Georgian, Flannery O'Connor, concerns herself with the deformed and the grotesque, most of whom are outside the average person's experience. Truman Capote, on the other hand, epitomizes the love of the morbid, of horror, and of the degenerate for its own sake. Representing the literary tradition of "the Southern Gothic gone to seed" and the worst to be found in both Carson McCullers and William Faulkner, Capote creates his own world of the unloved and the loveless, the grotesque and the eccentric. He aspires to poetic writing, poetic symbols, and a kind of specious literary excitement. Although he indicates a kind of insight into character, he is basically an exhibitionist.

From a completely different point of view, Paul Green, working in the 1920's with Frederich Koch and the Carolina Playmakers, produced a number of good regional plays. In the next decade, Lillian Hellman with her tightly-plotted, unsentimental dramas honestly faced the issues of the mid-twentieth century. Lillian Smith, dedicated to the social problems of her region, has focused her attention upon the position of the Negro and has raised a number of embarrassing questions about the practice of Christianity in the South. Two Negro novelists, Richard Wright and Ralph Ellison, portrayed the ugly vengeance not only of the whites but of Negro against Negro. And in still a different way, the novels of Eudora Welty and the work of Harper Lee make distinctive contributions to the understanding of life in the South.

Tennessee Williams is a part of this rich and varied literary tradition. He became a name immediately after the extraordinarily enthusiastic reception of *The Glass Menagerie* in New York City in March, 1945. The South obviously produced a winner; for since those halcyon spring days almost everything that he has said or written seems to have been set in type. Williams, who was born in Columbus, Mississippi, in 1914, spent about his first twelve years there; and he returned on occasion after he had decided to become a writer. He has capitalized on his heritage; but whether he has contributed to the stature of the Southern Renaissance, and in what ways, is still a controversial question. Since no figure on the contemporary literary scene has aroused so much critical disagreement and since his success is spectacular and popular, it is difficult to reach a balanced appraisal. Critics seem to agree that he is a writer of unusual talent, but many deplore not only his lack of artistic discipline but also his limited view of life.

He continues the southern myth in deploring the loss of an old aristocratic culture and its replacement by gross mercantile values. He shows sympathy for the decaying aristocrats whom at times he places in incredible situations. His portrayal of the businessman, usually a villain or a clown, is often a caricature created out of dramatic need or a theory. He has emphasized the idea, fostered by the new critics as well as inherited from a long romantic and classical tradition, that only the poet—blessed or marked at birth—can show modern man the way out of his confusion.

On the other hand, some of the characters are not southerners but imitations of a literary type. Some of them seem to have been inspired by the novels of D. H. Lawrence; there are the primitives: children, uncorrupted by middle-class proprieties, whose sexual communion brings them happiness and contentment; or reflections of a Lawrence hybrid: businessmen and effete intellectuals far removed from the natural man. Others seem to have a special personal significance, such as the series of itinerant heroes from the early Val Xavier to the war buddies in a later attempt at "serious comedy"; all of them rebel against what Williams considers American mediocrity. In spite of—or perhaps because of—his theories and his personal prejudices, he has created a number of striking theatrical characters. Whether or not he has contributed to an understanding of the South is still to be determined, but there is no question but that he has one of the sharpest senses for theater of any playwright in American dramatic history.

Although he echoes the tenet that only the poet is aware of cultural values and that only he can chart the way for others, Williams lacks the discipline and respect for form which characterize the Vanderbilt coterie. He is more closely akin to the romantic spirit of Thomas Wolfe, who wrote mostly of himself and his own experience. And again, although Williams' subject matter is quite different from that of Erskine Caldwell, he has from the very beginning veered toward the sensational and almost pornographic to create "something wild." Like Caldwell, he has achieved considerable financial success and international reputation—at the expense of the American image. Indeed, the result is that in Europe Williams is often considered the representative of American "culture."

Williams, at times, as in the variations of *Orpheus Descending*, attempts to portray the cross section of a southern town and its varied social strata; but he does not attain the characterization or the legendary quality to be found in Faulkner's Yoknapatawpha stories. Whereas Faulkner, from a blend of observation and imagination, has created characters, white and Negro, aristocratic Sartoris and materialistic Snopes, Williams has created from theory or prejudice a number of type characters whom he uses again and again. As with Faulkner, his work ranges from realism to involved symbolism, from simple narrative to a highly involved literary and stylistic writing. But neither Faulkner nor Williams, both respectful toward the individual Negro, is as dedicated as Lillian Smith to the serious social problem of which he is a part.

Like Carson McCullers, Williams has created his own special world and has an affinity for lost souls and out-of-the-way characters; like her, he also returns to revive old material, to wring from it the quality of myth. Both writers reach for the elusive quality of experience in character and try to catch the vaguely significant element in human experience. In his "Introduction" (1950) to Carson McCullers' novel, *Reflections in a Golden Eye*, Williams describes the world of the artist—and the lunatic—as outside that of the rest of society, and so his sense of the dreadful is different; it is not so tangible as the atom bomb or cancer—nothing visible or knowable. He speaks of the artist's sense of the dreadful in ambiguous terms, as a kind of underlying spiritual intuition. It is too dreadful to speak of and therefore incommunicable, so he says it is a mystery which inspires dread. Williams indicates that the "Sense of the Awful which is the desperate black root of nearly all significant modern art" may be expressed in "externals" or symbols—by the presentation of "diseased and perverted and fantastic creatures." There are times, however, when Williams bears close resemblance to Truman Capote—"the Southern Gothic gone to seed"—for both seem to glamorize decay in a kind of specious, poetic writing.

Tennessee Williams is a consciously literary writer whose

work shows an increasingly clever manipulation of words for their emotional impact. As we have suggested, he seems repeatedly at a loss for new material so he returns either to the old shorter pieces or to very personal experience and works to give them cosmic significance. Some of the earlier writing seems to reflect life in the South, but the later seems to be excellent material for some future biographer. He has written profusely about the craft of writing—some pronouncements have little to do with his own work, some are rather pretentious, some merely rhetorical. But his statements will be interesting material for some critic seeking to discover the effect of early brilliant and financial success upon the development—or the distortion—of a fine talent.

Anything that Tennessee Williams says or writes seems to have been newspaper copy, and he seems to have flourished on controversy. For a brief time the New Critics whipped up a new battle of the books and became the literary arbiters. Their influence is still potent in academic and writing circles. It can also be said that in the theatrical world there has been a stormy argument about the validity not only of Williams' plays but of the special kind of world that he portrays. It is ironic that so controversial a figure should have become a kind of literary spokesman for his countrymen both at home and abroad. This has been due partly to his talent and his shrewd sense for supplying what the public wants, and partly to the high-pressured commercialism of the contemporary theater. The real contribution of Tennessee Williams to the stature of the Southern Renaissance remains to be seen.

CHAPTER 2

Search for a Medium

I Forms of Imaginative Writing

TENNESSEE WILLIAMS, in a preface to his own verse in *Five Young American Poets* (1944), wrote an amusing confession of his early literary efforts and admitted that he turned poet about the time of puberty. He admitted that his efforts were well received by high school students, women's clubs, and poetry groups in Mississippi and Missouri. In the years immediately after graduation from college he resisted a regular job as too monotonous and too dull; he chose, instead, the life of an itinerant. The early poems in this collection are a record of Tennessee Williams, as poet-vagabond and, if the autobiographical details are to be fully credited, as lover, as well. They are, by his own report, the product of six to eight years of nomadic life, and they reflect not only the personality of the writer but the ideas and images that fired his imagination. He began as a poet, and the increased symbolism of the later plays suggests that he still thinks of himself as a poet. The early verse, however, is of interest because in it appear many of the literary habits and attitudes, some of the affectations which have always marred his work, some of the same characters and even some phrases which reappear in the later plays.

Another confession about his early writing is recorded in the "Foreword" to *Sweet Bird of Youth* (1959). He said that at fourteen he had discovered writing as a kind of escape from the world in which he lived. The neighborhood "kids" and even his father thought him a sissy and gave him a girl's name. This is only one of a series of statements from the playwright to the effect that writing for him has been a cathartic for his psychological difficulties. Evidently, according to his statement, this early social rejection made him express himself verbally in violence and hysteria. He went on to say that he got thirty-five dollars from the magazine, *Weird Tales,* for a story adapted from a chapter in Herodotus. It was the anecdote about Nitocris, the Egyptian Queen, who invited her enemies to a large banquet and in the midst of the party ordered the sluice gates of the Nile to be opened. Her guests were drowned like vermin. With a note of pride Williams admits that he was a confirmed writer at sixteen and at that early age had already found the keynote for most of the writing that followed.

To those acquainted with his work the fact is well known that the name of Tennessee Williams burst into print as well as lights with the success of *The Glass Menagerie* in March, 1945. The real turning point in his career came when the Chicago critics, late in 1944, whipped a lethargic public into an enthusiastic audience and made of the midwestern try-out a future bonanza for both the playwright and his supporters. Before this success, however, he had written some poetry, a number of very fine short stories and one-act plays —which still represent some of his best work—and had also written several long plays. Since his early work not only suggests his stature as a writer but includes material which he used in later plays, it deserves attention.

One Arm and Other Stories (1948) is not limited to horror tales but ranges wide from the delicate and sympathetic to the violent and the perverted; and, like the poems, most of the stories reflect the wandering years through sordid rooming houses, city streets, and obscure corners where the derelict can be found. Some stories leave the reader with the uneasy feeling that the writer has been very close to the material from which he works, for they have the quality of confession. The volume is also an excellent key to the development of Tennessee Williams as a writer; it indicates his increasing skill in using words to evoke the emotional reactions he wants to arouse—sympathy for the unfortunate and frustrated, and horror for the macabre. The sense of values —or lack of them—about which there has been so much controversy, seems to have been formulated rather early.

The American Blues: Five Short Plays (1948), published

after the success of *The Glass Menagerie* and *A Streetcar Named Desire,* includes some of his earliest attempts at playwrighting. Williams won one hundred dollars in a one-act play contest for young playwrights, a small prize that marked an important milestone in his literary career because it brought him to the attention of literary agent Audrey Wood. The plays in *The American Blues* are short and fragmentary; but they indicate their author's keen sense for evoking the dramatic quality of a situation and for catching the essential quality of characters and their natural idiom. Williams showed very early that he could be a master hand at recording lively, characteristic dialogue—dialogue which contrasts to the sometimes flamboyant rhetoric that he imposes on certain characters.

In the more ambitious collection of one-act plays, *Twenty-Seven Wagons Full of Cotton* (1946), is included some of the best of Williams' dramatic writing. These plays foreshadow what he might have written in later years; but they represent also the kind of writing in which he did not believe enough when he courted the Broadway market. For that trade he turned with considerable finesse to "arty" motifs and theatrical tricks; he became fascinated with symbols, myths, and literary obscurities; and his plays became increasingly devious, personal expressions.

In *Battle of Angels* (1940), his first real bid for Broadway attention, he again made use of the itinerant years. Obviously pitching the tone for a commercial theater, he assumed that the erotic dreams of an adolescent are those that most adult American males never outgrow. He proved that, although he had a keen sense for theater and could write good scenes, he had not yet developed a technique for longer dramatic units. To cover up his inability to handle a more involved conflict, he resorted to rather shrill shock effects to maintain emotional tension. Most of the characters are symbolic, representing such ideas as freedom, dull mediocrity, or ruthlessness; they resemble, therefore, figures of an old morality play. The fancy and occasionally strained symbolism not to be found in most of the one-act plays has been laid on rather heavily. Some of the dialogue is good, but some of the rhetoric sounds as if it were written for a megaphone. There is a certain amount of posturing for ef-

fect, and a curious indirectness in the handling of a number
of scenes and characters which suggests that the playwright
was deliberately trying to mystify his audience. *Battle of
Angels* seems to have been a play which the dramatist could
not get out of his system because he returned to it repeatedly.

I Rise in Flame, Cried the Phoenix, published in 1951 but
with an explanatory note by the playwright dated 1941, is
an imaginative scene describing the last day in the life of
D. H. Lawrence; and it represents Williams' interpretation
of the British writer's views about life and art. It is of particular interest because the ideas projected in this one-act
play reappear in some of Williams' subsequent work.

He collaborated with David Windham to write *You
Touched Me!* Although not so overloaded as *Battle of Angels*,
it goes off in several directions at once. The play is important for the portrayal of the hero, one of the first of several
characters who reflect Williams' idea of the D. H. Lawrence
thesis about sex. The British novelist wrote of the basic
role that sex plays in life, but he deplored the way society
made relations between the sexes intellectual, hard, and
lacking in vitality. Man's reason for being was "perfect union
with a woman," since all other forces were dead. The ideal
of tender intimacy is to be found in all of Lawrence's novels;
but, as he perfected his art, he concentrated on the quality
of erotic experience as felt particularly by the woman. His
ideal of the submissive as opposed to the aggressive woman
who seeks to dominate is a recurrent contrast. The early play,
You Touched Me!, based on a short story by Lawrence,
anticipates the playwright's habit in later years of finding
a cue in a legend, a literary idea, a convention, or even a
painting; of incubating this idea; of producing his own art
object; and of not writing from observation of life and
people around him.

Tennessee Williams tried his hand, therefore, at several
forms of imaginative writing before he achieved sudden,
spectacular success as a playwright. Much of the early work
he combined and developed into the later plays which he
wrote and produced with tremendous energy. This body of
early work is important as a source of inspiration. It is also
important because it seems to indicate that his patterns of
thought have not changed too much during almost a quarter

of a century of writing. There has been, however, a considerable change in emphasis and in development of techniques.

II   *Five Young American Poets*

Tennessee Williams is represented in *Five American Poets* (Third Series, 1944)[1] by a group of poems in which appear certain themes and ideas worked over in later years; and these indicate that certain literary habits had already been established.

Tennessee Williams, who thinks of himself as a poet, repeatedly contrasts the sensitive poet with the commonplace person, the crude materialist, or the Philistine. In "Cried the Fox," dedicated to D. H. L., and written at Taos, 1939, he makes the fox symbolize the poet whom he describes as a lonely, pursued fugitive who calls the pack to follow. In another, "Lament for Moths" (Jacksonville, October, 1942), he tells about the enemies of fragile spirits polluting the air with their pestilent breaths. He makes a plea for the delicate moths who soothe the neurotic sickness of the poet. In another, "Intimations" (St. Louis, 1941), he describes the poet as enveloped in bandages to ward off the blows he anticipates, his timid fear of abuse, and an elderly female romantic poet whose verse is out-of-date. He cites as fellow heretics, three historical figures: DuBarry, described as a strumpet; the mannish Joan of Arc; and the ardent priest, Savonarola. With a flourish, as if to set it off for emphasis, characteristic of his inclination for the mysterious but suggesting also his habit of covering up an incomplete image or a seemingly incomplete thought, Williams isolates a final line: "Blue is such a delicate piece of paper." The poet, in "The Summer Belvedere" (Santa Monica, 1943), wants to remain detached from the world of suffering and hysteria, the dying, and the destruction of the war. It is an involved statement in images of softness and deceit, an early attempt to express in obscure symbols and strained metaphor what may have been a personal feeling.

In a rather pretentious poem, "The Dangerous Painters" (Manhattan, 1943), Williams indulges in a hodgepodge of bald generalizations and pseudo-poetic imagery and in sensational, lush descriptions of decadence. In this dramatic monologue between a youth whose purity seems to have been effortless and the initiated Williams' artist, the poet describes not only the pictures but the painters as well in rather fancy rhetoric, foreign phrases, exclamatory punctuation, and in occasional phrases that would seem to reflect personal experience. The poem repeats a frequently expressed theory that art is the by-product of disease, and reflects the writer's distaste of art circles and art patrons. In this poem, he again isolates a line to give it special significance: "All time cracked and admitted the truthful flowers." There is here not only a mixed metaphor but an attempt to be very mysterious as well.

Dudley Fitts, reviewing *In the Winter of Cities*, which includes most of these early poems, found in them "the weakest elements of his art—the self-consciousness, the pretty playing with symbolic devices and the gadgetry of sentimental color" and "an undisciplined flood of talk"—talk but no excitement. "The effect is a blur, like the uncertain syntax, and the impetus of the passage trips over the culminating cliché . . . and expires beneath an exploding exclamation point." Because of the many flat lines broken for no structural reason, it is rather easy to agree with this judgment of Dudley Fitts: "It is poetry, however, by typographical courtesy."[2]

In "The Beanstalk Country," an ugly ogre's world, the mad people are more perceptive than the normal. Not only the mad ones but children receive Williams' special blessing. Nostalgic memories of childhood and lost innocence seem to preoccupy him like an obsession, as critics of his later work have pointed out. Three poems in this early collection, "Towns Become Jewels" (Vero Beach, Florida, 1941), "Mornings in Bourbon Street" (Santa Monica, 1943), and "Marvelous Children" convey this pure and precious time before the corrupting effect of experience. The last of the three poems affords a number of examples of poetic posturing; in them the writer obviously was more interested in reaching for unusual and exotic metaphor than in creating clear imagery.

As a young poet Williams also sharpened his literary pencils to practice a few fancy filigrees over the ancient rites of sexual intercourse. "The Legend" (New Mexico, 1940) describes an aggressive girl and an acquiescing boy. Once initiated, their experience is given cosmic significance. According to Williams, their private sexual act was accompanied by a battle of angels, storm and thunder.

> They knew only
> the hot, quick arrow of love
> while metals clashed
> a battle of angels above them,
> and thunder—and storm!

This goat-germ of an idea and the accompanying noise the writer used again in his first attempt to reach Broadway, in *Battle of the Angels* (1940). "The Siege" (Gloucester, July, 1941) expresses in large, general, religious terms a disbelief in love. "The Angels of Fructification" (Summer, 1942) represents an increased sophistication and complexity, a play of humor and considerable spite. There is much ado about mountains and birds to decorate a coarse treatment of his favorite subject—sex.

Two poems in the early collection might be singled out. "Pulse" (Santa Monica, 1943) written in a series of images, suggests, without excessive decoration, the fragmentary and vivid quality of experience. In "Cortege" (Santa Monica, Summer, 1943) some lines picture a loveless, ruthless lawyer's home and his way of life, but others communicate the chill which surrounds the family. The mother, overcome by these brutalities, is dead; the children, marked by their father's ruthlessness, begin to anticipate other betrayals.

John Woods, in his review of *In the Winter of Cities*, said of the poems that, when the poet "has brought no more power to bear than the poem can hold," he is successful. "He has two qualities, an occult ability to find the poem and an exasperating insistence on burying it in extensions and assumptions and false moves." Of the nature of poetry Woods wrote: "But what I miss in most of these poems is that singing tension between formal and conventional rhythms, that music which is the authority of poetry."[3]

III *One Arm and Other Stories*

One Arm and Other Stories,[4] originally published in 1948 in a limited edition of 1500 copies, shows not only the development of a writer into a craftsman sure of what he is about but also indicates the wide range of theme and subject matter which interested Williams in these early years—material to which he also returned for later development. Some of his best work, as well as some of his most characteristic, is to be found in this volume; and for that reason a number of the stories warrant consideration. The characterizations are frequently handled with admirable economy and sharpness. Some of the phrasing is exquisite and beautifully apt—often striking in its precision and simplicity. So often Williams writes his best poetry when he is not self-consciously trying.

In "The Field of Blue Children" (1939) a college senior girl found release in writing poems at times of intense emotional feelings; they had the quality of religious exaltation. There seems to be an autobiographical touch in Homer Stallcup—what a name!—a shy awkward boy in love with the girl, a lad who wrote poetry, uneven in quality, difficult to read, some of it reminiscent of Hart Crane,[5] some of it as naïve and lucid as the verse of Sara Teasdale. There were lines, says the writer, of touching imagery and of originality. Their common interest in poetry brought them together; he took her to a place he calls the field of blue children, an acreage of blue flowers. The lover's tryst is delicately veiled with poetic lines about winds as soft as the hushed cry of small children at play, and about dancing flowers. After the lovers' rendezvous, the girl, more practical than poetic, returned the boy's poems, married the steady provider, had a momentary tinge of regret, and then settled into contentment. She is an early example of the kind of woman Williams later describes more harshly—the woman for whom love and poetry are not enough.

"The Important Thing," probably also an undergraduate story, describes the groping curiosity of a college boy, again a poet, and a sexless female intellectual, who talk about religion and art, but seek to find their answers in sex. Unsuccessful as lovers, they clasp hands as friends with the knowledge that each one is no longer completely alone and a stranger. In this early story of sexual impotence are two comments of interest. The poet says he has written a one-act play in which the symbolism is involved and hard to explain, a comment that might reflect Williams' credo. It is also stated that the girl put up a resistance to his sexual advances that was bred into her by a Kansan God of Judgment. This is an early statement of the idea of Puritan repression as a deterrent to happy sexual relations, an idea that was to become a theme for Williams.

"Portrait of a Girl in Glass," somewhat autobiographical and one of Williams' best, became the source of *The Glass Menagerie*. Rich in detail, the story communicates the quality of southern gentlewomen who are unable to cope with contemporary society. Abnormally diffident, Laura made no positive movements, but stood in the shade as if she dreaded what the world might offer. She hid in her room where two windows opened on an areaway called Death Valley. In this narrow passage a vicious chow trapped the defenseless kittens and tore them to pieces—perhaps there is an analogy between the alley tragedy and delicate Laura's experience with contemporary society or perhaps the violence and the brutality of the scene appealed to the writer. Laura kept the shades drawn so that there was perpetual twilight in this little room of dingy, ivory furniture, of a sentimental picture of Christ, effeminate and teary-eyed. The hundreds of little colored glass ornaments on the shelves, which absorbed the faint light from the windows on Death Valley, gave the room its soft, transparent radiance. Laura loved and washed and polished each object. She suffered with Gene Stratton Porter's *Freckles*, a novel about a one-armed hero; she reveled in victrola records such as "Whispering," or "Sleepy Time Gal," or "Dardanella"—souvenirs of a father who had abandoned his family.

The brother, as if modeled upon the author himself, made a secret practice of hiding in the warehouse lavatory and working out rhyme schemes. He turned to Laura after the day's monotony, for she could soothe a temperament racked by intolerable circumstances. His relationship with his mother was far from restful. Obsessed with a threat of even more degrading poverty, she cut expenditures to a minimum, made her family continually penny-conscious. This garrulous, oppressively thrifty mother, afraid of having an old maid on her hands, drove her daughter to business college; and, when she failed there, she forced her son to bring from the warehouse a prospective husband. Jim Delaney, a big red-haired Irishman, described as looking like polished and well-washed china—a not too happy description—received the brother's eleventh-hour invitation to dinner. Williams' description of the little party is well handled, and it was reworked successfully in the play.

There is also in *One Arm and Other Stories* a group of stories about derelicts, all of whom seem to be sex deviates, and who are described with sympathy and understanding. The particularity of some of the description may have helped to speed the early sales of the limited edition; but, when the stories are told in the first person, it is sometimes difficult for the reader to separate the imagined from the autobiographical. One of the less successful stories in this group is "The Angel in the Alcove"; the title refers to a mother image, reminiscent of a grandmother during her long illness; the memory of her image brings solace to the writer at the time of discouragement, before he had received recognition and when he had almost accepted the possibility of always being unknown and unsuccessful. Another, a somewhat arty, symbolic story, "The Poet," relates, in rather flamboyant language, the frenzy at the heart of the creative effort. Ironically, Williams' portrait would only corroborate the too-common Philistine notion that men who write poetry are irresponsible drunks and unsafe company for women and children.

The most sophisticated of the group is "One Arm," the title story, which describes a mutilated Apollo, a light heavyweight boxing champion who lost the center of his being when he lost his arm. It is implied that the injury is also sexual and moral. Rebelling against this mutilation, he knocks about the country looking for destruction; and, in the course of his vagrant adventures, he commits murder, is caught, is lionized by the newspapers, and rediscovers his own meaning of life just before he is executed. Because of its implied praise of the fugitive kind, a type repeatedly found in the later work of the playwright, it deserves particular attention.

Williams' professed interest in Rimbaud may be reflected in this story; for it suggests the Frenchman's distaste for the well-scrubbed, average family man and wage earner and his monotonous life; his praise of the irresponsible vagrant who walks alone in search of experience and high-pitched emotion and who indulges in self-loathing, self-worship, or self-pity. Although not apparent in this story, it is quite possible that Williams may have responded to certain literary habits of Rimbaud. In the later plays, Williams, like Rimbaud, indulges in fragmentary bursts of rhetoric, expresses intense emotion in single words and exclamation points, phrases ideas and images in disconnected sequence, and leaves them as recorded in the first heat of composition.

Most of the story of "One Arm" is given to description of homosexual adventures. Williams seems to suggest that Oliver Winemiller's contribution to society has been the great richness of experience he has unconsciously afforded his many sex clients across country. In the early days of this young Apollo's itinerant life, a New York vagrant made him realize that his sexual life was not over and taught him how to profit from "the gift" he had. The broken Apollo soon became accustomed to the underworld practices common to the area around Times Square and the parks. With the loss of his arm also went that sense of propriety by which he had formerly evaluated the whole range of sexual experience. Whereas at one time he had rejected the grossly ardent advances of an older woman, he now accepted the homosexual relationships with tramps who made him aware of the extraordinary excitement he aroused.

This phase of his career culminated at a drunken party on a broker's yacht off Palm Beach. He and a girl prostitute had been hired to perform a licentious bedroom sequence before the camera and a stud party. The two had slowly and drunkenly undressed and had gone through the series of intimate embraces usually played behind a closed door. For a reason that Oliver could not explain to himself, he suddenly revolted, broke up the scene, and fled from the room. This affluent chapter of his life ended when he split the skull of the sportsman, and again, did not understand why he did it. He fled and hid himself among the fugitives; but, when he was picked up, he fully confessed the killing within fifteen minutes. The representatives of the law, according to Williams, had not played fair by loosening with whiskey the blond Apollo's tongue.

Sentenced for murder, he waited in jail for the death penalty. The publicity given his trial and the display of his picture in papers across the country brought a deluge of letters. These male correspondents described the nights he had spent with them, spoke of the richness of the brief hour or two when they had been together as the best time of their lives. They recalled not only his youth and physical attractiveness but "the charm of the defeated" which made him irresistible. Because he was about to die, Oliver became for these men a kind of father confessor who listened unseen to their confessions of guilt. "The usual restraints upon the unconscious were accordingly lifted and the dark joys of *mea culpa* were freely indulged in." Confessions poured in upon him like a flood, as if he, like Christ, could assume all the world's sins and, through his own sacrifice, purify the sinners. This double theme of sexual indulgence and punishment through an overpowering sense of guilt Williams returns to many times in the later plays.

The broken Apollo was at first revolted by these uninhibited confessions. But as he began to realize how much he meant to hundreds of strangers—quite a numerical record for any normal or homosexual lover—he also began to perceive that he himself was indebted to them, not in money but in feelings. If this tardy realization had come to him before the yacht scene, he might have been saved. It might have given him a way toward integration, says Williams, since he had lost his equilibrium with his arm. The resurrection came too late. The letters roused his self-interest and, just as strangers' fingers had sought his body, he tried to make love to himself.

A lonely frustrated Lutheran minister, who is disturbed by the contradiction between the stories and the picture of the virile saint, a killer with a baby face, looks at the imprisoned man and recalls his childhood memory of a panther —a savage beast with eyes glowing with innocence—and the way he had cried himself to sleep in pity for the imprisoned animal. Then one night he had dreamed of the panther in a way that awakened and initiated him to Eros. (This persistent repetition of sex and sentimental feelings and innocence associated with childhood raises the question of how far back it is necessary for Williams to go to find a state of comparative purity. It may be that he believes that all children—as he is supposed to have said of himself—are small sensual monsters.) But, to return to the minister, whose sexual response is like that of the hundreds of homosexual lovers who have been writing letters, he is torn between his sympathy for the misunderstood and his terror before this innocent criminal about to be executed. He tries to soothe the prisoner with talk about Eternity—talk which the boy does not want. When asked, instead, to rub the sweat off the flanks and back of the convict, who calls himself a truly clean whore, the nauseated minister has to be carried out. Although Tennessee Williams is supposed to have been devoted to his maternal grandfather who was an Episcopalian minister, he consistently depicts every clerical figure with contempt or ridicule.

He describes the execution of the Apollo in grand poetic terms, an early experiment in embroidering the horrible. It is an exercise in rhetoric that reads well but suggests a great deal more than it says. It is about as appropriate as a poem on death and the possibility of immortality composed in jigging rhythms would be. Written with a cool detachment very much different from the sentimental descriptions of this derelict's hard luck, or the suggestive eroticism of his relationships with these hundreds of strangers scattered across the country, these rhetorical passages leave the impression that the writer was not sure just what he wanted to do.

The story, however, contains a subtle analysis of primitive strength, of the delicate quality of communication, of the terrible loneliness that imprisons so many, and of the almost mystical quality of giving which glorifies such personalities as this mutilated Apollo. There is also in the story an understated characterization of the rich sportsman whose concupiscence results in the murder of the broker, and of police officers who handle the case by the book, as if it were only a routine matter. "One Arm" might have been a distinctive story about the dark forces beneath man's so-called civilized mask if Williams had sharpened his focus, if he had approached his material with a sexually mature point of view, and if he had ruthlessly struck out the rhetorical and prosy affectations which he considers poetic writing.

"The Yellow Bird" represents a successful excursion into

humor and fantasy. It relates the story of the moral decline of a southern girl in whose blood runs two contrary strains: a grim Puritan tradition as old as the Salem witch trials; and its opposite, the Cavalier, which is aligned with the world, the flesh, and the devil. There is an autobiographical note implied in the conflict expressed here; Williams once described himself—as a child—as being externally a prim Puritan but at heart a carnal little beast. Supposedly a yellow bird named Bobo, representing the flesh, had served as interlocutor between the first Goody Tutwiler and Satan; and, though Goody was properly hanged, the bird's nagging kept the Puritan spirit flaming. The metamorphosis of the twentieth-century Alma Tutwiler from a shy mousy girl to a brazen thirty-year-old spinster determined to make up for lost time with any man in town or on the highway, indicates that she has a vigor for a free life comparable to that of generations of true reformers attacking sin. The idea of a refined girl becoming the town prostitute appears in later plays depicting southern gentlewomen. For all of her loose living Alma should have suffered, been punished, or died a horrible death; but, like all of Williams' orgiastic heroes and heroines, her face retains a look of bright, fresh innocence. In time she bore a glowing, lusty male child, who, after a few years—according to the fantasy—crawled out in the morning and returned in the evening with fistfuls of gold and jewels. After her death, her bastard son erected a curious monument depicting three sexless figures upon a dolphin, one carrying a crucifix, another a cornucopia, and the third a Grecian lyre. The name of the yellow bird, Bobo, was traced on the side of the fish. If there is a moral in this tongue-in-cheek fantasy, it most certainly favors the fleshly sinners.

"The Night of the Iguana," another story describing Puritan repressions, portrays the deterioration of a thirty-year-old spinster of a southern aristocratic family whose inheritance represents two types, already grown very familiar: among the over-sexed were those who had flowered into drunkards, poets, sexual degenerates, and gifted artists; the others had developed into old maids, male as well as female, both of them proper and squeamish. This spinster at a nearly deserted hotel in Acapulco tries to foist her charms on two young writers; she is miserably insulted but cannot leave because her curiosity has overcome ordinary good sense. Her intrusions become more and more indiscreet until the night when she discovers an iguana tied below her window; then she discards all her natural dignity. In her impassioned defense of the animal she moves herself and her belongings next to the men. She not only discovers their intimacies but overhears their bawdy ridicule of her. When her further intrusion isolates her with the older man who tries to rape her, she remains inviolate, protected, like the girl in "The Important Thing," by a terrible spirit of virginity. She seems to profit from the experience; for, like the iguana which had been freed, she had been released; in her case, it is freedom from "the strangling rope of her loneliness."[6]

The tortured metaphors in "The Night of the Iguana" mark a difference from the more effective and simpler observations of southern gentlewomen. The spinster is compared to a dainty teapot not expected to heat to the boiling point. The brief interlude of the attempted rape lies, apparently, between the clouds of immaturity shot with lightning and a murky decline to age. Williams bursts into rhetorical poetics as he describes the attempted rape; he plays with what might be a phallic bird image and the man who, like a bird, attacks her furiously.

Two stories describe timid little men who are victims of harsh circumstances and their own sensibility. "The Malediction" concerns Lucio, "a panicky little man" who finds shelter with a large-bosomed landlady, companionship with a stray cat, and financial support in the kind of factory work which occupies the hands but torments the mind. It is another story of those who have been rejected: the landlady's husband, injured at the plant and dismissed, lies at home a semi-invalid; a former renter, a Russian and the landlady's lover until his tuberculosis made him unwanted, is driven out; Lucio, the little man fired from his job, jailed by the police for vagrancy, is later ousted from his room when a willing lover arrives; the cat, the friend at first of the Russian and then of Lucio, is not only thrown out of the house, but is later found with its leg crushed; and the drunken old vagrant, who must depend on temporary shelter, shouts maledictions on an unfeeling world. What is most curious in the story is the comment that Williams gives to Lucio; it is another example of "moral paralysis" that characterizes a number of his heroes. He has Lucio, seeing God in his own image, say, *"God was, like Lucio a lonely and bewildered man Who felt that something was wrong but could not correct it, a man Who sensed the blundering sleep-walk of time and hostilities of chance and wanted to hide Himself from them in places of brilliance and warmth."*

"Desire and the Black Masseur," the second story about a timid little man, is a fiendishly clever piece of writing—a highly literary study in masochism. Timid little Anthony Burns, who at thirty still had a childlike quality in face and body, was of the nondescript kind of person who is easily submerged or swallowed up by his surroundings; he had unsuccessfully scuttled from one kind of protection to another and had found his greatest security in the movies—just like Tom Wingfield in *The Glass Menagerie,* a character who is supposed to be autobiographical. While at the movies, little Burns loved every one of the people on the screen and felt warmed by their presence. And yet his basic desire—for what, the writer prefers to remain mysterious—was so big that it swallowed him up.

Williams explains the moral dilemma of man as follows: "For the sins of the world are really only its partialities, its incompletions, and these are what sufferings must atone for." Man has a number of makeshift arrangements by which he can conceal these incompletenesses. Through his imagination he can turn to dreams and art; alone or in groups as nations, he can turn to violence as a compensation. Little Anthony Burns selected another kind when he surrendered himself to abusive treatment by others to purge himself of his own guilt. This principle of atonement through violence Williams was to illustrate in his later plays, *Sweet Bird of Youth* and *Suddenly Last Summer.*

The instrument of atonement is a Negro masseur who sensed a special quality about his white patron. During the first treatment the black giant struck his dark palm with a terrific force on Burns's soft belly, giving him a shock and then a feeling of pleasure. The masseur turned him over and began to pound his shoulders and buttocks; as the blows increased, so did the violence and pain. "The little man grew more and more fiercely hot with his first true satisfaction, until all at once a knot came loose in his loins and released a warm flow. So by surprise is a man's desire discovered."

The Negro, who sensed Burns's search for atonement, loved him for the opportunity he gave of venting his hate for white-skinned bodies. The violence and the bruises increased, so that by spring Burns suffered two broken ribs and, shortly after, a fractured leg. The manager, alerted by a cry of pain, ordered both of them to leave; he demanded that the Negro take away the perverted little beast. Williams contrives a complicated analogy between atonement, sexual aberration, and violence; and the involved ideas of atonement and purification are associated with the Easter season—an analogy he used again later.

The latter part of the story coincides with the Lenten season, and the illicit passion between the Negro and little Burns seems to be compared to the massive atonement in the church where preacher and audience, like crazed animals, are caught up in "the fiery poem of death on the cross." A house catches on fire—whether or not it is the Negro's is part of the mystery—but the death chamber is described with precious and sensuous touches: delicate white curtains and an overpowering reek of honey. The black man picks up the still-breathing figure of his victim, lays it on a clean table, and spends twenty-four hours devouring the flesh. When this is accomplished, the air of completeness is returned, which for Williams means a serenely blue sky, conclusion of the church services, ashes settled, and the clearing of sickening, honeyed air. He obviously is trying for an involved religious symbolism, and for him there may be some deep significance between homosexuality, cannibalism, atonement—and the crucifixion and resurrection.

There is calculated and clever writing in this story. It may be a comment on the sensuous perversions to be found in a certain kind of religious worship that demands atonement. It also includes a morbid sexual theme elaborated and embroidered in sensuality and its own kind of masochism. As is characteristic of many of his later plays, this story is not only deliberately obscured by its related meanings, but is dependent for its effect on violence and horror.

IV *American Blues: Five Short Plays*

The early and very short plays of *American Blues* (1948)
won for Tennessee Williams a contest prize and an introduction to his literary agent, Audrey Wood; they mark, therefore, the beginning of his career as a dramatist. One of them,
Moony's Kid Don't Cry, recounts the crisis between a nagging, sick wife and a husky, young, workman-husband who
champs at the restrictions of cheap living and a monotonous
job and who regrets that he had left a free woodman's life
in Ontario. Worried over bills and the expensive hobbyhorse
which Moody bought for the child, the wife in her turn regrets that she has settled for marriage rather than for her
boss's attentions. Moody recalls his first night in town after
six months in the woods: he held in his arms the girl, seduc-
tively dressed and perfumed, and waltzed her around a
cheap dance-hall floor. He accuses her of seducing him into
the notion that marriage was better than swinging his axe in
the north woods. The disillusioned wife shoves the sick,
month-old baby into his arms as he is about to walk out to
freedom, and then the young father abruptly becomes absorbed in his infant son. This short play is forcefully and
honestly written; the dialogue conveys anger and inarticulate
feelings, the disillusionment and disgust of every average
human being.

The Dark Room is an early attempt at a technique Williams
used repeatedly in later plays: the dramatic revelation of a
situation through delayed and piecemeal confession. A neat,
precise and seemingly unsuspecting social worker queries an
Italian of immense size about her delinquent offspring. The
mother has lost track of her older no-good sons; has the
young ones in school; and has hidden her pregnant daughter
in a dark room for six months. Max, the daughter's lover, has
been forced by his parents to marry another girl; but he
continues to visit the daughter in her room. Mrs. Pocciotti's
detachment, her lack of responsibility for her daughter, and
her seeming denseness about the enormity of the situation
contribute to the interest. She has faced officials before; she
is dumb; but she is never so stupid that she gives herself
away.

The Long Stay Cut Short, or The Unsatisfactory Supper

describes the hopeless position of an old family servant, an old lady who has been used by all the relatives and discarded because none of them wants the responsibility and expense of her last illness and funeral. Mrs. "Baby Doll" Bowman, an exotic, foreign-looking, blackhaired woman dressed in purple and heavy jewelry, argues with her heavy, slack, tooth-sucking husband, Archie Lee, who wants to get rid of this ancient. Old Aunt Rose, with a canny awareness of her shaky position, pathetically tries to please. Her childlike religious faith seems to have made these long years of service tolerable. She is a tragic figure, described without sentimentality. The final scene, however, is a facile conclusion which is not in keeping with the rest of the play: a sudden high wind blows her away—symbolically, without a doubt.

The Case of the Crushed Petunias,[7] dedicated to Helen Hayes in February, 1941, is obviously an experimental piece by a young Mississippian who adheres to the myth that Boston maids are prim and unaware of the tremendous possibilities that hover around them. The young man dedicated to rescue the young miss from a fate worse than death—virginity—proposes to meet her on Highway 77 for a couple of beers and a cheese sandwich and a ride in an open car to Cypress Hill,[8] the cemetery, where they can listen to the advice from the dead: live! The lady bookworm, easily won, looks for the romantic highway where people lose their inhibitions and live dangerously. This play is obviously a trial flight, an early effort to make symbols do the work of extensive dialogue.

A later play in this volume, *Ten Blocks on the Camino Real* (1948), makes much the same statement as *Camino Real* (1953) about man's journey in an unfriendly world. The play leaves the impression that the author, a convalescent on a Mexican beach, had just read Strindberg's *A Dream Play* and had written his own adaptation. More than half the play is given to an account of the amorous adventures of a literary prostitute, to an extensive seduction scene, and to a sentimental lament by two weary lovers about a life wasted on women. The remainder of the play— less than half—is a comment about the rest of life, which on Camino Real is a matter of Starvation, Frustration, Swindling, Brutality, Indifference, and Death. The human condition is conveyed through symbolic figures caught at dramatic moments; the mood is enhanced by musical accompaniment and off-stage noises.

A guitar player serves loosely as master of ceremonies and much of the action is symbolic. For instance, a peasant throws himself at the dry fountain and for some strange reason there is a mysterious clink of castanets. Why mysterious? The peasant is shot by an officer. The proprietor of the swank hotel, an imposing fat man, described as a silk glove artist and also, for some strange reason, completely sincere, comments on the prosperity of the clip joints. He is also given the big philosophic questions about the cosmic fireworks.

The literary courtesan, the aging Marguerite Gautier, confesses at length to the aging Casanova about her first night of love, an account embroidered with tango music, a choric dance, and the kind of line that might well have been deleted: "That was the night that was talked about in the poem, the one that says that 'The stars threw down their spears and watered heaven with their tears!'" Love on Camino Real is only a process of becoming used to one another, an observation which erupts in some rather incredible metaphors.

The little man, the defeated one, is Kilroy, the all-American boy and ex-boxer with a heart "as big as the head of a baby," who left an unjust world for a worse one. He is robbed, ridiculed, marked for a sucker, seduced, swindled, and disillusioned. When he dies, he is collected by the streetcleaners; has his golden heart removed by the clinicians; returns from the dead; buys girl-loot for his siren, but is rejected; and is finally taken away by that incorrigible old romantic in rusty armor, Don Quixote.

Tennessee Williams resorted to a number of old stage tricks, combined them with rather obvious symbols—the Streetcleaners, La Madrecita, the Gypsy, and Casanova, to mention a few—made use of Spanish names and titles, injected some none too profound philosophizing, bore down heavily on the sex theme, and presented an early draft of a play that might have had possibilities.

V *Twenty-Seven Wagons Full of Cotton*

A collection of one-act plays, *Twenty-Seven Wagons Full of Cotton*,[9] reveals the young playwright's increasing skill in the development of his dramatic talent, his ability to communicate sympathy for the derelict and the unconventional or the delinquent, and a marked advance in handling a variety of dramatic styles. This group of plays indicates that he first tried his wings in the realistic mode and seemed to have been interested in concise projection of character without resorting to poetic trappings or theatrical clichés. The honesty and the strength of most of these one-act plays gave promise of a major figure in the American theater.[10]

Three of the plays are studies of the prostitute—lucid and straightforward portrayals. *This Property is Condemned* is a study of a young delinquent girl who still clings to her doll but lives on contributions from a series of railroad men or from chance findings in garbage cans. A skinny child of about thirteen, she is innocent looking in spite of her heavily rouged cheeks and lips and her ridiculous party dress. The play is a recital to a boy slightly older than she of the two years since she quit school. Deserted by both mother and father, she tries to imitate her dead sister, Alva, the good-time girlfriend of a large number of railroad men. The girl, Willie, contrasts Alva's sordid, lonely death when her men left her like rats scuttling from a doomed ship to the Greta Garbo scene in *Camille*, a beautiful death with white flowers and violins playing. This study of a delinquent youngster, communicated through overtones of innocence and ignorance, evokes sympathy for this abandoned child who knew only one way of life. The dialogue, again a mixture of cliché and imaginative speech, is simply done. The poetic strength of the play lies in its insight into the life and limited ambitions of the girl.

Two other plays describe the relationship between landladies and aging prostitutes. *Hello from Bertha* portrays a large blonde, who is in the last stages of physical and mental decay, who is cared for by strangers and who angrily resists attempts to remove her from her dingy bedroom in the red-light district of East St. Louis. It is a grimly realistic picture of a diseased relic from a "good-time house" and of the patient care on the part of the landlady. In *The Lady of Larkspur Lotion*—an excellent title—a derelict writer defends an abandoned forty-year-old blonde against a landlady who has a hard time collecting rents but gets considerable pleasure from berating deadbeats. She orders the prostitute out of her room and sneers at her story about a Brazilian rubber plantation. She says that a landlady in the French Quarter learns not to see and not to hear but only to collect the rent. As long as the money keeps coming in, she says, she is blind, deaf, and dumb. The derelict writer breaks into her tirade with a plea of compassion for the woman who dreams of a rubber king, a dream that is necessary compensation for the brutal facts of her life.

When the landlady accuses him of perpetrating a lie about a 780-page manuscript, he passionately defends his living in his imagination—an outburst with a curious autobiographical note. He talks of wanting to be a great artist but lacking the power, of stumbling from one bar to another, and of returning to his lousy bed in this brothel. To make this intolerable existence endurable, he dreams of masterpieces and Broadway successes, and volumes of poetry about to be printed. Lies like these, he says, are real and a small defense against stark necessity. He pushes the landlady out the door and encourages the woman to continue her dreams with his gift—a pint of whiskey. He whimsically introduces himself as Anton Pavlovitch Chekhov. The very human escape into self-deception, from little white lies to imaginative exaggerations to the delusions of the mad, is a theme on which Williams played many variations. In the more extreme cases it seems to be part of his romantic view of life as an escape from the hard world of reality.

Others of these early plays also indicate Williams' talent for creating a variety of characters, of combining the fully delineated ones with more or less type figures. *The Last of My Solid Gold Watches* affords a good example of a contrast between a fine old drummer and a contemptible young "squirt." "Mistah Charlie" Colton—who has fifteen watch chains criss-crossed over his huge expanse of chest and belly, each chain attached to a gold watch, each watch representing his achievement as ranking salesman of the year for the Cosmopolitan Shoe Company in St. Louis—deplores the changes he has lived to see. This old warhorse, who has probably received the last of his solid-gold Hamilton watches, represents the vitality, the genuine respect for character, good craftsmanship, and the good manners of the South. As he tries to alert the indifferent, flabby, bad-mannered "young peckerwood" of a Bob Harper to the old traditions, he describes a world in which standards and character have given way to cheapness and commercialism. He speaks in terms of his merchandise. Not only have genuine leather and craftsmanship given way to substitutes and flashy appearance, but the old accepted qualities of character—self-reliance, independence, initiative—have been replaced by lack of respect, ignorance, rudeness. The contrast between the old drummer and the indolent youngster is a comment not only on the South but the country as a whole.

An obviously early one-act is *The Long Goodbye,* an experiment in the memory technique. A son recalls his mother's suffering from cancer and her suicide, and his sister's zest for night life and subsequent career as prostitute. In the talk between the son Joe, a sensitive young writer, and his fellow worker on the Project, the references to Harry Hopkins and the Royalist forces in Spain seem to date the play in the 1930's. It is an early experiment in realistic dialogue, spiced with four-letter words.

Lord Byron's Love Letter contrasts two impoverished women with a grotesque tourist couple. This slight one-act, told with bitter humor and irony, reveals how two desperately poor southern gentlewomen, a forty-year-old spinster and her grandmother, try to cash in on the dubious interests of the tourist trade during the Mardi Gras. They read to the Tutwilers, a commonplace couple from Milwaukee, fragments of titillating description about the touch of Byron's hand, excerpts which imply that more intimate details have to be passed by. Poets, poetry, and sentiment cannot hold Tutwiler when the band plays. The women, cheated of their fee, pick from the floor the letter written not by the grandmother but by the grandfather.

The Strangest Kind of Romance, contrasting a mild little man and a harridan of a landlady, is a dramatization of the story, "The Malediction," which is about the love affair between Lucio, who doesn't fit in a machinist's world, and a stray cat. There are a variety of scenes: a touching one in which Lucio feeds his cat; another in which the vulgar landlady solicits Lucio's favors; a violent one in which the Old Man, who looks like Walt Whitman, shouts his maledictions against profiteering business: "you niggardly pimps of the world! You entrepreneurs of deception, you traders of lies! . . . Devour the flesh of thy brother, drink his blood! Glut your monstrous bellies in corruption!" There are touching moments between the man and his cat, but the social protest is a bit bombastic.

Tennessee Williams calls *Auto-Da-Fé* a tragedy; its violence, however, and the murky characterization anticipate the later studies in decadence. The mother is a fanatic about household cleanliness and about soft speaking, practical hygiene, and a literal interpretation of certain rules; and, in a way, she anticipates Amanda Wingfield in *The Glass Menagerie*. The neurotic son is aware of the corruption around him—the brutality, the crime, the decay—and that only burning would bring purification. There is a dubious suggestion of his own corruption through the charge made by a roomer, Miss Bordelon, a reference to a lewd picture confiscated. Feeling overwhelmed by the conscience of all guilty, dirty-minded men, he sets fire to the house and the guilty trio, as if to make a retribution for their various kinds of guilt. There is in the play the suggestion developed later in the characterization of Brick in *Cat:* both men talk of the corruption around them when their disgust may stem from the corruption within themselves.

Portrait of a Madonna is a sympathetic study of the mental deterioration of a southern spinster; delicate, over-refined, and repressed, she is a lady whose life seems to have been circumscribed by her mother's rigid standards and by those of her church. A recluse since her mother's death fifteen years before, she has buried herself in her apartment with an accumulation of twenty-five to thirty years of debris, is supported without her knowledge by church contributions, and is watched over by strangers. An old porter with a sense of pity for this woman and an impertinent, wise-cracking elevator boy, who sees her as a disgusting old woman, keep her occupied until the authorities from the State Asylum arrive. The spinster, one of Williams' frustrated, affected,

and aging southern belles, is lost in the world of her own
delusions. Like the maiden lady in "The Night of the
Iguana" and a number of his heroines who flourished before
World War I, she has become sex-obsessed as a result of
a "fractious" southern Puritanism. She imagines that she has
finally won the man away from the Cincinnati girl he married and that she is expecting his child. "I saw him in the
back of the church one day. I wasn't sure—but it *was*. The
night after that was the night that he first broke in—and indulged his senses with me. . . . He doesn't realize that I've
changed, that I can't feel again the way I used to feel, now
that he's got six children by that Cincinnati girl—three in
high school already! Six! Think of that? Six children! I don't
know what he'll say when he knows another one's coming!
He'll probably blame *me* for it because a man always *does!*
In spite of the fact that he *forced* me!" This formerly
ardent church worker and fanatic defender of Episcopalianism talks of protecting her illegitimate baby against the
corrupting influence of the church, its teaching of sin and
the doctrine of the crucifixion. When the Doctor and
Nurse, performing their duty wearily but efficiently, come to
take her away, she believes that she is being arrested on
moral charges made by the church. This study of repression
and a sense of guilt is an effective short play and may have
inspired the final scene in *A Streetcar Named Desire*.

Twenty-Seven Wagons Full of Cotton (c. 1944)[11] is an
early attempt at humor, but it has the ugliness of a dirty
political joke. The frequent references to the "good neighbor policy" and an allusion to a speech by President Roosevelt
raise questions about the germ-idea of the play; furthermore,
the general tone is somewhat reminiscent of the hatred and
contempt heaped upon that American. Sometimes the teller
of a good sexy joke glories in the elaborations and accretions
he can devise for each new listener; Tennessee Williams
wrote a whole play and made of the joke a study in sex and
sadism. This "Mississippi Delta Comedy" tells about the rape
of a huge, childish woman by an avenging little Italian and
about a husband too stupid to see what is going on. The critic
in *Time* wrote of the 1955 production: "*Twenty-Seven Wagons Full of Cotton* reveals that for Tennessee Williams life
had dirty fingernails from the outset. . . . The plot is rowdy

Erskine Caldwell with a crueler edge; already, eleven years ago, Williams could make a smoking car story constitute a criticism of life."[12]

The play takes place on the narrow front porch of the Jake Meighan cottage. There is perhaps significance in the Gothic-styled door and windows and the incongruous white curtains tied with baby-blue satin bows, a suggestion of a southern doll's house—an incongruous residence for the Meighans. As the first scene opens, sixty-year-old Jake, described as a grossly heavy and purposeful man, rushes out the door and around the house, carrying a gallon can of kerosene. His large and simple-minded wife, Flora, who is complaining about the loss of her white kid purse, is soon startled by the sound of a muffled explosion. Jake returns almost immediately; she whines in a petulant, babyish tone that he forgot to drive them to the White Star Drug Store to buy Coca-Cola. He tries to drive home the idea that he has not been off the porch since supper; but his Flora stupidly answers: "You didn't go off in th' Chevy. (*slowly*) An' you was awf'ly surprised w'en th' syndicate fire broke out!" As this scene closes, Flora, still complaining about her lost white purse, stands at the steps "with an idiotic smile." She starts to walk down like a baby experimenting with his feet, one step at a time, and Jake inside the house smugly sings the old popular song about his loving baby.

At noon the following day, Jake's cotton gin is busy and lint drifts in the air. He gloats over destroying the gin of Silva Vicarro, superintendent of the once-prosperous Syndicate Plantation, one of Williams' first virile men, an Italian, a Roman Catholic, and a *persona non grata* in the decadent South. The old husband brags to Vicarro that he prevented marital trouble by marrying a huge woman, a tremendous baby doll. Very sure of himself, he says to his heavy dumb wife, "Baby you keep Mr. Vicarro comf'table while I'm ginnin' out that twenty-seven wagons full of cotton. Th' good-neighbor policy, Mr. Vicarro. You do me a good turn an' I'll do you a good one!"

Flora tries to fill in the silences with accounts of her pre-marital misadventures with the Peterson boys; but Vicarro, one of Williams' early contemplative males, brooding over his misfortune, calls himself the type that prefers his own thoughts. Observing the white purse in her hands, he pontificates about woman's role of motherhood, a kind of defense against loneliness and a feeling of emptiness; but this endlessly repeated Williams theme is too abstract an idea for Flora. She pines for a Coke and inadvertently involves Jake in the affair of the burned-out cotton gin.

Vicarro's suspicions are aroused. He defines arson in dictionary terms that mean very little to the slow-witted Flora. Her confusion, however, confirms his suspicions; and an ugly idea explodes in his mind. Jake's remark about the good-neighbor policy takes on a new significance since, as he says, the world is built on a principle of vengeance, an eye for an eye. Very deliberately, Vicarro begins to get even with the arsonist. He flatters the heavy, dull-witted woman; works on her until she is so fuzzy-headed that she almost admits that her husband set the gin on fire; then sweet talking, but with his whip in hand, he drives the hysterical woman into the house. As the scene closes the sound of the gin pumps can be heard in the distance. A wild cry of despair comes from the house; a door is slammed; and the cry is heard again but more faintly. The scene is deliberately built for its appeal to those in the audience wanting sex and sadism. It is an off-stage bedroom rape scene that Williams was to develop even more fully in *A Streetcar Named Desire.*

The third scene takes place at nine o'clock the same evening. Williams heightens the mood of dubious excitement by having the ravished Flora appear highlighted by the ghostly brilliance of a full moon. She is the heavy, slow-witted woman who has been bruised and raped. Her hair is loose and disheveled. She is naked to the waist except for a torn strip about her breasts. Dark stains on her shoulders and cheeks and a dark trickle of dried blood from her mouth give evidence to the ugly revenge. But Williams has not written the scene as a comment on brutality; he has achieved what he aimed for—a masochistic shock.

Jake, the other brute in the woman's life, enters, tired from a day's work, but bragging, "I drove that pack of niggers like a mule-skinner. They don't have a brain in their bodies. All they got is bodies. You got to drive, drive, drive." Completely deaf to the innuendo in his wife's comments about her own day and maddened by her giggling laughter, he spits out his contempt about her size and helplessness. Smug in his certainty that he has outsmarted Vicarro, he never tumbles to her remark that the wiry little Italian will bring another twenty-seven wagons the next day and each day after that for the rest of the summer. Jake exits to the toilet. Flora, no longer Baby but Mama, drags herself to the edge of the porch. With a smile on her ravaged face she cradles the big white purse in her arms and begins softly to croon a lullaby. The Williams' implication was to become a commonplace in the later plays: virile Italian, sterile Anglo-Saxon.

Flora is not the usual pregnant woman who often evokes Williams' lyricism, but a ravaged, slow-witted woman. It is difficult to accept the brutal violation of a large, simple-minded female as having any relationship to the comic. The characterizations are sharp, for Meighan is one of the best of Williams' ignorant brutes. There are also vivid details about life in rural areas, which are brought quite casually into the dialogue. These details from observation give the play a certain amount of authenticity.

The Purification is very different in subject and in tone from *Twenty-Seven Wagons Full of Cotton*, but it is similar in its attempt to achieve a more sophisticated dramatic technique. Seemingly inspired by literary ideas rather than by observation, it is more contrived, more self-consciously written to evoke emotional response. Structurally, the play involves the gradual and rather dramatic unfolding of truth— a technique as old as *Oedipus Rex*—to discover not only evil but its causes. Williams seems to have been fascinated with the quality of evil and the nature of corruption. The characters are symbolic expressions, sometimes very carefully spelled out; at other times they are made suggestive and mysterious. Much attention has been given to costume and color; to tableaux, pageantry and pantomime; and to mood, music, and dance rhythms. Since the play is about sexual indulgence, frigidity, and incest, there is considerable imagery about birds and bird songs, favorite symbols for Williams.

Set in the clear breath-taking country around Taos, New Mexico, this poetic drama unfolds, during an informal trial, a story of incest, murder, retribution, and purification. The guitar player and the chorus, neighbors of the people involved, contribute in their dance and music to the highly charged emotion of the scenes. It is to them that the Judge first states a theme of honor as opposed to human law:

> I do not believe in one man judging another:
> I'd rather that those who stand in need of judgment
> Would judge themselves.

The Judge observes that a crime has been committed and allowed to go unpunished—the analogy to *Oedipus Rex* is obvious—and that the country is parched from the lack of rain. Not only is rain needed for the land but truth—which Williams also compares to rain—is needed for men's spirits as a kind of purification.

The Spanish Father and the Castilian Mother speak circumspectly of their murdered daughter, Elena; but it is the son and brother, Rosalio, who can really describe this sister. The dead Elena of the Springs (symbol of life) appears during the trial, supposedly visible, at first, only to Rosalio. The Indian woman, Luisa, tells how five of her goats drank of the purest water and died—crystal water polluted at the source, an account obvious in its symbolic implications. She reports how she came upon the naked brother and sister—exposed in a kind of "dance"; she thus confirms the relationship whispered about in the kitchen. The Mother defends her son as "victim of an innocent rapture"—just as she herself had been in her youth. When the Judge asks for the truth, Rosalio refers to the enigmatic truth of music or of the uncaptured song of a bird torn by a falcon, obvious erotic symbolism. Williams then breaks the mood of this highly symbolic recital with a blunt description of the effect of the bird song: "Our genitals were too eager!" The Father, on the other hand, demands the Rancher's death for the murder of his daughter Elena, who had been the Rancher's wife.

The Rancher, the "former repair man," is almost like the later, rising, young businessmen in Williams' plays; he is a man who is possessive, domineering, and destructive of love. Like an echo from a concept of D. H. Lawrence, this type of unsuccessful lover becomes a symbol of death. As the Rancher tells about his marital life with this woman who did not love him, the Desert Elena (symbol of death) appears. Dressed in a tight coarse sheath, her hair wrapped close to her head, she carries a cactus in one hand, and in the other a wooden grave cross wound with dusty artificial flowers. She is visible only to the Judge and the Rancher who likens her to the desert-bearing cactus, for she is barren. But he is non-Latin, and a man of property—not a lover. Against the slow dance by the chorus and the beat of the drums and guitar music, the Rancher gives a lyrical account of Elena's flight, a romantic description of drunken abandon. His account also has evaded the whole truth.

A little more of the truth emerges when the Judge describes the ominous smoldering character of the Rancher, who as a gentle boy withdrew from the world:

> This reticence, almost noble, persisted through youth,
> but later, as you grew older,
> an emptiness, still unfilled, became a cellar,
> a cellar into which blackness dripped and trickled,
> a slow, corrosive seepage.
> Then the reticence
> was no longer noble—but locked—resentful,
> and breeding a need for destruction.

The key terms used to describe his character are worth noting—reticence, emptiness, resentment, destruction—for there is something reminiscent about them. In the "Preface" to *Sweet Bird of Youth* Williams confessed his own youthful inadequacy and his need to express himself in violence. To the Judge, the Rancher confesses the turbulent state of his own being, his need for his wife, her rejection, and his violence upon discovering the lovers. Rosalio, the son, curses him for trying to defile "this quicksilver girl." As the vision of Elena of the Springs (life and love) returns, guilty Rosalio plunges the knife into his breast. As in "Desire and the Black Masseur" when the air is cleared after the so-called "retribution," so in this one-act after the guilt has been exposed and the guilty ones dispensed with—and the guilt is again sexual—the rain begins and the people rejoice. As a final gesture of retribution the Rancher gratefully accepts the knife from the Mother, his feeling expressed in symbolic terms: "As one who has suffered over-long from drought."

The Judge closes the play with the comment that honor goes deeper than law with these people. The whole theme of freedom and honor is stated only in sexual terms; and the abnormal relationship of the brother and sister is described as sensitive and fine as opposed to the ugly lovelessness between husband and wife. There seem to be echoes of the playwright's own character in both Rosalio and the Rancher—the love of freedom and worship of sexual happiness in the former and the almost neurotic reticence and its expression in violence in the latter. Although the lines are set off as poetry, many of them are only prose lines with words repeated or synonyms added. Rather easy symbols have been substituted for metaphor. But the play is important in the study of the work of Tennessee Williams because symbols and private significance have been substituted for observation of common experience. It also anticipates later plays in which the dramatist is preoccupied with half-told truths—a literary mannerism that he likes to call "mystery"—and with theatrical devices which serve very well to cover up either a lack of thought or inadequacies in dramatic writing.

These early plays, like the short stories, reveal an interesting new talent; and they justified the enthusiastic support and encouragement given the playwright. Themes and dramatic techniques that were to be used later had already been tried; and in these plays are to be found not only skillful, articulated scenes in which dialogue flows in beautifully phrased idiom but also a more artificial, contrived style of writing that is an attempt to break from realism. On the whole, some of Williams' best writing is to be found in these short plays.

VI *Battle of Angels*

Tennessee Williams describes *Battle of Angels*,[13] his first attempt to reach Broadway but a play which did not get beyond the unhappy Boston tryout, "a lyrical play about memories and the loneliness of them." This may be the stated theme but the play really concerns a sexually attractive itinerant who walks into an old-fashioned southern town and causes considerable excitement. The range of characters suggests that Williams may have been trying to imitate Faulkner's delineation of the various levels of culture that are part of his Yoknapatawpha County, but Williams has combined so many different elements and precipitated so much violence that he has allowed little time for the development of a dramatic sequence.

The play is set in a mercantile store, as "harsh and drab" as reality. It attracts the traffic of a small Delta community: the commonplace, overdressed housewives who are snoopers, gossips, and choir-singing good women who savor mortuary information; and their pin-headed, bulky mill-hand husbands who are dangerous when drunk. In contrast to these dull grotesques are a number of originals and eccentrics such as the decadent aristocrat, gun-toting, heavy drinking, sex-obsessed girl, Cassandra Whiteside, who delivers some rather heady and prophetic words. A symbol of rebellious freedom, she is described as if she were a delicate translucent relic of a bygone culture, the residue of intensely burning emotion. Vee Talbott, the wife of a brutal, race-violent sheriff, is a barren, frustrated woman and apparently, a symbol of the consequence of Puritan repression. As one of Williams' favored mad people she has visions, and out of those visions she creates her primitive paintings. Jabe Torrance, dying of cancer, is an ugly version of a southern businessman, not so much a character as a caricature. Myra, his wife, was "bought" twenty years previously after her father, "the wop," was burned in his wine garden because of his racial tolerance; scarred by this tragedy, as well as by a loveless marriage, she broods over broken dreams.

The town comes to life with the arrival of poet-itinerant-lover Valentine Xavier, who wears his snakeskin jacket, a symbol of freedom. This twenty-five-year-old, like the Williams-D. H. Lawrence heroes, is virile and handsome, a primitive uncorrupted by a mercantile society, and the epitome of sex appeal. The main business of the play concerns Val's amorous adventure with the lady proprietor, Myra. A moment before these lovers meet, Sandra[14] asks him caustically, "Don't you know what these women are suffering from: Sexual malnutrition! They look at you with eyes that scream 'Eureka!'" For some crazy reason, perhaps to symbolize her freedom, she laughs and saunters casually to the door, raises her revolver, and fires two shots into the sky. Bedlam breaks loose—the women snooping upstairs come tumbling down, one of them falling; the pregnant one deplores such excitement for one in her condition (her sixth or sev-

enth expectancy). Myra enters to face a strange man with
a gun. Myra is Italian, a race—according to Williams, who
beats that one note continually—naturally ready for love.
Like so many of the heroines she is older than the lover,
a woman of thirty-four. Her face showing the ravages of a
traumatic experience years before, she is somewhat tense and
hysterical when alert or suspicious, but she is girlishly tender
and soft when she relaxes.

Val applies for work, talks of the book he is writing about
"life," and rebukes Myra for her heartless unconcern about
him; and, in a very short time he charms her into laughter.
Sometimes jealous and caustic and at others sympathetic,
she is not an easy employer. But the Lawrence radiant primitive wants to settle down. He tells her that he is weary of
his roving life and lonesomeness and everlasting association
with strangers. He wants to belong somewhere and live like
other people, and that, of course, is his fatal mistake. For all
Williams' heroes, the sacrifice of any freedom is like entering the outer gate of hell. But Val says he is tired of being
the fox chased by hounds, an image the playwright had used
in a poem when describing D. H. Lawrence.[15]

His talk wins Myra's sympathy and the relationship
changes fast, very fast indeed. In a series of illogical scenes
Val has an argument with the Sheriff over the rights of a
Negro, makes a confession about being "Wanted for Rape
in Texas," talks about his fear of touching Myra, and his
determination to leave. Against the sound of the cotton gin
in the background, which increases in volume as she pleads
with him to stay, they reach one another in "a compulsive
embrace" and then rush into the back room. This is one of
the early exit-to-the-big-double-bed scenes that came to be
Tennessee Williams' specialty.

Val's problems with the decadent young aristocrat are
somewhat different. The tension between Sandra and Val,
which apparently rises from some kind of mutual understanding, is immediate and violent; she is provocative; he,
antagonistic. Early in the play, after a brief exchange—very
brief, about six lines, in fact—she wants to take him out
dancing—juking—drinking—cohabiting in the graveyard on
Cypress Hill; or, as she calls it, "just one word—live!" By
her own confession, she represents the third generation of

women who claim to have a secret communication with the birds, meaning that she is the Williams' type that belongs to the sensual Cavaliers rather than the Puritans. Although Val doesn't respond to her proposition, he has to fix her car. She rewards him with a hard slap on the face; he had ignored the "Male at Stud" sign she had hung on him. In a highly rhetorical speech she expresses the Williams' thesis that the free spirit is badly restricted in the contemporary world, that both the primitive and the aristocrat are derelicts from a better society. "You must be blind. You—savage. And me—aristocrat. Both of us things whose license has been revoked in the civilized world. Both of us equally damned and for the same good reason. Because we both want freedom. Of course, I knew you were really better than me. A whole lot better. I'm rotten. Neurotic. Our blood's gone bad from too much interbreeding. They've set up the guillotine, not in the Place de Concorde, but here, inside our own bodies!"

She again returns to Val after the officers have confiscated the light-colored Negro chauffeur with whom she was caught on Cypress Hill. She pleads with Val to go with her. "You an' me, we belong to the fugitive kind.[16] We live on motion." In this scene that mixes sex and prophetic hysterics and cosmic significance, Williams does, indeed, achieve "something wild." Sandra crosses to him, loosens her red velvet cape, lets it drop to the floor, and stands close, her white evening gown clinging nakedly to her body.

VAL: Don't stand there in front of me like that!
SANDRA: Why not? I'm just looking at you. You know what I feel when I look at you, Val? Always the weight of your body bearing me down.
VAL: *Christ!*
SANDRA: You think I ought to be ashamed to say that? Well, I'm not. I think that passion is something to be proud of. It's the only one of the little alphabet blocks they give us to play with that seems to stand for anything of importance. . . . They've passed a law against passion. Our license has been revoked. We have to give it up or else be ostracized by Memphis society. Jackson and Vicksburg, too. Whoever has too much passion, we're going to be burned like witches because we know too much.

> MYRA: What are you talking about?
> SANDRA: Damnation! You see my lips have been touched
> by prophetic fire.

In drunken excitement she concludes profoundly that time
has run out, and that catastrophe is imminent; and, clasping
her ears, she melodramatically shouts, "A battle in heaven.
A battle of *angels* above us! And *thunder!* And *storm!*"[17]
She concludes in her fatalistic, melodramatic way that since
there's nothing one can do, he might as well seize whatever
is near with both hands—and roughly at that. Having uttered
this gloomy philosophy, she kisses Val with abandon. This
overloaded scene would seem to indicate that Tennessee
Williams' mind was not playing with philosophic concepts—
for all his talk about battling angels and revoked licences.
Sandra would seem to be another example of "moral paralysis," the condition which characterizes so many of Williams'
romantics.

Val's great search for philosophical truths seems to have
been very early handicapped by his sexual attractiveness to
women. He makes full confession of his sex life to the interested Myra. Since he was fourteen, when he had run away
from his sharecropper heritage, to live like an animal on
Witches' Bayou, he had felt that something important was
going to happen to him. He had kept his senses alert for
the answers to his question, why. Then he had been thrown
off the track by the naked and lonesome girl he saw standing
on the dogtrot. On a bed made of cypress and moss, an idyllic
rendezvous to be sure, he had taught her some words like
love. After a period of sexual contentment he had decided
that she was just a woman and not the answer to questions
he had not yet formulated. He had hit the trail again; and,
after ten itinerant years doing odd jobs, he had settled down
in Waco, Texas. Another woman. He confesses to Myra that
he is wanted for the rape of a plain-looking wife of the oil-
field superintendent. She was the aggressor, evidently. She
came into his cabin when he was drunk and what happened,
he says casually, was accidental. The trouble came when
he tried to get away and she screamed bloody rape.

Women, always women. As a shoe clerk he cannot keep
his hands off women. Strumming his guitar, he tells Myra

how much trouble his hands have caused him, and how he restrains them till his muscles ache. There is also a scene with Vee Talbott, the religious fanatic who hoped to "save" Val. She has been describing to him how she painted the red steeple on the Church of the Resurrection; and, as she talks, the passionate clerk massages her knees. She grows a bit hysterical and makes a weaving exit. Val may deplore his unmanageable hands; but it is soon obvious that, as a shoe salesman, he has the right touch. With Val's treatment the shoe business becomes very brisk. These scenes indicate that, Williams, when not straining for effect, has an excellent sense for the comic.

But he packed too much into one play, and he substituted hysterical action and rhetoric for the natural development and the excellent dialogue of the one-acts. As already suggested, he overlays a simple tale with symbols, some of them rather far-fetched. The confectionery, redecorated to imitate the old Moon Lake Casino, suggests the return of romantic dreams; and Myra's pregnancy is represented by a dress described as ecstasy blue. Vee Talbott, in deep black and even deeper in her crucifixion complex, brings her latest picture: Val as Jesus on the Cross. One wonders by what stretch of the imagination the oversexed poet-vagabond-lover is equated with Jesus, and whether the "crucifixion" isn't necessary to the plot—Williams' kind of plot—rather than an outgrowth of dramatic development. Just as in the short story, "Desire and the Black Masseur," there is also here a connection between sex and crucifixion. The hideous final scene takes place on Good Friday morning, anticipated by a symbolic gesture: the old Conjure Man holds out an ominous claw hand. There's a storm, an unholy row between the two females, Myra and Sandra, over the radiant male, Val; and a jubilant shout from Myra that she is pregnant. Jabe, the moribund husband, lumbers in—suggesting a prince from hell —mouths curses, and plugs bullets into his faithless wife. The woman from Waco enters with a crowd carrying pine torches; but they are stopped by the Conjure Man holding up the snakeskin jacket, the symbol of *the hard, immaculate challenge of things untamed.*

As if there hadn't been violence enough in the last act, the "Epilogue" concludes on a shriller note. It is reported that Cassandra's car plunged into the river and that she was lost. The snakeskin jacket—described as a "shameless, flaunting symbol of the Beast Untamed!"—stays fresh and clean; but Val, stripped of his clothes, was lynched—as Vee Talbott's picture had anticipated. She becomes insane; the Waco woman disappears; Jabe dies of cancer; and only the gossiping females remain—to catch scandal-hungry tourists—a note reminiscent of an early one-act, *Lord Byron's Love Letter.* Val spoke a line that might have been developed, if sex and violence and symbolism had not taken over, "We're all of us locked up tight inside our own bodies. Sentenced—you might say—to solitary confinement inside our own skins."

This early play seems to idolize the happy itinerant of the early poems, short stories, and one-act plays. It also seems to adopt ideas the dramatist may have picked up from D. H. Lawrence: the artist in disagreement with society; the artist as a proponent of sexual freedom; and such ideas as that of equating sexual fulfillment with resurrection, or that of equating middle-class virtues with all that is stultifying and mechanical. Tennessee Williams developed several variations of these ideas in his later plays. He rewrote *Battle of Angels,* which had an unhappy reception in Boston,[18] many times; he called a later version *Orpheus Descending* (1955); and the film script of the same play is *The Fugitive Kind* (1958).

VII *I Rise in Flame, Cried the Phoenix*

The one-act play *I Rise in Flame, Cried the Phoenix*[19] is an imaginary portrayal of the last day of D. H. Lawrence's life, but the tiger's fury is still raging in his emaciated body. The play communicates the vitality of this rebel against prudery, and it vividly dramatizes the conflict between the sick man and his dominant wife, Frieda. It is also of particular interest for a number of ideas about Lawrence which caught Williams' imagination and which reappear in his later plays. Lawrence is made to regret that his life was expressed in books rather than action, violent action. Williams has him confess to a pretense of waging war with bourgeois ideas of morality, prudery, intellectuality and other kinds of abstract external forces. What he is really fighting, he admits, is his own prudishness, the old maid in himself, a confession that has a personal ring from the playwright. Williams also has the novelist define art in terms close to his own heart; the artist loves life with such intensity that the love is turned to hate; he wants his art to embrace the whole world; the world, like a woman, has to be taken by storm and so the artist doubles his fist and strikes; he painted as he wrote, colorfully, fiercely and shamelessly, for that is what life is to an artist.

According to Williams, Lawrence feared that at the moment of his death he would be surrounded by women, all kinds of women, the oversexed and the undersexed, women who considered him the prophet of their sick, confused libidos. Williams has Lawrence describe woman as the aggressor in the sexual act, the description at first in frankly sexual terms and then repeated in bold symbolic terms: the bright male sun is seduced by the harlot of darkness who tries to devour him—the cannibal image again. According to the rather hysterical description, the sun will climb out of the belly of the harlot of darkness and there will be light—universal light. Thus, the symbolism, in sexual terms, is given cosmic significance.

In this short play Tennessee Williams has communicated the complexity and strength of this literary personality which seems to have influenced his own work so much. From the introductory statement, this play was written about 1941 though it was not published until ten years later.

VIII *You Touched Me!*

You Touched Me![20] written in collaboration with David Windham and suggested by a D. H. Lawrence short story,[21] is an early work of writers who have contempt for Ibsen's realism. The play goes off into three different directions: part of it is romantic comedy; part of it intellectualizes about "frontiers of the mind"; and another part is like the slapstick farce often found in undergraduate variety shows. The characters are symbolic figures and much of the action appears to have symbolic meaning.

Captain Cornelius Rockley—exponent of freedom and sex, a raucous, lecherous-tongued old soak who traded his ship, the *Polar Star,* for a barrel of rum—carries on a feud of "epic fury" with his bossy tabby-cat sister, Emmie, who symbolizes frozen Virginity. As a protection against this ominous female, the Captain had adopted years before a "charity boy" called Hadrian, who is currently a fighter pilot on leave from service in World War II. This boy with a philosophical turn of mind is a natural son of Pan. The Captain's daughter, Matilda, a dreamy, man-shy lady who idolizes Hart Crane and writes poetry of her own, is caught between the two compelling forces of sterile Virginity, symbolized by Emmie, and Life, represented by her father and the young Pan in uniform.[22] The side of Virtue is flanked by the Reverend Guilford Melton, a little man of mincing refinement and limited intellectual endowment, who seems to be edging toward "spiritual companionship" with the virginal, slack-witted Emmie. The maid Phoebe, when moments are dull, shrieks when she is poked, tickled, and chased by the inebriated Captain.

At the heart of the play is a significant and universal theme: the human need for sympathy and understanding, natural qualities often obstructed by puritanical virtue and propriety. For years Hadrian has tried to break down the diffidence which imprisons the fearful Matilda. He believes, as does the Captain, that warmth and tenderness can be expressed in the touch of the fingers, an idea which arouses Emmie's disgust. These opposing views about ways of life are expressed briefly in the third act when the Captain tells of the destructive power of a so-called good woman; he is speaking to his sister:

CAPTAIN (*yelling at her from the foot of the stairs*): You want to do with my daughter what you did with my wife?

EMMIE: Protect her from you? That's right!

CAPTAIN: Turn her into a lifeless piece of clay!

EMMIE: That's an astounding statement.

CAPTAIN: True! You weaned her from me. Holy, holy, holy! Nothing but helping others in your dear brain. Some people have got that power—of turning life into clay. You're one of that kind, Emmie.

EMMIE: Insane babblings!

CAPTAIN: But others have got a different kind of power. Their touch turns clay into life. Hadrian's one of that kind.

The Hadrian-Matilda romance has been likened to the old fable of the sleeping beauty, but the Williams-Windham version has been complicated by symbolism and a number of extraneous elements. The girl, mistaking the reclining figure of Hadrian for her father, places a loving hand on the man's forehead. This romantic scene is played at the same time as Emmie's angry "gunning" of the fox in the chicken coop, where she ineptly shot "the Stoneyfield rooster," the ribbon winner, and thereby reduced masculinity by one.[23] The morning after "the touch," young Pan-fox-pilot-philosopher Hadrian urges Matilda to accept change and the challenge of the future: "The future is not conceited [sic] . . . it pauses to look the old things over and pick out . . . such things as music—poetry—and gentleness." This young Pan, talking rather casually of the prison guard he knifed in order to gain his own escape, asks the girl, "Do these impress you as being dangerous fingers? Do they look fierce and cruel?"

At the right moment Matilda changes into *"a delicate, filmy blue-green dress and a pair of feather slippers"*—and becomes a Williams heroine in love. Emmie, who can spot the first signs of liquor and of love, locks her in her room. The Captain urges Hadrian to lay siege: "Virginitiy is mostly the consequence of bad environment an' unfavorable social conditions." And so the manly pilot, in an incredibly naïve scene, scratches at the girl's door and whines like Flora, the Pekinese. The lovers are reunited, but the shy girl walks through a rainy night brooding over her predicament. She returns in the morning, suddenly assertive, speaking a "damn" or two, and rudely asks her suitor: "What's—stopping you, you fool?" The second embrace is accompanied by music and tinkling bells and by some rather precious lines from the pilot: "Little silver Matilda, little bells, little bells!" The bottle-happy Captain, a bit ashamed that he might have ruined by his gross behavior Emmie's marriage to the Reverend, but more afraid that he may have risked his own freedom, reiterates his tearful line, "The bird of remorse—has got his beak in my heart."

Joseph Wood Krutch found the best scenes to be "those in which the hero and heroine try to understand the ardor of the one and the fears of the other. The worst are those in which the attempt is made to give this personal drama some significance both political and cosmic. . . . There may be some connection between phallic worship and a new league of nations, but it is not to me a very clear one. Almost at his first appearance we see the hero playing a penny flute, and no reader of Lawrence needs to be told what that means. Very shortly thereafter he is in the midst of a passionate speech about a new world order, and to me it does not become quite clear whether society is to be saved through better international understanding or whether, as Lawrence sometimes seemed to think, all we need is more and better copulation.[24]

The whole range of Tennessee Williams' talent and the uses which he made of it are represented in his works before the success of *The Glass Menagerie;* for this reason, these early pieces are of particular significance.

CHAPTER 3

The Southern Gentlewoman

I *The Southern Gentlewoman*

TENNESSEE WILLIAMS first achieved widespread recognition for *The Glass Menagerie* (1945) and its portraits of southern gentlewomen: Amanda Wingfield and her
daughter Laura. He continued this study with Blanche Du
Bois of *A Streetcar Named Desire* (1947) and with Alma
Winemiller of *Summer and Smoke* (1948).

The hypersensitive Laura, the girl who retreats into her
special world of glass ornaments and phonograph records,
he had already described in the story, "A Portrait of a Girl in
Glass." In a number of briefer portraits the southern lady
had already appeared to represent the conflict between normal emotions and the repressive ideals of the Puritan tradition—a high-tensioned lady unable to harmonize the world
of her dreams with reality. The early poem "Intimations"
(1941) presents the vignette of the spinster poet who is far
behind the times. In the short story, "Night of the Iguana,"
the spinsterish artist is presented as a sexually frustrated
woman whose need undermines her ordinary good sense. In
the one-act play, *Portrait of a Madonna,* an aging nice girl,
a psychotic on her way to an asylum, is described as a
church-trained woman obsessed by the conflict between her
religious teaching and her sexual dreams.

All of these portraits are studies in frustration of women
of a culture and refinement associated with the Victorian
era that disappeared during the decade of World War I.
These women are several degrees superior to the domesti-
cated housewives and gossips who frequently appear as carbon copies of a type that symbolizes Williams' antipathy for

[70]

the average. Along with the gentlewomen's refinement seems to go a kind of prissy affectation that is sometimes only a mask for a passionate but frustrated nature. There is either much talk about beaux or an unladylike aggressiveness toward unattached men. They are all out of touch with the world around them, and they live in worlds of their own making: one of soft sentimental dreams about their own charms, or one about their own past and successes with men. In some cases, because of the conflict within themselves, they are unaware of their own unseemly behavior. In spite of his ruthless exposure of their dreams and delusions and deceit, their affectations and pretenses, Williams seems to have sympathy for them all—except for Amanda, whom he describes as a carping, garrulous bore. Amanda, a dominating mother, was anticipated by Mme. Duvenet who torments her son in *Auto-Da-Fé;* she was developed more unpleasantly as Mrs. Venable in *Suddenly Last Summer* (1958) and as the wealthy southern spinster, Miss Cornelia Scott in *Something Unspoken.* In the last two plays heroines appear without any psychotic tendencies; attractive young women, they seem to have made sane adjustments to their difficult situations.

The men who appear in these plays are not so much southern gentlemen as developments of a theory. The epitome of the monotonous, average male reappears in all three plays: Jim O'Connor, Laura's secret love, is a normal, unimaginative hireling of the business world; Mitch, a workingman of a decent sort and Blanche's last hope of security; Roger Doremus, Alma's effeminate boyfriend, companion at the ladies' literary circle. In contrast to these rather nondescript men are the glorious uninhibited youths who are uncontaminated by any association with the Episcopalian church or any other institutions of a mechanized society. These red-blooded rebels have much in common with the D. H. Lawrence derivatives: Hadrian is the Pan worshiper in *You Touched Me!* and Stan Kowalski in *A Streetcar Named Desire* is the epitome of full-bodied male pulchritude and Williams' most radiant symbol of virility. John Buchanan in *Summer and Smoke* is another Apollo who seems to have wasted his youth on the town but is unmarked by his excessive drinking and wenching.

II *The Glass Menagerie*

The Glass Menagerie[1] is a memory play, a series of seven sharply remembered scenes of the son who finally escaped from a nagging mother and from an exquisitely fragile sister whom he could leave but not forget. It represents Williams at his best in brief, highly charged scenes. But neither the incidents nor a well-developed plot holds the play together: the mood and the emotional excitement arising from the characters do so. Even though Williams expresses contempt for realism, his portrait of Amanda Wingfield, the mother, addicted to bromides and delusions, is incisively delineated and one of his very best.

She is a middle-aged southern belle, garrulous and silly, narrow and spinsterish in her attitudes toward life. Wrapped up in delusions of her girlhood conquests, she is often unaware of the realities of the world around her. The picture is as caustic as a Daumier print. Her husband, present only in the blown-up photograph over the mantle, is described as a telephone man who fell in love with long distance and left for good. Years before she had been deluded by his uniform, just as she currently deludes herself about her girlhood and her youthful gentlemen callers, men now grown rich. She keeps reminding her children that a particular Sunday afternoon seventeen gentlemen came to call, an exaggeration typical of her delusions. Ironically, she is proud of her conversational talents, as her son and daughter know only too well. It is obvious that for years she has overworked the charm.

Just as willfully she ignores present reality; she refuses to admit Laura's shyness and her crippled leg and forces her to attend church socials where she might meet men. When Laura fails to attract a husband, her mother drives the girl into secretarial school where she may learn the means of self-support. Although she insists that Laura not refer to herself as a cripple, that she speak only of a little physical defect and distract attention from it by developing charm and vivacity, she is not entirely blind to the situation. She has known firsthand what can happen to a southern girl without a home of her own. Her cry comes from experience. "I know so well what becomes of unmarried women who aren't prepared to occupy a position. I've seen such pitiful cases in the South—barely tolerated spinsters living upon the grudging patronage of sister's husband or brother's wife!—stuck away in some little mouse-trap of a room—encouraged by one in-law to visit another—little birdlike women without any nest—eating the crust of humility all their life!"[2]

During the play she makes another attempt to provide for her daughter by asking Tom to find a clean-living, non-drinking suitor. When from his limited acquaintance he invites to dinner a warehouse friend, her hopes skyrocket. Tom admits that he has said nothing about Laura and tries to make his mother be a little more realistic:

> TOM: Mother, you mustn't expect too much of Laura.
> AMANDA: What do you mean?
> TOM: Laura seems all those things to you and me because she's ours and we love her. We don't even notice she's crippled any more.
> AMANDA: Don't say crippled! You know that I never allow that word to be used!
> TOM: But face facts, Mother. She is and—that's not all——
> AMANDA: What do you mean, "not all"?
> TOM: Laura is very different from other girls.
> AMANDA: I think the difference is all to her advantage.
> TOM: Not quite all—in the eyes of others—strangers—she's terribly shy and lives in a world of her own and those things make her seem a little peculiar to people outside the house.
> AMANDA: Don't say peculiar.
> TOM: Face the facts. She *is*.

Refusing to listen, Amanda with grim feminine energy works to change Laura into a pretty trap; on the ill-fated evening she makes the girl so sick that she cannot eat dinner and then crudely isolates the young man and her daughter. When she discovers that this plan has also failed, because the man is engaged, she forgets all her silly lies and sees the humiliating position of herself and Laura for what it is. She brutally castigates Tom for what has been her own folly. She accuses him of allowing them to make fools of themselves, spend money recklessly—a new floor lamp, a new rug, a new dress for Laura—forgetting that Tom had tried to talk to her. Her carping accusations of his being selfish and thoughtless, her hysterical disappointment over another plan gone wrong, and her mawkish self-pity are ruthlessly exposed. She lacks the charm she talks so much about.

Amanda, though at times proud of her son, is insensitive to his position. She carps at him continually, his eating habits, his smoking, his going to the movies, his late hours. The continual friction between this young man and his mother indicates her lack of understanding. Almost every talk leads to a quarrel. She insists that Tom should either find adventure in his warehouse job or do without it. When he tries to explain that basically man is by instinct a fighter, a hunter, and a lover, she nearly explodes. It is the word, "instinct," that has set her off, a dirty word to her and one belonging to animals and not Christian adults. The conflict between body and spirit, as it reflects the southern Puritanism of the early twentieth century, is symbolized in the attitudes of these two people. According to Amanda, for whom the word instinct is a term only for monkeys and pigs, Christian adults should be concerned with things of the mind and spirit.

Another argument in the same vein arises over the D. H. Lawrence novel which Tom brought home from the library; Lawrence is a writer who offends her sense of propriety and whom she considers insane. Exasperated by this everlasting carping and her nagging about his running away to the movies, Tom bluntly tells her how much he detests the life he is leading. He is appalled by the idea of spending fifty-five years cooped up in a celotex room with fluorescent lights for sixty-five dollars a month; of waking up every morning to his mother's maddening cheerfulness; and of going back to recording numbers again, over and over again. He'd rather be dead. The intensity of these lines reflects the disgust of Williams' own two-year experience with the shoe company and may, in part, account for the contempt he always expresses for the businessman whom he characterizes as a ruthless, loveless automaton.

On the other hand there is a reflection of attitude from the novelist that Tom was reading. Williams' adoration of the lover and contempt for the businessman, his full treatment of the man of blood in contrast to his summary type casting of the man dedicated to industry, a man sexually impotent and almost symbolic of death, recalls the D. H. Lawrence characterizations in *Lady Chatterley's Lover*. Mellors, if only a miner's son, is nevertheless a man, alive and passionate, a whole human being. He is symbolic of the source of life, of vigor and of tenderness, a character who reappears in Lawrence. By contrast Clifford Chatterley, physically impotent from a war injury, an effete intellectual, cared for by his nurse, a kind of mother substitute, is described with contempt. He belongs to a series of men dedicated to business and power rather than to love, whose lives represent success in industry but failure in bed. They are embodiments of Lawrence's contempt, caricatures of an idea rather than delineated characters. The same contrast of full characterization and type casting is to be found in Williams.

Tom Wingfield belongs to neither of these categories, but to the itinerant-dreamer like his creator. Trapped by two women and his own indolence, he is the narrator who sets the scene as taking place in the thirties. He describes Americans as going their blind way, dancing, making love, and being mildly disturbed by labor troubles at the time that the Spaniards were being methodically slaughtered at Guernica. He is evidently a lonely soul, ignored and slightly ridiculed by his fellow workers at the plant until the big Irishman, Jim O'Connor, paid attention to him. There is considerable talk about his writing poetry but it seems to be a kind of escape from a very trying life. It is not Tom's poetry nor his world view but his patience with his mother and his sensitiveness and deep affection for his sister, Laura, that give him a certain stature. He is about as frustrated as they. Fired for writing poetry on the boss's time, he takes off, as did his father, to find an escape. But in every city there is a reminder of his sister. "Oh, Laura, Laura, I tried to leave you behind me, but I am more faithful than I intend to be! I reach for a cigarette, I cross the street, I run into the movies or a bar, I buy a drink, I speak to the nearest stranger—anything that can blow your candles out!"

The shoe factory job, the poetry writing, the cramped living quarters and the very close relationship with the sister are all echoes of Williams' own experience.[3] These autobiographical touches perhaps explain his own identification with this character. As a poet-narrator who likes to speak in symbols, he controls the scenes although they usually do not need his explanations. There is imposed on the characterization of Tom himself a rather precious symbolism—the type that Williams associates with the "poetic" but that is often so simple or so pretentious as to be like a parody. For instance, when Tom returns from the movies about five o'clock in the morning, somewhat alcoholically inspired, the church bell is striking the hour. According to the stage directions Tom is to shake a little rattle and this gesture is supposed to symbolize the spasm of a little man in contrast to the dignity and power of God—the church bell, undoubtedly.[4]

When Williams says the play is not realistic, but is intended to be a sentimental, evocative piece, he must be thinking of Laura, the morbidly shy, overdelicate sister who is as fragile as the little glass ornaments and phonograph records which are her escape. It is upon Laura that Williams has not only spent sentiment but pathos and tears; he has oppressed the girl with much more sad biography than was included in the short story which first presented her in fiction; the pathos is not needed in the play.[5] But the fact that this expenditure is not readily apparent is a credit to Williams' capacity not only for writing some of the most beautiful dialogue that has come from any American dramatist but also for creating delicately emotional scenes and an appealing character. For, through her timidity, her suffering from the friction between Tom and Amanda, and her retreat into the world of dreams, Laura evokes genuine sympathy; she is the appealing one of those who must be cared for, loved, and understood. Her charm and delicacy win the audience—just as they won her brother Tom.

Perceptive of others' feelings, Laura senses her mother's need to romanticize her own past and so stands between the mother and her son; and it is she who suffers over the ugly wrangling that breaks out between the two. Williams has made her not only sensitive and shy but also a cripple forced to wear a clanking brace—a torture to one abnormally self-conscious. During her final semester in high school she becomes nervously ill, flunks her final exams, and does not graduate. When her desperate mother spends fifty dollars for a secretarial course for her, Laura becomes nauseated during the typing speed test. But the same unimaginative mother forces her to join a young people's church group where she might meet some nice boys. Because Laura won't or can't talk, she suffers another humiliation. Furthermore, she has been secretly in love with a high school boy and has dreamed of him for six years; and, thanks to the long arm of coincidence, he is the gentleman caller Tom brings home at his mother's urging.

Some of Laura's best scenes are with Jim O'Connor, the gentleman caller, who is to her a hero and not a dull extrovert or a paragon of the ordinary. Tom describes him as a high school hero; he was evidently one of those dynamic extroverts whose youth, looks, and enthusiasm won him the vote as the boy graduate most likely to succeed. Time and his failure to produce have proven otherwise. Jim seems to represent the average, unimaginative American—a contrast to the more perceptive Tom.

Amanda's planned evening, begun in panic for Laura, becomes her dream come true. After she brings out the annual with all the romantic memories and after something of the old excitement is restored to the disappointed hero, he brashly analyzes Laura—much as Amanda might have— as a victim of an inferiority complex. He talks to her as if he were addressing his public speaking class in evening school, thinking of himself, making his point, completely insensitive to his little one-girl, wide-eyed audience. He urges her to forget her crippled leg and the brace she wears. No one ever noticed it, he lies. Her imagination has magnified her trouble when she ought to forget it and think of herself as superior in some way. Jim then talks in big terms about his own future plans, becomes a little abashed at his own egotism, and then remembers his evening-class lesson that success comes from interest in other people. Williams through these few lines has given simply and most effectively the character of an unimaginative, ambitious, and very average young white-collar worker.

Laura responds to the encouragement, and shows him her precious glass collection. She picks up her dearest treasure, the thirteen-year-old unicorn, points to the single horn on his forehead and admits that he is extinct, but she loves him because he must feel lonesome. The little glass figure is a living thing to her; she talks about his accepting without complaint his companions—horses without horns. The unicorn is obviously a symbol for Laura who is also a delicate translucent being, out of place in the contemporary world. In this scene is some of the best dialogue that Tennessee Williams has written.

LAURA: Hold him over the light, he loves the light! You see how the light shows through him?
JIM: It sure does shine!
LAURA: I shouldn't be partial, but he is my favorite one.
JIM: What kind of thing is this one supposed to be?
LAURA: Haven't you noticed the single horn on his forehead?
JIM: A unicorn, huh?
LAURA: Mm-hmmmm.
JIM: Unicorns, aren't they extinct in the modern world?
LAURA: I know!
JIM: Poor little fellow, he must feel sort of lonesome.
LAURA: (*Smiling*) Well, if he does he doesn't complain about it. He stays on a shelf with some horses that don't have horns and all of them seem to get along nicely together.

Laura is carried away with the conversation, but Jim's attention is soon distracted by the music played across the alley. He gallantly asks Laura to dance; they take a few steps in a clumsy waltz and hit the table. There is a shatter of glass. The unicorn is broken.

LAURA: Now it is just like all the other horses.
JIM: It's lost its——
LAURA: Horn! It doesn't matter. Maybe it's a blessing in disguise.
JIM: You'll never forgive me. I bet that was your favorite piece of glass.
LAURA: I don't have favorites much. It's no tragedy, Freckles. Glass breaks so easily. No matter how careful you are.

Jim is won by Laura's unique charm, but he is more obviously impressed by his own power. He sets out to build up her confidence in herself. Like the clumsy stumble-bum who broke the unicorn, and unaware of what is happening to the

girl, he talks about making her proud and not shy and blush-
ing. He kisses her and realizes his mistake; for, seeing her
bright, dazed look, he dimly senses her feelings. He pops a
mint into his mouth and bluntly explains that another girl
has strings on him. Unaware that he is destroying all the
self-confidence he had so casually built up, he indulges his
own egotism. He talks of what love has done for him, and
of the power of love, which made a man of him. He voices
his creator's own theory that love can change the whole
world—romantic love, that is—and so he becomes a mouth-
piece for the line or two of rhetoric that is supposed to give
cosmic significance to a scene that needs no pontificating.

This scene is one of the best that Williams has written.
It closes, however, on a symbolic and precious note, incongruous in spirit. The playwright mixes up romantic love and
religion—as he was to do so often in later years—and he mixes
his metaphors as well. He refers to Laura's face as an altar
and speaks of the holy candles being snuffed out; he then
describes the altar of her face as having a look of desolation.
This is posturing, not poetry. The symbolic action which follows is more nearly to the point. Laura gently places the
broken unicorn, which is no longer like her but like an
ordinary animal, in the hand of the big Irishman and closes
it around her once favorite ornament. Jim stupidly asks her
why she does that. He has not only broken her unicorn but
also her heart.[6]

In his production notes Williams makes a rather patroniz-
ing comment to the effect that since the play is episodic,
it might seem fragmentary to the audience. If the basic
structure of the play is obscured, he says testily, it is not
the fault of the play but the lack of attention on the part
of the audience. In his attempt to keep them awake, he proposes a series of screens with titles suggesting the main idea
of the scene. He makes some strange miscalculations. He
would give the title—in French—of François Villon's famous
tribute to beautiful women to the scene in which Amanda
talks of her seventeen callers. Or, during the scene when
Amanda describes the role of dependent spinsters, one of
her best speeches, he would have a legend about the crust
of humility, a sentimental note that is incongruous. Or again,
when Tom has voiced his contempt for women's magazines,

he would flash on the screen a glamor cover, a detail that would belabor the obvious.[7]

This tendency toward precious writing and theatrical tricks a sensitive director can minimize or ignore, but these devices are worth mentioning because they represent the playwright's inability to allow his simply told play to stand on its own. Joseph Wood Krutch, sensing that Williams had a weakness that might damage his work, gave him a bit of sage advice: "whenever you have written a line you like especially well, strike it out."[8] But the greater part of the dialogue is the work of a sensitive writer who listened to and caught the subtle nuances of speech. And although the dialogue is not in meter, the play does return poetry to the theater. There is a good blend of imagination and realism, and the overtones are more complex than are readily apparent.

Tennessee Williams should be everlastingly grateful to the director and actors who projected his first play, for they set an excellent pattern for the later productions: Eddie Dowling, Laurette Taylor, Julie Haydon, Anthony Ross.

III *A Streetcar Named Desire*

In *A Streetcar Named Desire*[9] the southern gentlewoman, the last representative of a dying culture, is too delicate to withstand the crudeness and decay surrounding her. The conflict between her standards and those represented by the primitive laborer finally destroy her. It is the study of this final descent into madness, with all its implied comment about the two codes, that seems to interest the playwright. It is characteristic of Williams, however, that he does not take a stand, for he romanticizes both the natural man and the decadent aristocrat.

Blanche Du Bois, the last relic of the decayed southern plantation, "Belle Rêve," enters the Vieux Carré section of New Orleans: her first line seems to give a clue to the theme of the play, that life is equated with passion, and its opposite is death. Actual trolley names provide Williams with appropriate symbols. Blanche was told to take a streetcar named Desire, transfer to one named Cemetaria, and get off at Elysian Fields—nomenclature that mixes Freud and classical mythology. It would take a Tennessee Williams to place the sex-happy adult children of the New Orleans slums in the Greek Isles of the Blessed. In this Gulf Coast heaven which lies between the river and the tracks, and where the "Blue Piano" in the bar around the corner symbolizes the easy mingling of Negro and white, there lives a colony of married couples whose lives represent sexual contentment, uninhibited and unashamed.

The entrance of Blanche, delicate as a moth and dressed in white—all of Williams' sexual deviates are dressed in immaculate white—and looking as if she were about to take cocktails or tea in the best drawing room or garden, is an incongruous and shocking intrusion. This is her first visit to her sister, Stella, who is married to a Polish-American mechanic, Stanley Kowalski; contented with her commonplace life, Stella is undisturbed by the vulgarities of her friends and neighbors. The contrast between the two sisters —Stella as the normal, happy, and average woman; Blanche as the refined, hypersensitive, and decadent aristocrat—is soon obvious. It is also apparent that the arrival of this older sister, a representative of the civilized world and one most critical of the primitive mores of the Vieux Carré, will threaten the happy marital arrangement between Stella and Stan.

The explanation of Stella's happiness and willing descent to the cave apparently rests in the sexual charm of the man she married. Stan is a particularized characterization of the primitive hero who bears some similarity to the D. H. Lawrence type as exemplified by Mellors in *Lady Chatterley's Lover*—a type which Williams tentatively portrayed in Hadrian in *You Touched Me!* and partly in Val Xavier in *Battle of Angels*. The playwright's romantic ecstasy has a wistful note, for he indulges in a paean to virility that epitomizes the romantic admiration of the little man for the vigorous virility of a male hero. This deification of sex is the most enthusiastic passage in the whole canon of Tennessee Williams and is one statement which indicates where his heart is. Stan is the epitome of the pleasure an animal enjoys with his body, an aggressive, indulgent, powerful, and proud expression of sex. Williams describes him:

Animal joy in his being is implicit in all his movements and attitudes. Since earliest manhood the center of his life has been pleasure with women, the giving and taking of it, not with weak indulgence, dependently, but with the power and pride of a richly feathered male bird among hens. Branching out from this complete and satisfying center are all the auxiliary channels of his life, such as his heartiness with men, his appreciation of rough humor, his love of good drink and food and games, his car, his radio, everything that is his, that bears his emblem of the gaudy seed-bearer. He sizes up women with a glance, with sexual satisfactions, crude images flashing into his mind and determining the way he smiles at them.

The clash between Blanche and Stan is inevitable, for they represent two opposite views of life. The play, however, is not a simple, clear-cut conflict between two equally strong forces but a subtle and sometimes rather confused study of character; rich in overtones, the play is sometimes weighted with significance implied rather than expressed. A play that has moments of greatness, it misses being great because the playwright had no clear idea of what he was trying to say. The complicated and rather contradictory characterization of Blanche, the failure to follow through and dramatize the conflict, and Williams' inability to resist writing "something wild" instead of extracting the fullest significance from his materials—all of these factors exhibit a weakness in the playwright's handling of the material.

The first clash between Blanche and Stanley arises over the loss of the plantation which he dreamed of owning.[10] He suspects that she has squandered the property. He yanks out of the trunk, which dominates the kitchen, showy pieces of clothing and costume jewelry which he thinks are expensive. When he touches a sheaf of papers, Blanche's contempt is immediate; she says that the touch of his hands contaminates them. She gives the first hint of her private sorrow when she identifies them as poems of a dead husband whom she hurt as badly as Stan would hurt her. She says that she is protected because she is no longer young and vulnerable. She vaguely suggests that the plantation was lost on mortgages; she tells about family history which is part of her heritage. In highly exaggerated language she tells how the plantation was eaten away by spendthrift grandfathers and uncles and father and brothers—Williams loves so much these exaggerations—who over the years mortgaged the land to pay for their "epic fornications." Blanche's sexy by-play at the beginning of this scene rouses Stan's suspicion about his sister-in-law and gives him an early clue for his mode of revenge. The unsteadiness of her mind is suggested by the way she flits from one subject or one feeling to another, always, however, coming back to her own delusions about herself.

The next clash occurs when Stella and Blanche return about two-thirty in the morning to interrupt the men's poker game. The scenes with Stan and his poker-playing pals, where the characterizations are vivid and the dialogue a brilliant imitation of the idiom of an elemental people, are well handled. Williams makes an interesting comment on the early writing of the play: "I settled for a while at Chapala to work on a play called *The Poker Night* which later became *A Streetcar Named Desire.*"[11] If the third scene was the beginning of the play, then the southern gentlewoman theme must have been a later addition. The description of the poker scene, inspired by a Van Gogh picture of a billiard parlor, is a good example of the way Williams uses contrasting colors for dramatic effect. The scene calls to mind lines which he gave to D. H. Lawrence in *I Rise in Flame, Cried the Phoenix;* the British writer claimed for the artist the right to express himself in violent colors. But though Williams notes especially that the colors are those raw ones from childhood's spectrum, his characters represent coarse men at their physical prime—men as powerful as primary colors. Almost as if by habit Williams places together childhood innocence and sexual prowess. Part of the confusion in the play arises not only from his glowingly wistful admiration for Stan and his friends and for their capacity for unlimited physical pleasure, but also from his sentimental support and sympathy for Blanche who degenerated pitifully with the same kind of physical indulgence.

In the poker scene a number of elements intrude in the inevitable Blanche-Stan conflict. Blanche singles out Mitch as the one seemingly respectable player and stops him on his way to "The Little Boy's Room," as she calls it. She speaks pathetically of her great sorrow, of her need to cover

up ugly truth—with a Williams' symbolic touch, she asks him
to cover a naked light bulb with a paper Chinese lantern—
and of the aesthetic problems of an English teacher working
with "bobby soxers and drug-store Romeos." When she turns
on the radio to encourage Mitch to dance, Stan in a drunken
fury seizes the radio and hurls it out the window. He brutally
strikes his wife, Stella, who tries to send the men home. In
the brawl that follows, the women escape and the poker
players soothe their violent companion. When he realizes
that his wife is gone, Stan throws back his head and howls
like a dog, yelling out her name. When she returns quietly,
tears in her eyes, they rush together moaning like animals.
He falls to his knees, presses his face against her delicately
rounded belly, and she with tenderness raises him to her.
He lifts her into his arms and carries her into the dark flat.
The sight of this connubial bliss, following so closely upon
the scene of drunken brutality, stuns Blanche for a moment.
She soon, however, focuses her attention upon Mitch, the
one unattached man who may offer the kindness that she
needs.

The following morning Stella is serene and happy. Williams compares the tranquility on her face to the narcotic
inner peace reflected on the images of Eastern idols—a very
fancy way of glorifying pregnancy. It recalls his habitual way
of equating sexual intercourse and religious rites. Stella explains to Blanche that the row wasn't serious, and she assures
her sister that she is not in anything that she wants to get out
of. Nevertheless, Blanche, living in her delusions, babbles on
about telephoning an old beau, Shep Huntleigh, now a rich
oil man and married, to plead for an escape. Blanche tries to
impress upon Stella the depths to which she has sunk in
her marriage, and unaware that Stan overhears her, she describes him as she sees him. She vents her contempt for a
man who eats, moves, and talks like an animal—an interesting
contrast to the playwright's paean describing Stan as a glorious male. Blanche calls him a sub-human, an ape, a survivor
of the stone age bearing raw meat home to his mate, a throw-
back after thousands of years of civilization. She pleads melodramatically with her sister not to return to the brutes, but
the plea is wasted on Stella who has a very different feeling
about Stan.[12]

Stan avenges these continuing insults as he begins to confront Blanche with veiled questions about a man named Shaw, the hotel "Flamingo," and the town of Laurel. Stan has obviously struck a sore spot, for Blanche later explains herself to her sister in half-truths. Her sentimentally expressed lines anticipated the lurid confession which comes later.[13] She explains that soft people have to seek the favor of hard ones, have to play a seductive role, be soft, resort to magic—to pay for a night's lodging. She explains that she's been running from one shelter to another trying to escape the storm, that she has depended on men's lovemaking to give her a sense of existence. To Stella, whose approach to sex is frank and simple, this talk is only morbid.

In spite of her pretty explanation, Blanche senses that her welcome is wearing thin and that her last refuge lies in marrying Mitch. Blanche—who flirted so indecently with Stan; who exhibited herself before the poker players; who called a strange young man collecting for papers a young Arabian prince and kissed him softly on the mouth—plays as prim and coy with Mitch as if she were sixteen and pure. At the same time, this southern gentlewoman sets the scene as if for a seduction—perhaps Williams' way of indicating that the lady is slightly confused. And then, a chance remark from Mitch about loneliness—there would seem to be more loneliness in the plays of Tennessee Williams than in all the lonely crowds of the entire United States—elicits her confession about her early marriage.

The boy she married, though not effeminate looking, had something different about him—a tenderness, an unmasculine softness, and nervousness. He had turned to her for help, she found out later, but she did not realize it. She describes him as struggling in quicksands and herself as slipping down with him. Then she found her husband with an older man in an unmistakable situation. Because of her expression of disgust, Allan shot himself. Blanche, desperate for a home, pours out this confession in a drunken, half-dazed condition. This recital is accompanied by sounds associated with the tragedy —a locomotive whistle and polka music—and suggests her present psychological state. Mitch takes her in his arms and she says, "Sometimes—there's God—so quickly!"[14]

On a September afternoon Stan returns armed with revenge against the sister-in-law who called him sub-human. He reports to Stella that Blanche is not the modest white lily she pretends to be but a liar; that she was so famous at the "Flamingo Hotel" that she had to turn in her room key; that she was fired from her teaching job because she became involved with a seventeen-year-old boy. He also tells Stella that he has reported his findings to Mitch, a war-time buddy and his best friend, and that he has bought a return bus ticket for Blanche—to Laurel. All this information is reported to Stella who refuses to believe; she is remembering the older sister she knew as a child. It would seem that Williams threw away a naturally dramatic scene when he did not allow Stan to face Blanche directly with her lies. It represents the culmination of his revenge and the reason he has needed to clear his home of the unwelcome visitor. The scene could logically have precipitated the insanity which is evident in the closing scene.

Aware that disaster is closing in on her, Blanche tells the angry Mitch how much she needs him, and her deteriorating mental condition is conveyed by the polka music. In another confession scene she spills out the full hideous story of her degradation: her intimacies with strangers after her poet-husband's death, the affair with the seventeen-year-old boy, and her dismissal from her teaching job. She needs Mitch, she says, as a refuge from the world. She tells him of the endless acquaintances she has had with the dying. Then she adds another unsavory chapter to her biography: not far from the plantation was an army training camp. On Saturday nights the soldiers would return drunk from town, stagger across her lawn, call her name, and she would slip out to answer their calls. Later the paddy wagon collected the boys and returned them to the camp. Such a biographical account, even with the widest possible stretch of the imagination, hardly seems to belong to the delicate, moth-like, mentally unbalanced Blanche Du Bois.

Mary McCarthy wrote that Williams "is addicted to the embroidering lie" in his characterization of Blanche. "But the thin, sleezy stuff of this character must be embellished by Mr. Williams with all sorts of decorations. It is not enough that she should be a drunkard (this is in itself plausible); she must also be a notorious libertine who has been run out of a small town like a prostitute, a thing absolutely inconceivable for a woman to whom conventionality is the end of existence." In addition to her "interesting biography," which Miss McCarthy finds incredible, "she must be a symbol of art and beauty, this poor flimsy creature to whom truth is mortal, who hates the feel of experience with a pathological aversion . . . she who has never spoken an honest word in her life is allowed, indeed encouraged, to present her life to the audience as a vocational decision, an artist's election of the beautiful, an act of supreme courage, the choice of the thorny way."[15]

Mitch has the same ingenuousness as that other gentleman caller, Jim O'Connor. He talks of his heavy perspiration and of his fight against getting soft in the belly, but he has a code of honor and a diffidence about women that make him a little awed before the seemingly aristocratic Blanche. When he discovers what she really is, he is not so much shocked as hurt—the extent of her degeneracy seems not to have destroyed his love for her. Nevertheless, he reproaches her as not clean enough to present to his mother. As the bashful boy turned rake, he makes tentative advances to the prim prostitute who effects his speedy exit by yelling, "Fire!" It may be that Williams' real interest in the scene was in the symbolic, decorative elements—a blind Mexican woman peddling tin flowers, the kind displayed at funerals, and calling out in Spanish that she is selling flowers for the dead. It is against the old woman's mournful cries that Blanche insists that she never lied in her heart. Her legacy has been death, all the hideous, ugly manifestations of the dying that she faced alone. The opposite of death, she says, is desire. Richard Asselineau reported that during the time he was writing *Streetcar* Williams fancied that he had cancer and it was the good friendship of Carson McCullers that helped him to recover from his moribund imagination. He said that it is not surprising, therefore, that the play is so permeated with ideas of death.[16]

Stan returns from the hospital to find a very much confused Blanche decked out in a crumpled, white satin evening dress and shabby silver slippers, and wearing a rhinestone tiara on her head. In her drunken exhilaration she talks of a Caribbean cruise with her one-time sweetheart, now a millionaire; she plays the role of the aristocrat, the woman of intelligence, refinement, and beautiful spirit and refers to Stan and Mitch as swine. Angered by her superiority and pretensions, Stan flatly tells her that it is all lies, conceit, and tricks. He tells her to face the facts, to look at herself and her rag-picker outfit, and to recall that she may think of herself as a queen but she has been swilling his liquor. The speech gives an interesting contrast between the blunt realist who sees the powder and perfume and the paper-lanterns over the light bulb for what they are and the romantic dreamer who lives in her imagination.

The rest of the scene is fever pitched. Blanche, like a cornered animal, makes desperate and pointless calls to Western Union. The state of Blanche's mind is pictorially suggested by the lurid reflections, grotesque and menacing shadows, that appear on the walls; the mood is intensified by off-stage noises symbolizing inhuman jungle cries. The excitement is heightened by offstage pantomime. Through the transparent back wall can be seen a portrayal of the struggle between a prostitute and a drunk, a scene interrupted by a policeman's whistle.

Stan emerges from the bedroom dressed in his silk wedding pajamas, grins at her deliberately, corners her. She tries to get away—in the background the "blue piano" begins pianissimo and increases to the roar of an approaching locomotive—erotic symbolism, perhaps, but a good stage trick. Stan moves stealthily toward her. Frantically she breaks a bottle and threatens to twist the broken end in his face. He springs toward her, snatches her wrist. Then come the beautifully loaded final lines of the scene: "Tiger—tiger! Drop that bottletop! Drop it! We've had this date with each other from the beginning! (*She moans. The bottle-top falls. She sinks to her knees. He picks up her inert figure and carries her to the bed. The hot trumpet and drum from the Four Deuces sound loudly.*)" Perhaps this situation is the culmination of Stan's "revenge," or only an incident in Blanche's decline into insanity, or perhaps this is a necessary culmination of many "come-on" scenes Blanche has played, suggesting an equivalent to the old dramatic cliché of the long-delayed rape. One thing is certain. It makes brilliant use of all the old theatrical devices. It has the quality of a big finale, loud brass and full percussion. It also has that unmistakable, profitable, high-keyed, emotional box-office appeal.

In the final scene which occurs weeks later, Blanche, now obviously deranged, dresses to leave as if she were going to dinner with Shep Huntleigh. She immediately recognizes that the doctor is not the man from Dallas; but, when he speaks softly to her and smiles, he is another suitor; she is won. The lurid reflections fade, the inhuman voices grow quiet. Clinging to his arm, she leaves quietly: "Whoever you are— I have always depended on the kindness of strangers." Broken by her excursion into Vieux Carré and its brutal realities, she escapes completely into her own mad world—and she ironically does so like an aristocrat.[17]

Blanche in a number of ways resembles Amanda—her pretentions to gentility, her legend about her former suitors, and her habit of lying to herself and to others. But also, as with Laura, Williams has been overzealous in his explanation of her pitiable condition. Too many factors have contributed to her insanity. Her frequent references to death-bed responsibilities, her girlhood marriage to a poet-homosexual, the fear of poverty and loneliness, her frustrated need for love and companionship could explain her condition. But on the other side, the nymphomatic tendencies which she seems to have inherited, her almost pathological care of her body, her pretenses to virtue and her exhibitionism at the slightest excuse, and her eagerness to tell her whole lurid story—all these add up to something theatrical and deliberately sensational. As if that were not enough, she is the last aristocrat of an old order, an intellectual of sorts, something of a poet by nature, and the easy mark for the insensitive. As Mary McCarthy has implied, there is no wonder that confusion arises about the playwright's intentions.

The controversy that has stormed over Tennessee Williams can be very well illustrated by the widely different reactions to this play. The drama critics recognized a distinctive talent, were intrigued by the scope and the complexity of the play, but were disturbed by the ambiguities and the pretensions. Brooks Atkinson in his review of the stage production found the play "almost unbearably tragic." The audience, he reported, came away "profoundly moved. . . . For they have been sitting all evening in the presence of truth, and that is a rare and wonderful experience." Without flatly stating that Blanche is closer to the theater than to life, he kindly said: "Since she is created on the stage as a distinct individual, experiences identical with hers can never be repeated. She and the play that is woven about her are unique."[18] Joseph Wood Krutch stated that, in spite of the sensational quality of the story, "the author's perceptions remain subtle and delicate and he is amazingly aware of nuances even in situations where nuance might seem to be inevitably obliterated by violence." He believed Williams' stories "enable him to communicate emotions which have special, personal significance," so that it can be taken for granted that "his plays will be immediately recognizable by their familiar themes and a sensibility as unique as that of a lyric poet."[19]

A Streetcar Named Desire won two major awards and became big business. A two-year run on Broadway and roadcompany productions for approximately three and a half million American theatergoers—and packed houses in London, Rome, Stockholm, Copenhagen, and Mexico City—afford solid proof that Tennessee Williams can reach a wide and varied audience. It became one of the best-known plays in the midtwentieth-century American repertory, partly because of its originality, but also because of the heated arguments over morality and art that it aroused.

IV *Summer and Smoke*

In a setting reminiscent of the broken walls and interiors of a Chirico painting, Williams mounts his "tone poem" and underscores his theme in *Summer and Smoke*[20] with two symbolic pieces: on the public square, a stone angel with wings lifted and hands cupped as for a drinking fountain; in the doctor's office, an anatomy chart. These are outward symbols of an inner conflict between soul and body, spirit and flesh; and these symbols in turn are represented not only by the southern gentlewoman Alma Winemiller, a too faithful adherent to Puritan negations and the daughter of an Episcopalian minister, but also by a virile young doctor, John Buchanan, Jr. The play is set in the years before 1916.

Alma is a delicate blue-stocking whose responsibilities

require thankless care of a peevish mother and help to her father, a minister in the Puritan tradition. She has mannerisms of refinement such as a broad Oxford "A," a self-conscious nervousness when she sings, and a habit of indulging in verbal affectations. Above all, she is a lady. Williams describes her as having gestures and mannerisms that are exaggerated but graceful; she is a lady more at home in eighteenth-century France than in twentieth-century Mississippi where she would be accused of snobbishness and affectation.

Part of her hysteria arises from her frustrated love for young doctor John Buchanan, who seems to feel respect for her but little else. She rebukes him for his sensual indulgence and his lack of spiritual depth. In a rather literary pretentiousness she likens a nobler kind of satisfaction than his to a Gothic cathedral. Giving voice to her own soul, symbolized in her name, she expresses the idea that man is continually aspiring to higher things, beyond the limits of human existence. This sincere expression of man's reaching for perfection, a theme that hovers around the edges of a number of Williams' plays, seems to be the essential quality of the character of Alma Winemiller. Having expressed herself, she wistfully asks John if he does not want a lady for his wife and the mother of his children, but he has other ideas of connubial felicity.

John Buchanan, another beautiful body, whom Williams calls a Promethean figure in a stagnant southern town, maintains his heroic freshness in spite of his dissipations. Amused and bored by Alma's rather prissy and tentative approaches, he prefers Rosa Gonzales, the daughter of the Mexican who owns the Moon Lake gambling casino. A Williams' original, Rosa conveys a mysterious atmosphere like a wind on the palmettos and is dressed in garish finery, feathers, and flashy jewelry. She is a colorful figure, and might be Mexican— or Negro, if the playwright had dared. When John protests that his dusky mistress can never make love without scratching or biting, she explains that she is trying to "hold him," that she needs him to raise herself from the sordid life in which she grew up.

Rosa gives an account of her life in a one-room house with a dirt floor and of the five people, three geese, and a game-cock who lived there. Her account of her papa's love-making, recited to guitar accompaniment, is the kind of anecdote which Williams might have told at his Greenwich Village spots before he acquired his larger audiences. The account adds nothing to the play.

In her attempt to prevent John's complete involvement with the Mexican glamor girl, Alma intrudes; and, in a somewhat illogical sequence, she causes John's father's death, The continued argument of John and Alma over the spiritual and physical life is climaxed in an anatomy lecture, a rather awkward statement injected into a play of sometimes beautifully easy, natural dialogue. John defends his emphasis upon the physical side of life: "Now listen here to the anatomy lecture! This upper story's the brain which is hungry for something called truth and doesn't get much but keeps on feeling hungry! This middle's the belly which is hungry for food. This part down here is the sex which is hungry for love because it is sometimes lonesome. I've fed all three, as much of all three as I could or as much as I wanted—You've fed none—nothing. Well—maybe your belly a little—watery subsistence—But love or truth, nothing but—nothing but hand-me-down notions!—attitudes!—poses! (*He releases her.*) Now you can go. The anatomy lecture is over." When John confesses later that he never could have taken her,[21] Alma learns what his feeling for her has been: "I'm more afraid of your soul than you're afraid of my body. You'd have been as safe as the angel of the fountain—because I wouldn't feel *decent* enough to touch you."

In another illogical twist John, after the murder of his father, suddenly returns to medicine and finishes his father's research problem; in a single sentence he stamps out the fever and gets himself covered with glory. In still another sudden reversal—a change involving the whole structure of the play but hardly more than suggested—Alma and John exchange character positions; she becomes the advocate of the physical life; he, of the spiritual. It is a strange and violent kind of conversion that is neither motivated nor explained in terms of action; it is merely talked about in rather precious, symbolic terms. John, commenting about their infrequent meetings, says that each was trying to find in the other person that something he needed, neither one of them knowing quite what it was. In a symbolic gesture John strikes a match and they both stare at it with mixed undertsanding. This simple symbolic act inspires lines that articulate what might be the heart of the play; it is the kind of dialogue that needs to be extended—the idea underscored and re-peated.

JOHN: You couldn't name it and I couldn't recognize it. I thought it was just a Puritanical ice that glittered like flame. But now I believe that it *was* flame, mistaken for ice. I still don't understand it, but I know it was there, just as I know that your eyes and your voice are the two most beautiful things I've ever known—and also the warm-est, although they don't seem to be set in your body at all. . . .

ALMA: You talk as if my body had ceased to exist for you, John, in spite of the fact that you've just counted my pulse. Yes, that's it! You tried to avoid it, but you've told me plainly. The tables have turned, yes, the tables have turned with a vengeance! You've come around to my way of thinking and I to yours like two people exchanging a call on each other at the same time, and each finding the other one gone out, the door locked against him and no one to answer the bell! (*She laughs.*) I came here to tell you that being a gentleman doesn't seem so important to me any more, but you're telling me I've got to remain a lady. (*She laughs rather violently.*) The tables have turned with a vengeance!

The way this idea is projected into action, however, does not do justice either to the idea or the characters. However, Brooks Atkinson, noting in this play another variation of a familiar theme, wrote that again the insight to character is intensely perceptive. He pointed out that the play is slight in content, written in brief scenes, for a few characters. At-kinson called Williams "a writer of superb grace and allusive-ness" who is more concerned with the sound of ideas than their meaning.[22] It is for these reasons, perhaps, that the play collapses under analysis. For instance, the play closes on an improbable and grotesque note as John marries Nellie, the girl who does not need an anatomy lesson; and Alma takes up with a traveling salesman she meets at the stone fountain—the first, apparently, of her bedroom adventures. Alma has rejected the purity and refinement which kept John at a distance; flesh being stronger than the spirit, she seems to have been completely converted by the anatomy lecture. If the earlier statements about man's reaching for the stars are to be taken seriously, this abrupt shift at the end would seem to be closer to the theater than to life.

There are several striking minor characters: Mrs. Winemiller, senile and mean, with a childish passion for fancy hats and ice-cream cones; the Reverend Winemiller, harried by this childish wife and a daughter he cannot understand; Roger Doremus, Alma's effeminate suitor and a participant in the literary meeting of the pseudo-intellectuals; Mrs. Bassett, the nosey, right-thinking neighbor who forces Alma to report young John's riotous living; Nellie, the giggling teen-ager whose mother is too well known in the town; and a few incidental figures such as the drunken Gonzales, who is dragged in to despatch the old doctor—and to save the plot.

Summer and Smoke was obviously resurrected from the author's trunk after the success of *The Glass Menagerie* and *A Streetcar Named Desire*. Harold Clurman observed that "the naturalistic details of portraiture in 'Streetcar' are so right that the audience accepts and enjoys them on their own terms whether or not they follow the author's ideological intention, which, to begin with, is intuitive rather than analytic. In 'Summer and Smoke' so much time is given to a conscious exposition of theme that Williams loses the specific sense of his people."[23] Joseph Wood Krutch described the play as "more like the fable or allegory" and the characters as "a bit more suggestive of the protagonists in some old morality play."[24] The playwright often allows himself to be distracted from his main theme either by time-consuming scenes, by irrelevant action, or by symbols which are sometimes a bit obvious. For instance, the ladies' literary club uses up precious time. In the scene in which John is trying to discover Alma's trouble, a scene which has much to do about buttons on a blouse, the main point is dissipated. A play like this one—obviously directed to the Broadway market and necessarily an expensive production—calls attention to the shameful and tragic absence of small theaters where a playwright might be able to write honestly—and survive.

CHAPTER 4

Southern Wenches

I *No Inhibitions*

ANOTHER GROUP OF PLAYS concerns a very differ-ent type of southern woman. Unlike the frustrated and rather excessively refined lady of the decadent aristo-crats, she is full-bodied—an uninhibited matron who seems to represent the conviction that lovemaking is the major rea-son for existence. Serafina della Rose and her daughter in *The Rose Tattoo,* Margaret in *Cat on a Hot Tin Roof,* and Baby Doll in the film script of that name belong to this group. It is a neat question whether this girl is really from the South or whether, like the primitive and glamorized heroes, she is not the feminine counterpart of the D. H. Lawrence sexually contented male. One thing is sure, perhaps partly because of the nature of these women: the main line of action in each of these plays leads directly to the big double bed. There is no artificial standard to thwart the design, for none of these women has been blighted by the outmoded proprieties of a Victorian culture or by the bri-dling restrictions of a southern Puritanism. Each of these healthy women seems to know instinctively that sex is the only valid expression of life; and, without having to read Sigmund Freud, she understands perfectly that the opposite of passion is death.

These southern goddesses of love have much in common with the sister of Blanche, Stella Du Bois of *Streetcar* who escaped the many dyings at "Belle Rêve" to marry the bellowing Stanley Kowalski. Although he beats her when he gets drunk, his lovemaking is evidently delicious balm for the bruises. A pregnant woman, she is contented, forgiving, at peace with the world. In *Summer and Smoke* Nellie Ewell, who escaped an Episcopalian training in her childhood and is the daughter of a good-time mother and herself a "natural" adolescent of the same type, is also paired off with the glamorous hero, John Buchanan. In the same play Rosa Gonzales, the romantically garish daughter of the Mexican casino proprietor, satisfies the young doctor before he becomes "spiritual" and seems to represent the same thesis— except that she has achieved professional status. In the amusing short story "The Yellow Bird," an Alma Tutwiler beats the frustration out of her Episcopalian heritage and devotes her life to men. Unlike Blanche Du Bois and Alma Winemiller, she discards all notions of gentility; but evidently, like other characters of her persuasion, she retains the innocent look of a fresh May morning.

Although Tennessee Williams describes Serafina della Rose and her daughter in *The Rose Tattoo* as Sicilians, they have much in common with Stella Du Bois; but they are much more vocal about their dedication to physical passion. Maggie, the Cat in *Cat on a Hot Tin Roof*, is not only vocal but determined; she is a strong-minded woman mated with a cool, indifferent husband. Baby Doll Meighan, of the film play, *Baby Doll*—a variation of the dumb blonde of *Twenty-Seven Wagons Full of Cotton*, but more attractive—is Williams' comedy version of the willing but untutored wench who needs only to be awakened—and the dramatist cooperatively obliges with a variant of his already successful, virile hero.

II *The Rose Tattoo*

In *The Rose Tattoo*,[1] its hymn of praise to love-making is sung by a Sicilian mother who finds as much beauty in bed as she does in religion—a refrain most familiar to the followers of Williams but one suitable not only for herself but her daughter as well. The playwright transplanted a newly acquired enthusiasm for Italy and set his play in a village on the Gulf Coast between New Orleans and Mobile where Sicilians had collected. Although the mother and the daughter may have been inspired by Tennessee Williams' sojourn in Italy and although the role of Serafina was written with Anna Magnani in mind, these women are repetitions of his idea of the Cavalier tradition—which, according to the play-wright, means dedication to the flesh.

When Serafina della Rose's husband dies, she goes into a three-year, slatternly decline; fights rumors that her amorous mate was unfaithful; isolates herself because of a fanatic distrust of men; suddenly discovers that her husband really was not true; goes to bed with another truckdriver who reminds her of her dead mate; and, unable to justify her irregular conduct, sends her passionate daughter off to a hotel room with a sailor.

This rather slender line of action is embellished with considerable "romantic" overtones, with musical effects, and with as many erotic symbols as Williams could crowd into one play. There is some rather beautiful dialogue; but the play also has some of the usual rhetoric and regrettably adolescent vulgarity; characters who appear briefly when needed; and a rather large number of processions, introduced seemingly, when action or "poetry" failed to carry the momentum or excitement. Much of the play is again built around memory sequences. The full-bodied Serafina, whose image of Rosario is a lyrical tribute to his virility, is contrasted to man-crazy women who will settle for boys or bald-pated, pot-bellied men. Much to the amusement of the late George Jean Nathan—who noticed that Williams, for all his preoccupation with sex, was a bit short on his biology—the playwright has Serafina say that from their marriage night until the day he died, they never skipped a night of love. She has even been able to keep count: four thousand-three hundred-and eighty nights of lovemaking.

Serafina is "a rich and lyrical portrait of an Italian peasant, but she is also an embodiment of a credo, the affirmation of sex as the root feeling of a complete existence."[2] She is deeply religious, but not entirely in the way the priest would like. Passionately devoted to her beautiful daughter, she is also unreasonable about her; and she is so grief-stricken over the death of her husband that she retreats with her memory of him into a world of her own. The scenes depicting the inconsolable grief of the widow, although her late husband was not all she believed, are serious material and worthy of serious interpretation. Williams almost achieves the depth and tone of this situation in the earlier scenes. Serafina, in her suffering and in her delusion, might have been a character of considerable stature if the playwright had not intruded.

Williams introduces an incredible character with Estelle Hohengarten, an aggressive stringy blonde and gangland doxy, who is supposed to have seduced the amorous Rosario. Williams also brings in, for contrast to his attractive widow, two female nit-wits, Flora and Bessie, who jeer at the widow for being a "female ostrich" and who give her the first hint of her husband's infidelity. These two grotesques are on their way to the American Legion convention in New Orleans where they hope to pick up stray men. By way of comment about the usual American marital relationships, Serafina says: "They make the life without glory. Instead of the heart they got the deep-freeze in the house. The men, they don't feel no glory, not in the house with them women; they go to the bars, fight in them, get drunk, get fat, put horns on the women because the women don't give them the love with its glory.—I did, I give him the glory. To me the big bed was beautiful like a religion. Now I lie on it with dreams, with memories only!"

The tone of the play changes completely with the introduction of another truckdriver, Alvaro Mangiacavallo (Alvaro Eat-a-Horse), a man with a body like that of Serafina's husband but with the face of a clown—a clown with big ears. But just before he enters, there is a curious scene, obviously representing Williams' idea of the business world. Accompanied by music satiric in tone, a vulgar, cheap-talking salesman accosts Serafina. He is red-faced, a fat man in a seersucker suit heavily stained under the arms. Obviously any ordinary man could enter after that. Nevertheless, conquering hero Alvaro is given special treatment. The sound of timpani, which begins pianissimo when his voice is first heard, rises to a thrilling climax as he meets Serafina. A twenty-five-year old Italian—for again the heroine is a much older woman—Alvaro is supposed to be as handsome as a young bull. The radiant male has only changed nationality. Henry Popkin has noted that Williams uses foreign names to symbolize characters who are alive in contrast to the sexually unexciting Anglo-Saxons. Vicarro, the avenging representative of "life" is followed by other Italians: Myra in *Battle of Angels;* Serafina and the new truckdriver, Alvaro, in *The Rose Tattoo.* There is Stanley Kowalski in *Streetcar,* and Dr. Kukrowicz, another noble Pole, in *Suddenly Last Summer,* to name a few.[3]

In the scramble that follows Alvaro's entrance, the salesman's article explodes in Serafina's face. Alvaro, cursing the traveler for crowding him off the highway, is called macaroni, spaghetti, and greaseball. The salesman adds insult to humiliation by kicking him in the stomach. Alvaro starts crying like an injured child; Serafina joins in a wail; and, after a few tentative conversational starts, these adult children are on their way to love. Both have had their troubles, and confidences flow. Williams sentimentally compares their growing, fumbling intimacy to lonely children making their tentative acquaintance. Alvaro talks of his dependents and his matrimonial plans—and his dream bride is as sumptuous as Serafina. She talks of her husband, retells her legend of the rose that appeared on her breast, and furtively eyes this new hero with the heavy torso. After the curious, rather arty introduction involving the salesman, the scene becomes natural and effective—one of the best, really natural comedy scenes that Williams has written in spite of bursts of rhetoric that he could not resist. For instance, Alvaro, who since his entrance has lost his job—by telephone, of course—can offer only his heart: "Love and affection!—in a world that is lonely—and cold!" This may be a theme line of the play—because of the way it is pontificated.

In the scene that follows, Williams reveals a growing technique in developing emotional excitement. The retreat to the big double bed is inevitable. The only deterrent to the widow's immediate exit is her stubborn loyalty to her dead husband; but the newly shaven, newly scented trucker is a powerful temptation. When Alvaro phones Estelle Hohengarten, her strident voice, loud and clear, dispels all the widow's doubts about Rosario's infidelity; Serafina flings the sacred ashes to the floor and with them her three-year loyalty. Williams, in spite of his contempt for the realistic mode, must find it a bit difficult to justify her reaction to the telephone call as a reasonable way of settling Serafina's problem; perhaps, since the play is "romantic," no sequence needs to be logical.[4] In any case, the three-year, sex tormented widow discards the memory of the man of the roses, turns out the lights, and directs Alvaro how to leave and return secretly so that the neighbors will not suspect. The erotic symbols pile up thick and fast: there is the goat bleating an accompaniment, a squawking parrot, harsh bird cries, a shriek of Negro laughter in the distance while in the moonlight the two innocents continue their "conversation."

The next scene at daybreak pictures daughter Rosa returning from the high school picnic with her sailor boy, Jack Hunter, two other grave innocent children—as they are described.[5] When Rosa pleads for him to take her, Jack has to fight not only his own urgency but her insistence and his promise to Serafina to protect her virtue. To the accompaniment of a rooster's crowing, Rosa pleads forlornly; "No, but —I think it could just happen once, and if it don't happen that time, it never can—later. . . . (*A rooster crows. They face each other sadly and quietly.*) You don't need to be very old to understand how it works out. One time, one time, only once, it could be—God!—to remember.—Other times? Yes—they'd be something.—But only once, God—to remember. . . ." The "innocent" Rosa asks about hotel rooms; her worried young man asks: "You want to buy me a ten-year stretch in the brig?"

Against this scene is played the one in the house with Serafina's long sighs, and later a long-drawn cry, "Ohhhh—Rosario." The theater-wise playwright has Rosa make comments like, "Oh! That's Mama dreaming about my father," or "She wanted me not to have what she's dreaming about," or "Listen to her making love in her sleep! Is that what she wants me to do, just—*dream* about it?" There are times when Williams keeps the image mysterious and vague, and there are other times when he works rather hard to underscore the obvious.[6]

Rosa at fifteen is reported to be so good a student that she was awarded "The Digest of Knowledge" at graduation even though she didn't show up for the final examinations. She is also described as a "sweet and refined young girl" who is so beautiful that even her own mother is overwhelmed by her beauty. Jack's praise seems to have evoked this unusual radiance, just as his attention at the school dance opened for her the whole world of boys. Seemingly it is she that must teach him that little word, "*bacio*"; and, when she kisses him desperately, "*he forcibly removes her face from his.*" Considering Serafina's warm-blooded Sicilian ideas about men, it is to be expected that she would lock up her daughter and her clothes as well, as she did early in the play. But it is a Williams' touch to have the girl described as standing nude at the window, and it was a Pollyanna touch to have her cut her wrist only enough to bloody a handkerchief slightly —a loving memento for Jack.

Williams' portrait of these two ardent Italians and their lovers is contrasted to middle-aged adolescents of arrested development and other unattractive women—accompanied, of course, by his usual theatrical devices. A spinsterish high school teacher, an old herb peddler, a forbidding goat woman, and mocking neighbors like a swarm of attacking birds—biting, satiric vignettes—all make fleeting appearances when needed. The healthy normal side of female life seems to be represented by the happy mothers and their happy children. The Strega, a wild, grey-headed, hairy-legged woman, seems to evoke the superstitions of these simple people. A black goat crashes the scene and bleats whenever the sexual theme needs to be emphasized. Among other stage noises, the cackles of women suggest the conventional rejection of Serafina's idea of the good, full life; there is a witch cackle when the mother forces the sailor boy to kneel and vow to keep Rosa's virtue, a scene in itself genuine.

When Williams seems to have trouble with the plot or needs to break up an extended conversation, he sometimes resorts to a scene of wild commotion that may give symbolic weight to the scene. For instance, in the first courtship scene between Alvaro and Serafina a goat breaks loose, undoubtedly to symbolize the increasing compulsion in the relationship. There is so much crazed exultation that Serafina, suspecting the evil eye of the Strega, retreats to the Madonna for protection. Despite all the "souped-up" sexual excitement there is considerable comedy in the scene. The goat is running madly about the house. Alvaro runs out and joins the chase. A little boy beats two tin lids together. Wild cries of the children mingle with the goat's bleating. But what is happening to Serafina inside the house suggests an animal in heat. Standing half-way between the shutters and the protecting Madonna, she furiously imitates the bleating goat, and her face becomes distorted with desire. This is a not uncommon scene of confusion—again "something wild," frankly theatrical, and obviously symbolic.[7]

Williams has worked the erotic rose symbol into the play with many variations and repetitions. Serafina refused to buy powders of the ancient herb peddler Assunta, considering that an insult to Rosario. She tells of the night she woke with a pain on her breast and discovered the rose of her husband. She knew that she had conceived. It is later spitefully reported that Rosario had a rose tattooed on his chest and that his stringy mistress acquired one too. Serafina calls her dead husband "a rose of a man," and, seemingly unaware of the significance, gives to the new trucker-about-to-be-lover the rose silk shirt ordered by her dead husband's mistress and never collected. It is probably for Williams her symbolic encouragement to the new male; and also symbolically the playwright has Alvaro make much of the time of roses as the time of love. When Serafina laments that "the time of roses" is over for her, Alvaro assures her that not only for her but for the whole audience and everyone it is always a "time of roses"—and this may be Williams' way of giving his play a cosmic significance. Before the play closes, Serafina again feels the burning pain and ecstatically shouts Williams' paean to pregnancy.

Unsure of what he wanted to say and apparently wanting to appeal to various tastes, Williams dissipated his energy. What might have been a simply told, sensitive, poetic drama has been overlaid with a tragic mood and pathos; with comedy and low farce; with rhetorical outbursts; and, at times, even with obscenity. Williams also obscured his very distinctive talent for characterization with theatrical devices that do not add to his stature. He is at his best when he continues in the vein of his early work, and he does greatest injustice to himself when he becomes the self-conscious artist who sacrifices characterizations for symbols.

III *Cat on a Hot Tin Roof*

Cat on a Hot Tin Roof[8] bears some resemblance to the story "Three Players of a Summer Game,"[9] a study of the deterioration of Brick Pollitt and the increasingly mannish domination of his wife, Margaret. In the play it takes Margaret the Cat three acts to get Brick, her long-drinking husband, into bed with her; and she achieves this ambition only by destroying his liquor supply and setting her own conditions. Margaret's father-in-law, Big Daddy, jubilant over the phony report that he does not have cancer, dreams about the women he'll take; but, soon wracked with pain, he succumbs to the ministrations of the wife he detests. Gooper, his older son and another of Williams' caricatures of businessmen, has fathered out of a commonplace female five noisy brats, and another is on the way; he connives to get his hands on the family wealth. Whether these characters grew out of the playwright's observations in the South or whether they were born of his own disgust and sympathy remains an interesting question. Behind this complex of sensationalism lies the domestic problem of communication: the subtle and often abrasive antagonisms within a family that lock various members inside their own shells and prevent them from knowing one another. There is much talk of finding the truth that motivates people's actions—an insight that might explain the tragic waste or unhappiness of their lives.

Maggie the Cat, like some of Strindberg's women, is of the stronger sex; but she is a bit more attractive than those of the Swede. She does not talk like a southern gentlewoman but like a mid-twentieth-century modern without inhibitions. Deeply in love with her husband in spite of his distaste for her, she feels certain that he will again see her as other men do. She is a plucky little outsider in a family that is concerned only with whether or not she breeds an heir to the estate. Of the strange menagerie in this plantation house she is most closely akin to Big Daddy—as frankly sensual and as high-strung and vital; it is a pity there is no scene between them. She is the one character in the play who seems unafraid to tell the truth, the only one who isn't living behind the protective covering of a lie. She is discarded by her husband for speaking out—for exposing the falsehood that seems to have made his life tolerable. With the same candor, she aggressively works to keep for herself and Brick a fair proportion of the inheritance because she has known what it is to be desperately poor. It is her lie about pregnancy that seems finally to have penetrated her husband's thick consciousness—or was it merely his awareness that she controlled his liquor supply? The two qualities in Maggie which appear in other women characters of Williams are her frankly sensual nature and a cunning mercenary drive. She is a lively character indeed.

The relationship between husband and wife is expressed somewhat symbolically:

> MARGARET: *I feel all the time like a cat on a hot tin roof!*
> BRICK: Then jump off the roof, jump off it, cats jump off roofs and land on their four feet uninjured!
> MARGARET: Oh, yes!
> BRICK: Do it!—fo' God's sake, do it. . .
> MARGARET: Do what?
> BRICK: Take a lover!
> MARGARET: I can't see a man but you! Even with my eyes closed. . .

Maggie has other ideas about their marriage; she is sure that their sex life, cut off so abruptly before its natural time, will revive if Brick will ever look at her as other men do. She is supposed to move her hands slowly over her breasts and hips and speak in a child's voice—sexual excitement and innocent childhood again—and this erotic pose, according to the playwright, should be of such intensity that she can grip the audience until the first intermission. This would seem to be putting considerable pressure on both sides of the curtain.

The theme of homosexuality, introduced early, is played upon throughout the entire action. The marriage break came when Margaret told Brick the truth about his relations with Skipper, a college friend too close to the man she married. Then comes one of the most curious "confessions": she and Skipper made love together so that both of them could feel closer to Brick, who expects too much of people who love him. Maggie seems really to be in love with Brick, whom she calls a son-of-a-bitch and "an ass-aching Puritan" as well as a godlike being. If there is any stature whatsoever in his character, it exists in the mind of his wife whom he has rejected. When Maggie had forced Skipper to admit to homosexuality, he had turned first to liquor and drugs and then to suicide.

Brick, holding his wife responsible for his death, looks at her with contempt—and keeps on drinking.[10]

As another part of "the truth," Maggie tries to explain to the angry Brick that she understands the relationship between the two men. She compares it to the homosexual—a word that she and the playwright very carefully avoid—attachment in the Greek legends as being ideal and beautiful. According to her account, the relationship was beautiful because Brick is such a god-like being, a quality that is hardly evident in this cool, detached, "good looking" young man. When Brick accuses her of naming his pure friendship with Skipper as something dirty, she insists that any impurity was on Skipper's side. The discussion of the homosexual relationship in the "mysterious" overtones that Williams employs, Brick's resentment over its being brought out into the open, and Margaret's understanding and almost lyrical approval of a relationship more precious than the normal—approximately this same treatment of the subject is repeated in the second act between Brick and Big Daddy.

The second narrative element involves the impending death of Big Daddy from cancer; and since he has not made a will, this sharpens the rivalry between Maggie and the grotesques, Gooper and Mae, who are everlastingly descending on the house with their five noisy brats. The Gooper clan hopes to settle Brick in "Rainbow Hill," the refuge for alcoholics—and themselves on the plantation. Since the inheritance seems to rest on progeny, the rivalry between the fertile Mae and the childless Maggie is bitter and occasionally comic. Maggie, who knows what it is to be desperately poor and who also realizes that money is needed to buy her husband's liquor—daintily but realistically called "Echo Springs" —has no intention of being frozen out of the estate.

There is never a doubt that Brick is the favorite son of Big Mamma who blames Maggie for not having children. Pointing to the big double bed which dominates the scene, she says bluntly that it is in bed that marriages are made or broken, an ironic comment in view of Big Daddy's distaste for her. Simple-minded, garrulous and coarse, and given to "horseplay," she is described as a short, stout woman of sixty years and a hundred and seventy pounds, who is as tense as a Japanese wrestler. And when Williams calls a woman tense, that is the end of her. She appears overdressed and heavily jeweled as if she were the showcase of her husband's millions. Devoted to Big Daddy in her simple-minded way, she rejoices in the report that he does not have cancer but a slight indisposition called "a spastic colon," a phrase she reels off repeatedly as if she—or the playwright—were getting a "kick" out of it.

Big Daddy, who appears only in the second act, attempts a father-son talk with Brick; and the attempt at communication harshly rips from each man his own protective covering of lies. Big Daddy's only devotions have been the plantation and his son Brick with whom he has never been able to talk. The seeming compatibility between the two, a vital produc-tive father and an effeminate alcoholic son, sometimes seems to rest entirely on a love of four-letter words. The father's great bounding love of life, restored now by the doctor's lie, and his vitality that built a twenty-eight thousand acre plantation and stashed away ten millions besides, now make him dream of making up for what he lost by scruples and convention—pleasure with women, and lots of it. It was the shadow of death, he says, that made him realize how he had wasted his virility on Big Mama, whom he had never liked. When he tries to find out why Brick throws away his life in drink—life, that most precious thing that Big Daddy cannot buy with all his millions—Brick explains that it is because of mendacity: lies and liars, nothing definite, no identifiable person, no definite thing, just a vague, general, overwhelming disgust. The god-like Brick prefers to keep it "mysterious."

Big Daddy's answer is a guffaw: "What do you know about this mendacity thing? Hell! I could write a book on it! . . . and still not cover the subject. . . . Having to pretend stuff you don't think or feel or have any idea of? Having for in-stance to act like I care for Big Mama!—I haven't been able to stand the sight, sound, or smell of that woman for forty years now!—even when I *laid* her! . . . Pretend to love that son of a bitch of a Gooper and his wife and those five same screechers out there like parrots in a jungle? Jesus! Can't stand to look at 'em! Church!—it bores the Bejesus out of me but I go!—I go an' sit there and listen to the fool preacher! —Elks!—Masons!—Rotary!—*crap!* . . . *I've* lived with mendacity!—Why can't *you* live with it? Hell, you've *got* to live with it, there's nothing *else* to *live* with except mendacity, is there?"

When Brick answers that he can avoid mendacity in alcohol, Big Daddy again explodes into four-letter vituperation and asks why he should support a worthless bottle-happy drunk. Brick, quite indifferent to all this embroidered explosive, swirls the drink in his glass and waits for the click in the head. Big Daddy, trying to get at the root cause of this favorite son's deterioration, is frustrated. Neither man is honest with the other, and something is not clearly brought into the open. Then Big Daddy casually mentions that his son had started drinking when his friend Skipper died and that Gooper and Mae had suggested that there had been something not exactly normal in the friendship. He thus voices the same suspicion the expression of which has shattered Brick's marriage with Maggie.

This is the dramatic point in the play—one that needs to be more fully spelled out if the dramatist is playing fair with the audience and not being deliberately "mysterious." But Williams resorts to a vague and somewhat precious explanation.[11] He speaks of the way in which the two men approach the forbidden topic; for Big Daddy it is timid and painful, for Brick it is violent. If it existed, both men would have had to deny it to "keep face." Williams writes as if he himself did not know the physical and moral condition of his hero and the reason for his collapse; he speaks in terms of "if" and "may be." He professes not to hope for the solution of this one man's psychological problem. He says that what he is trying to do is to catch the momentary and electric clash of human beings caught in a moment of crisis. The playwright uses the word "common" as if this kind of crisis were a universal and frequent occurrence—which it is not.[12] He then goes on to say that there should be an element of mystery in every dramatic characterization because there is that element in life. At the conclusion of this extensive paragraph of exposition which dodges the issue, Williams says that a playwright should neither be obscure nor too facile in his definitions.

Brick erupts into an almost voluble hysteria following Big Daddy's question. He is shocked that his father thought him a "queer" and that he suspected illicit relations with Skipper. Big Daddy had proved it earlier, however, when he had put Brick and Maggie in the room where the old homosexuals, former owners of the plantation, had slept and died. When Big Daddy assures his son that nothing can shock a man who has returned as from the dead and that he has grown as much tolerance as cotton, Brick dramatically mouths his own defense. He wonders why exceptional friendship between men can not be thought of as decent, why they must be called fairies. He curses Gooper and Mae for their talk and lies, and Maggie for her destruction of what he calls something clean, something better than normal, a very true and rare friendship.

Then Big Daddy asks why, if—as Brick says—the relationship was so very rare and so very pure, both Skipper and Brick cracked up. Williams then has Brick face the audience, standing as if he were a tragic figure, to give his version of the "truth." He recounts the story of Skipper, Maggie, and himself; he places the blame, however, for the friend's death on Maggie. Big Daddy ridicules this preposterous story, accusing his son of lying to himself. He says candidly that Brick drinks continually because he is trying to obliterate his disgust with himself. He tells his son that all the talk about mendacity is only a disguise to cover up his disgust with himself.

Big Daddy has apparently told the truth and struck a sore point. Then Brick, who has been described as being noble as a Greek god, whose ideals of perfection make life difficult for his friends—according to Maggie—gets his revenge in a despicable, spiteful way. He faces Big Daddy with the lie the doctors have been telling him to make his last days endurable—to cover up the truth about cancer. He urges him to leave the twenty-eight thousand acres to Gooper and Mae, his idea of an ironic joke, because they appear to him another illustration of a world of mendacity. And just as casually and rottenly as he dispenses with the estate, he tells his father that the basis of friendship is truth telling. The second act closes with Big Daddy's shocked reaction to his own true condition and his cursing of all liars. And to the analytic viewer or reader, there is very little reason to call Brick a tragic figure. He has nobility only in Maggie's imagination;

his treatment of her and his father is like that of a small peevish boy striking back. When Joseph Wood Krutch says that there is no tragic nobility in the plays of Williams— only an "unsavory mess"—he could well be referring to Brick Pollitt.

The third act of *Cat* is a poor thing after the dynamic father-son, truth-telling scene. Some of the padding is given to the Reverend Tooker, another of Williams' inconsequential reverends who is described as "all hawk and no spit." Babbling about memorial windows and air-conditioned churches and interrupting the father-son conversation by asking for the toilet, he makes a jittery exit at the moment a minister is needed, when Big Mama staggers from the truth about her dying husband. More emphasis is given to Gooper and Mae, who are obviously eager for Big Daddy's death—the sooner it comes, the more profitable for them if their plan operates. But Big Mama orders Gooper to put away the inheritance documents before she tears them up. She sentimentalizes over her drunken son who is just about to achieve the click he has been waiting for since the first-act curtain went up; she—or Williams for her—sees in him the little boy coming home from play, all sweaty and glowing and tired.

This charming son with his charming detachment drops ice cubes into his glass as carefully as a chemist works out a formula. When Big Mama tells him that his father dreams of a grandson like Brick, it is not the son who answers but Maggie. It is the quickest lie in the play; it is mendacity dramatized: she announces that she and Brick are going to have a child. The comic hullabaloo that follows, the bawdy family row over her pretended pregnancy, makes curious contrast to the offstage cries of agony from Big Daddy and to the indifference of Brick who smiles to himself. He has achieved what he has been waiting for—the click in the head. In the little argument about going to bed, Maggie wins by cutting off the liquor supply and by asserting her superiority. She has become the stronger of the two since Brick has taken to drink, and she now feels that she can love him even more. In the concluding scene, one that combines death and sex, Big Mama desperately calls for help to relieve Big Daddy's torment; and Margaret tells Brick that she will bring back the liquor when they make the lie come true—her pregnancy. Williams' tribute to weakness comes in Margaret's last line: "Oh, you weak people, you weak, beautiful people—who give up.—What you want is someone to—take hold of you.—Gently, gently, with love! And——"

Williams wrote a third act for the Broadway production at the suggestion of his director, Elia Kazan,[13] who had a number of reservations: he felt that Big Daddy was too important a character to be abandoned after the second act; that Brick should indicate some change after his father's exposé; and that Margaret should be made a more sympathetic character. Williams had fallen in love with his own Maggie and so agreed to that suggestion but he did not want Big Daddy to overshadow Brick: "I didn't want Big Daddy to reappear in Act Three and I felt that the moral paralysis of Brick was a root thing in his tragedy."

The Broadway version of the third act is hardly an improvement. When asked why Big Daddy shouted "liars," Brick answered that he did not lie to his father but only to himself—the nearest approach to a clear-cut statement that Williams allows his character to make. Brick agrees that perhaps it is time for him to be taken to the asylum for alcoholics. Gooper and Mae are even more despicable in their determination to disclose the clinical report about Big Daddy. There is an even more pronounced squabbling over the estate and more noisy interruptions by Gooper's monsters—comparable to the "rhubarb" chase scenes that Williams makes use of so often. Big Daddy enters to tell an old story about a female elephant in heat; and he does so with so much emphasis on his way of telling it—lest he lose one precious vulgar overtone—that it had to be deleted to avoid trouble with the law. Maggie announces her pregnancy as a birthday present to Big Daddy. When the row over that lie breaks out, Brick rises to Maggie's defense and finally expresses admiration for her—the only positive stand he takes in the play: his defense of a lie. Her last speech is an even more romantic eulogy to what she—or Williams—calls beautiful weakness.

There can be little quarrel about Williams' perceptiveness; but, again, he obscures his good characterizations with posturing and some very cloudy resolutions; and, like a small boy showing off, he weakens fine dialogue with too much four-letter vulgarity. Because he translates all experience in terms of himself, his view of the world reflects his own nausea. It is curious that he has Maggie, when recounting her own testing of Skipper say, "Brick, I'm not good. I don't know why people have to pretend to be good, nobody's good." Big Daddy voices his cynical opinion that man is a beast without pity for anyone even when he himself is dying. As if to illustrate his contempt for the human animal, Williams has much business about a peephole through which Gooper and Mae spy to see if Brick and Maggie sleep in the same bed. He had Daddy tell of the vulgarity of a naked five-year-old Arab girl urged on by her mother. And there are questions about "how good" the various characters are in bed—impertinent questions even in the world of Tennessee Williams.

Brooks Atkinson, always the most sympathetic and formidable supporter of the playwright, wrote: "The drama is thoroughly subjective on the part of Mr. Williams; it is also subjective on the part of the characters. Seldom has there been a play in which the expression of thought and feeling has been so complete. . . . Although Mr. Williams is writing about hidden motivations and other elusive impulses, he is extraordinarily articulate. Being crystal-clear in his own mind, he speaks directly and vividly to the minds of the theatergoer."[14] The reviewer in *Time* commented that the revelations that spill out during family scenes "about sex, illness, greed, dislike" make it a harsh and bitter play. "Yet the play, closing on a lame, stagy note, lacks stature. Perhaps there is a little too much of everything: Williams is not only lavish of suffering, but voluble in articulating it. There might well be less emotionalism and should certainly be fewer words, particularly profane ones: the profanity often seems to relieve Williams' own feelings rather than his characters! But more important, *Cat* never quite defines itself as chiefly a play about marriage, about a family, or about a man. And if it means to be a complex of all three, it needs sharper form, greater unity, a sense of something far more deeply interfused. . . . The play, in exchange for abounding in theatrical trap doors, loses the slow, relentless, stair-case-climb of drama. Too much explodes, too little uncoils: much more is highlighted than truly plumbed."[15]

Eric Bentley called the father-son scene one "in which a new and better theme for the play is almost arrived at: that the simple old family relationships still mean something, that, in the midst of all the filth and incoherence and impossibility, people, clumsily, inconsistently, gropingly, try to be nice to each other."[16]

The question of whether or not Brick is homosexual was much discussed. Walter Kerr wrote, "There is, however, a tantalizing reluctance—beneath all the fire and all the apparent candor—to let the play blurt out its promised secret. This isn't due to the nerve-wracking, extraordinarily prolonged silence of its central figure, to his merely repeating the questions of other people rather than answering them. It is due to the fact that when we come to a fiery scene of open confession—between a belligerent father and his defiant son—the truth still dodges around verbal corners, slips somewhere between the veranda shutters, refuses to meet us on firm, clear terms."[17]

The playwright answered Walter Kerr partly by quoting the very evasive discussion which interrupts the climax of the second act. He then talked about how well he knew his characters and about how consistently they acted. Then he concluded with the familiar Williams' rhetorical evasiveness— the mystery of character. He spoke of his play as being "allusive" and "elusive" and of how he wanted the audience to leave the theater wondering and asking the same old philosophic question which represents the depth of his own profundity—the question, "Why?" Arthur B. Walters reported an interview with the playwright: apparently Brick was definitely not homosexual, but yet, again, on the other hand, there might have been tendencies not quite normal.[18] There is a kind of murkiness that increasingly pervades the writing of Williams as he concerns himself more and more with that special area of human experience, homosexuality. In his later work he cloaked this special concern in a dubious kind of symbolism or obscurity, perhaps to tease the public interest, perhaps to protect himself from the guardians of public taste.

Robert Hatch quietly voiced what he called an old-fashioned complaint: "I wish his play weren't so disagreeable. I left it feeling that I had spent the evening with a group of corpses that had had very little to recommend them when they were alive. Villainy in the theater is a splendid, stimulating force, but this cold second-rateness seems to me the negation of drama. Where is the suspense, if no soul is worth saving? Sex and death and money preoccupy Williams' characters; in the face of death, the sex is regulated to get money. . . . What ruins it for me is my inability to care whether anyone in the company sinks or swims. Let them die, let them breed, let them grow fat on the wealth—it is none of my business and I don't have to watch."[19]

IV *Baby Doll*

The film script of *Baby Doll*[20] is based on two one-act plays, *Twenty-Seven Wagons Full of Cotton* and *The Long Stay Cut Short*, or *The Unsatisfactory Supper*, both of which portray rather unsavory poor whites in Mississippi. The heavy, stupid Baby Doll who appears in each play becomes a thumb-sucking curvaceous blonde, rich in sex appeal, and appropriately equipped with a fourth-grade education but with very definite ideas about social status. Archie Lee Meighan, her husband—like Jake Meighan in *Twenty-Seven Wagons Full of Cotton* and Archie Lee in *The Long Stay Cut Short*—is a heavy-drinking, shiftless clod who hates Negroes and "wops." Since he cannot make a living honorably, he lives precariously on installment buying; and he is intent upon getting rid of Auntie Rose Comfort, the eighty-year-old servant whom he considers useless. Auntie Rose contributes ineptitude to the confusion in a run-down plantation house, but she is cheerful with her hymn singing and her roses. Silva Vacarro—the spelling has been changed—is not the evil avenger of *Twenty-Seven Wagons* but another of Williams' virile lovers. Until Archie Lee turns arsonist, Vacarro is a successful operator in a territory hostile to foreigners. He may be the whip-cracking sensualist; but, nonetheless, he has acquired movie-idol virtues. He prefers spring water to Archie's whiskey; he walks and leaps with the spring of a healthy animal; he is kind to the old servant; he is disgusted with the decayed plantation house; and he is nauseated by the garbage-strewn yard.

After a few brief scenes which portray the low-mindedness

of the southern businessmen and officers of the law and which take care of Archie's trick of setting Vacarro's mill on fire, the play turns to its real business: the sex play between Baby Doll, who has locked her husband out because she is not ready for marriage, and the attractively male Italian, who seems to be more interested in chasing arsonists than women. In one of the longest scenes of the play Williams writes a variation on his old seduction routine; but he has changed the tone completely from that in *Twenty-Seven Wagons.* The injured Vacarro sets out to practice the good-neighbor policy on the willing wife; he works up considerable expectation on the girl's part—and curiosity on the part of the audience. But, as in so many instances, when the talk begins to drag, Williams takes refuge in a chase—this time into the attic amid the falling plaster. Out of this "action" comes a revelation of the pursuer's honorable intentions—he was not after Baby Doll's virtue but her husband's dishonor.

The emotional quality of the scene is a curious mixture, and the scene itself has the characteristic ambiguity of so much of Williams' writing. Although considerably lessened, there is something of the ugliness found in the original, and this quality keeps the Vacarro scenes from being truly comic. Not only is the man determined to get revenge on the arsonist through this witless baby doll, but he goes after her cracking a whip. Williams, knowing the audience response he seeks to evoke, cleverly calculates the movements in this love game: a weak lock on the door, a push from the manly shoulder, falling plaster, references to the whip which the Italian strikes against his boots, and possible red marks on the lovely white skin, talk about a pencil, paper, and an affadavit—a word not in Baby Doll's vocabulary—Silva's references to his Sicilian background to make it clear that he is the lover type, a shriek and a shower of plaster when he pushes the door open and stands before the girl. There is also the skittery business of pushing the paper toward her, another fall of plaster, her hysteria and hasty scribbling on the paper, his satisfied laugh and polite acceptance. The hero then straddles the bannister, slides down and, like a healthy, agile animal, leaps to the floor. Baby Doll is nonplused, disappointed that he is about to leave. She cannot believe that he only wanted the scribble. The confused, "innocent" child asks if that *was* all he wanted, her confession that her husband set fire to the cotton gin. He tells her that she is only a child, and he is about to leave to go home for a nap. She says that he can take a nap in her baby crib—a deep, deep symbol to save the playwright from writing too many words.

This adventure seems to have been a major experience for Baby Doll; she suddenly grows up, becomes articulate, and is sexually awakened by the Italian. This sudden reversal recalls the very abrupt change in the character of Alma Winemiller in *Summer and Smoke.* In the wild melodramatic windup of *Baby Doll* the sweaty husband, drunk and hysterical, shoots the old servant and is taken off by the police; and the "shy children," natural sexual mates, are free to go off to celebrate Baby Doll's readiness for marriage.

There is considerable ado about a baby crib, the wife's favorite bed—the symbol is obvious—and for a brief time, Vacarro's. Baby Doll, awakened to love and typical of Williams' heroines in that state, emerges in a snug sheath exotically described as a lovely blue. During a good part of the play, however, she runs around in her slip, a damp slip at that; and, considering her sumptuous figure, the possibilities are evident. The old hymn-singing servant, who forgets to light the fire under the greens, gathers roses which she calls nature's poems. The background atmosphere varies from rooster crowings and hymns—sex and religion again—to machinery noises, apparently a symbol of the corrupting forces of industrial society. There is the usual traffic to the bathroom that seems to obsess the playwright; in this play, there is also a fight in a urinal. One amateur psychologist, concerned about what preoccupies Tennessee Williams, has offered the opinion that an accurate assessment of his early toilet training would throw considerable light on some of the "more difficult" problems of the plays. In *Baby Doll,* as is true with most of the plays, the necessary exposition is conveyed by telephone or through characters arbitrarily brought in.

Auntie Rose is one of the few real characters among the minor figures, grotesques and types, who appear when needed; among these are the "mendacious" businessmen and marshals or southern hangers-on who are contrasts to the natural sexmates. Silva Vacarro reproaches Archie Lee for his callous dismissal of Old Auntie Rose in an artificial, clumsy and pontifical line such as often interrupts natural, idiomatic dialogue: "Mr. Meighan, when a man is feeling uncomfortable over something, it often happens that he takes out his annoyance on some completely innocent person just because he has to make somebody suffer." And when Auntie Rose gives an account of what her life has been, the sketch recalls Amanda Wingfield's observation about homeless southern women: "I've helped out my—relatives, my—folks—whenever they *needed me to!* I was always *invited!* Sometimes—*begged* to come! When *babies* were expected or when somebody was *sick*, they called for Aunt Rose, and Aunt Rose was always—ready. . . . Nobody *ever* had to—*put me—out!* If you—gentlemen will excuse me from the table—I will pack my things! If I hurry I'll catch the nine o'clock bus to——" Vacarro heroically comes, however, to her rescue. This emotional scene is a contrast to the comedy of the attic pursuit and also the grotesque scenes between husband and wife, who are such in name only. On the other hand, Williams has introduced such issues as race prejudice, duplicity, and brutality—all of which are much too serious and evil for laughter.

Having skyrocketed into money and fame with two successes like *The Glass Menagerie* and *A Streetcar Named Desire*, Williams had set for himself a very difficult assignment if he wanted to continue in the theater. And having had his plays most advantageously interpreted by distinguished actors and actresses, it is not surprising that he should write afterwards not so much from observation as with the idea of providing a "vehicle" for certain performers. The plays represented in this chapter—though not all of his work between 1947 and 1956—show an advance in technique, a more sophisticated handling of situations for their dramatic and emotional effect, and an even more self-conscious use of theatrical devices, not entirely as a means of conveying characters and "life," but to arouse certain responses.

CHAPTER 5

The Desperate Heroes

I *Lonely Fugitives*

THE FREEDOM of an "unattached and nomadic exist-ence" has stimulated the imagination of Tennessee Wil-liams almost from the beginning. It epitomizes his romantic view of life. The man who lives uncommitted to the mores and to the responsibilities of American society stands above the average money-mad, sex-starved, high-tensioned, and un-happy job holder. For his independence he must pay, natu-rally; and Williams often makes him the victim of stereo-typed figures representing Business, the Law, the Church, or just Goodness masquerading as heavy-set, gossiping house-wives and their adipose husbands. Or the hero walks by himself, a lonely misfit in an artificial society, an outsider misunderstood by his contemporaries. He is lonesome, always lonesome.

He is often the man asking the Big Questions; groping for an answer; and, something of a poet, seeking to be articu-late. Because he refuses to conform, punch a time clock, and collect a pay check, he may carry worldly goods on his back or as a memento of some past achievement. By ordinary standards he is a failure. His physical attractiveness distin-guishes him, for he is usually described as "good looking" or as "very good looking"; and his sexual charm attracts not only women but men. In some cases this personal magnetism seems to be of so great force that it attracts admirers as if they had been hypnotized. And perhaps because of this highly charged sexual attractiveness, he often is presented as an adolescent, or at least as quite young.

There are a number of terms that might apply to this type of male character which appears so often. He might be called the Defeated, or the Derelict, or the Lonely Misfit, the Outsider, or the Rejected, or, perhaps, just Lonesome. He is a type for which Tennessee Williams has had repeated affinity, a character who has been "trapped by circumstance" to live in an industrialized society or in a small-town hell where mediocrity or dullness, bigotry and evil destroy any kind of originality or the first sign of humanity. The small-town hell of *Battle of Angels*, the surrealistic hell of the Plaza on Camino Real, the even more symbolized hell of *Orpheus Descending*, and the hell described by Catharine Holly in *Suddenly Last Summer* suggest the persistence with which the idea has preoccupied the playwright.

There is the shy, awkward poet, Homer Stallcup, in the early short story, "The Field of Blue Children," who is rejected by his girl in favor of a steady provider. The diffident college boy in "The Important Thing" fortifies himself with a quart of wine before he approaches his girl. Itinerants and sensitive men are the key figures in "The Angel and the Alcove" and "The Poet." Also in this group is Oliver Winemiller, hero of "One Arm," the broken Apollo and "baby-faced killer" who wears "the charm of the defeated" and who attracts a public like a matinee idol. There are panicky little men like the discarded millhand in the short story, "The Malediction," and in the dramatized version, *Strangest Kind of Romance*, or like the timid little Anthony Burns who is methodically devoured by the Black Masseur. Two writers, making sacrifices for their craft, belong to this special class: Joe, the young writer in what must be an early play, *The Long Goodbye*, and the ardent speechmaker in *Lady of Larkspur Lotion*. Moony, the Northern woodsman in *Moony's Kid Don't Cry*, anticipates the rebellion against timecards and shiny pants.

Heroes of romantic temperament, handsome primitives uncorrupted by the sordid and the mean in American civilization, take an increasingly important part in the plays. They may derive from Williams' admiration of D. H. Lawrence or from some facet of his own character. An early experiment in this type is the brother, Rosalio, in *Purification*. Val Xavier in the early play, *Battle of Angels*, the lover-itinerant-poet-philosopher, is the first full-dress description of this figure and a very important figure, perhaps, for those interested in the personal story of Tennessee Williams. He appears again —a bit older and more cynical—in the many-times revised version renamed as *Orpheus Descending*, and in the same as a script renamed for the film version, *Fugitive Kind*. The Val Xaviers of Tennessee Williams' world seem to retain a purity in spite of the vice in which they have wallowed during their meandering search for the Big Answer. It is their art, apparently, that keeps them uncorrupted.

The frustrated Tom Wingfield of *The Glass Menagerie*, a poet-dreamer-escapist to the movies, finally in desperation joins his itinerant brotherhood. Although he is not distinguished for his success with women, he shares some of the qualities of Val Xavier—and particularly a distaste for what is average American. There is also Kilroy of the short play *Ten Blocks on Camino Real* who is an adolescent adventurer in an ugly world and who reappears in *Camino Real*, the extended version. A lonely traveler, immersed in self-pity and sentiments of the "sweet-used-to-be," he faces a rough and sordid initiation on the so-called royal way of life. Trusting and innocent but always asking *why*, he faces one defeat after another; but he remains good in spite of continued humiliation. The Brick Pollitt of the short story "Three Players of a Summer Game" is married to an aggressive and socially prominent southern girl and degenerates into a kind of soft and "senseless amiability." The same character, given more complexity in *Cat on a Hot Tin Roof*, is in one way a perennial adolescent who never outgrew his college sports. The blame for his deterioration is placed upon his wife and also upon a number of vaguely defined causes: to homosexuality, to the exposure of illusions that men live by, and possibly even to his own moral inertia.

The desperate husbands of the serious comedy *Period of Adjustment* bear a number of resemblances to the frustrated men in this group of defeated charmers. They grow restive on a routine job, and they dream of freedom in the great open spaces. One of them, like Brick, seems weary of a passionate wife; the other fears impotence. They talk almost continually about sex as if it were the major fact of their lives, and sometimes they use the crude language of adolescents. They are neurotics, each in his own way; and their problems hinge upon physical adjustment to marriage.

All of these men seem to have in common a certain "charm of the defeated" and are a contrast to the radiant primitives: Hadrian, the charity boy; Stanley Kowalski, the Polish laborer; Alvaro-Eat-a-Horse, the Italian truckdriver; or John Buchanan, the young medico who suddenly reforms. All of the failures have been suffused with the playwright's sympathy. Friendship, love, and understanding, expressed in not quite the usual ways, take on a rather special significance.

II Camino Real

When Tennessee Williams reworked the short play *Ten Blocks on the Camino Real* (1948) into *Camino Real*[1] (1953), he deepened the symbolic meaning of his main character Kilroy whom he made two years older; and he attempted to give universal significance to the experiences of this lonely misfit trapped in a surrealistic world of decadence. He widened the suggested area of the Plaza; developed a Terra Incognita out of the rather indefinite "Way Out"; and extended the action to the apron of the stage, to the balconies, and to the floor of the theater itself. He made of the longer version a play within a play; for his incorrigible Don Quixote, the lonely romantic, is seeking a soul mate: "In a place where so many are lonely, it would be inexcusably selfish to be lonely alone."[2] He added several other romantics, a few sexual perverts, a number of symbolic figures of evil, and a kind of chorus represented by the Street People. He also resorted to a number of obviously symbolic stage tricks, gave cosmic significance to occasional scenes, and in others, edged toward the pornographic. There is—in this play—something for every taste.

The short play was reported to have been written during an illness in Mexico,[3] but between 1948 and 1953 Williams had traveled not only to Europe but to the northern parts of Africa. And it was during these years that American freedom was being polluted by the indecencies of Senator McCarthy and his intemperate followers, a condition which may be reflected in some of the senseless brutalities in the play. And yet this does not appear in Williams' explanation of his intended meaning; he wrote in the "Foreword" to *Camino Real:* "My desire was to give these audiences my own sense of something wild and unrestricted that ran like water in the mountains, or clouds changing shape in a gale, or the continually dissolving and transforming images of a dream."[4] He professed to have taken great pains with the construction of the play, more so than with others, so that it would have form. When the play was revived seven years later, Williams explained that it "was written to combat a despair" and that it had served him "as a spiritual purgation of that abyss of confusion and lost sense of reality that I and those others [sympathetic listeners] had somehow wandered into."[5] This is another of several statements in which he admits that writing has been an antidote for psychological difficulties.

The plaza of Camino Real, "the royal way" or "the way of life," seems to suggest any romantically decadent seaport from Tangier to Shanghai. The symbols are obvious. The luxury side is represented on the left by an elegant hotel, Siete Mares, and Skid Row on the right, by the Gypsy's stall, the Loan Shark's establishment, and a flea-bag hotel known as "Ritz Men Only." At the back of the plaza a flight of stairs mounts an ancient wall to "Terra Incognita," a wasteland between the town and snow-capped mountains in the distance. In the center of the stage is a dry fountain. The scene of action, since the play encompasses Tennessee Williams' world-view of man, takes place also on the stage apron, in the orchestra pit, in the aisles leading to the back of the theater, and in the balconies just above the stage.

Camino Real is a kind of dead-end street, a grand avenue that has deteriorated, where the inhabitants are desperate transients. A desolate world, its elements are meant to symbolize the worst in contemporary society. All that is decent is gradually destroyed. It is also a world where the power of money makes sincerity, love, or kindness impractical. The rich suffer from fatigue and boredom, and they furtively ask questions as if they were fingering pornographic postcards. A poor man asking for a drink is shot by the guards. Death, symbolized by busy and giggling Streetcleaners, is treated with indifference or cynicism. There is no compassion on Camino Real, for there the word "brother" is forbidden and even the wild birds have been tamed and put in cages. It is a world viewed through a dirty brown bottle by a man sick of everything and of himself as well.

Williams' prefatory quotation from Dante's *Inferno*, "In the middle of the journey of our life I came to myself in a dark wood where the straight way was lost," would imply that Camino Real is his own version of hell. Unfortunately he has not the clarity of Dante's vision nor his gift for imagery. He has imitated Dante by using historical and literary figures but without the Italian's subtle references. Most of the men are romantic adventurers or lovers—of various descriptions—and the women, with the exception of the Pietá symbol, are prostitutes.

What happens in this modern inferno is supposed to be the dream of that arch-romantic, Don Quixote, who wears a bit of faded blue ribbon to remind himself of distances gone and those yet to go, of the green country, and of the spirit in his heart which responds to such words as "truth," "valor" and "devoir"—words heightened by the playwright's capital letters and exclamation points. When Sancho deserts him, Quixote, sensing the loneliness of the plaza, speaks the already quoted line which Williams calls a key to the play: "When so many are lonely as seem to be lonely, it would be inexcusably selfish to be lonely alone."[5] He lies down to sleep and to dream. He describes this dream as "a pageant, a masque" and expects to derive new meanings or recall old ones from this experience. This would seem to be another— one of several descriptions or definitions—statement from the author to explain his play.

Gutman, proprietor of the luxurious Siete Mares, manipulates the sixteen short scenes in a way imitative of the Stage Manager in Thornton Wilder's *Our Town*. A caricature of a businessman and symbolic of the power of money and brutality, he views people as thieves, prostitutes, mendicants, and vendors; and he considers use of the word, *Hermano*, a ready excuse for riot. With the help of his stooges, he destroys any signs of independence, the intolerable spirit of anarchy. One of his victims, the aging Jacques Casanova, retains his pride in spite of poverty and the pressures to conform. When Gutman is about to hurl his portmanteau from an upper window of the hotel because Casanova can-

not pay, the lover cries out dramatically, "Careful, I have
—fragile—mementoes . . .—And so at last it has come, the
distinguished thing!"[6] This is another of the lines, like those
lines in the early poems which were set off to suggest some
deep significance and in which the dramatist attempts to
to be profound. Casanova's love for Marguerite Gautier,
which is not returned, one of the few heartening relationships
in the play, prevents his leaving the plaza.

Another romantic, Lord Byron, contributes a soliloquy
about the human heart and the role of the poet; and then
he escapes into the free blue yonder. With shocking particularity he describes the burning of Shelley's corpse: the
bursting of the skull, the splitting open of the body, and
Trelawney's snatching the heart. A curiously morbid description, it is obviously inserted for shock effect; and it tells
more about Williams than about the hell he means to portray. Byron, who is made to speak directly to the audience
about listening to the "pure stringed instrument" of his
heart, expresses sentiments which would seem to have a
very personal reference for Williams: "That was my vocation
once upon a time, before it was obscured by vulgar plaudits."
Williams has Byron admit, however, that fame and fortune
alleviated the frightening loneliness of the poet's lot. As if
blaming the public for the kind of writing he did during this
lush period, he makes a veiled comment on the demoralized
character of the times. Only he uses the strange word "declivity." As if speaking through Byron, Williams says, *There
is a passion for declivity in this world!*" As indicated here,
Tennessee Williams makes use of curious and devious ways
of answering his adverse critics. Baron de Charlus, an old
fop and sybarite, a homosexual masochist from Proust's *Remembrance of Things Past*, is trailed by an exotically beautiful young man. He admits he wants to be followed. To
those who call his condition corrupt, he answers that it is
only simplification; the obvious suggestion is that he escapes
the sordid world through homosexuality. Shortly afterwards
he is strangled, apparently not because of his "sins" but his
lack of money.

Most of the women seem to be aging prostitutes. Two of
the overpainted, overdressed grotesques are literary figures,
Prudence Duvernoy and Olympe, friends of Marguerite Gau-

tier. A particularly hideous old prostitute, Rosita, continually pulls down her blouse to expose her sagging breasts, and shuffles around calling her ware, love; she is easily one of the most unsavory of Williams' sex peddlers. Most of the attention is given to the heroine of Dumas' *La Dame aux Camélias*, Marguerite Gautier, a drug addict, an escapée from a sanitarium, but still beautiful for all the advancing years. Times for her have changed. Whereas she used to be paid for the pleasure she gave, she must now pay for the "love" which she hopes will retard the onslaught of age. She mouths the playwright's cynical view of love, that it is not tenderness but only two people's becoming a habit with one another, deriving a vague kind of creature comfort. Bored with the devotion of Jacques Casanova, and offering for another her "cabochon sapphire," she sends for a young gigolo who finally robs and insults her. In her final loneliness she turns to the mortally ill Casanova, and it is this late-blooming companionship that inspires the symbolic—and "poetic"—final curtain line: *"The violets in the mountains have broken the rocks!"*

The Gypsy and her daughter Esmeralda, the subject of much prattle about virginity, are brought out on the stage whenever the Street People need to be distracted from injustice or brutality. There are three symbolic figures of corruption: the Gypsy's stooge of a son, Abdullah; A. Ratt, manager of the flea-bag hotel; and the Loan Shark. They work with the women to cheat any susceptible customer. On the wealthy side of the plaza Lord and Lady Mulligan are caricatures representing the special privileges of rich and dreary old money bags. The Street People, sometimes starving, sometimes cowed, sometimes hypnotized by the domination of Gutman and his gang, seem to serve as a chorus. The blind singer, La Madrecita and her Son, figures which seem out of place in this "phantasmagoria of decadence," symbolize the infrequent evidence of love and pity. There is also a guitar-playing character called Dreamer who seems to accompany the Pietá.

The Dante in Williams' inferno seems to be the whole-some, American, eternal G.I. A young twenty-seven-year old vagrant, he carries a pair of boxing gloves around his neck, and wears a memento of better years, a belt with the word,

CHAMP, studded with rubbies and emeralds. This self-pitying itinerant complains of his troubles at length: tropical fever on a ship without medical care; forced retirement from the prize ring because of a bad heart—a heart symbolically described "as big as the head of a baby"; forced renunciation of liquor, smoking, and sex; and a loving wife afraid of a big hard kiss. Kilroy not only recalls the mutilated Apollo of "One Arm" who lost the center of his being when he lost his arm, but is reminiscent, because of the accumulation of difficulties, of the tearful biographies of Laura Wingfield and Blanche Du Bois. Kilroy becomes an easy mark for the roughnecks on Camino Real. He is robbed; makes friends with Jacques Casanova who, like Val Xavier, is looking for something he knows not what; and is forced into a clown outfit with a red wig, a bulbous nose that can be lighted, horn-rimmed glasses, and a big footprint on the seat of the pants, an outfit that obviously signifies man's loss of dignity. His resistance to the forces of order which label him as a "queer" is expressed in a noisy "rhubarb" of a chase over the stage, theater, aisles, and balcony, ending in a wild leap upon the stage. There are three such noisy spectacles in the play; substitutes for action, they are characteristic of Williams' failure to develop a dramatic theme. Or in other cases, as in the brother-act between Kilroy and Casanova, Williams, instead of dramatizing his idea, resorts to obvious symbolic gestures; each romantic removes the other's sign of ignominy.

There is a seduction scene that was obviously written for the box office. Kilroy's escape from Camino Real is thwarted by the cunning bawd, Gypsy, who offers her baby-faced daughter, Esmeralda, about whom there is so much virginity talk. According to the legend the full moon continually restores her purity. She is carried on the stage reclining on a divan. The description recalls the *femme fatale* of the silent movies—a veil over her face, a girdle below the navel, a diaphanous skirt, green snakes over her breasts. Kilroy looks upon this glittering daughter of Eve and gets dizzy. He asks in Tennessee Williams' capital letter excitement if her speciality is tea leaves—an amusing crack and a welcome relief. Mama the Gypsy orders Nursie, a male attendant, to "clock him," and sets out for street adventures of her own. When the silent and "innocent" siren does not talk, Kilroy describes

the romancing customary in the States. Esmeralda then
stuns her suitor with some heady comments which are more
likely the acid observations of her creator than ideas from her
own little head: "They say the monetary system has got to
be stabilized all over the world"; or "How do you feel about
the class struggle?" or "How do you feel about the Mumbo
Jumbo?"—Mumbo Jumbo refers to God—"We think there has
been so much of the Mumbo Jumbo it's put Him to sleep!"
Kilroy prefers a more intimate kind of conversation. When
Nursie pointedly warns the lovers that they have only fifteen minutes, he is sent to bed. Then the fun begins, sweet
fun, in what might be called symbolic or "poetic" dialogue.
It is another variation of the Williams' seduction scene that
becomes more and more conspicuous in these later plays. This
one has the same strange mixture of the comic and the very
sensuous as its parallel in *Baby Doll.*

This courtship scene, part of the "fertility rites," is a conglomeration of innuendo and the blatantly obvious, the
precious and the corny, the silly and the sentimental, the
caustic and the humorous. It seems to be the playwright's
comment about American women, sex-obsessed and ruthlessly
cunning, and wholly incapable of love. After this symbolic
bedroom scene between a mercenary doll and a disillusioned
American boy, Kilroy describes love as no better than the
four-letter word which youngsters scribble on fences when
they run away from school. He talks about being gentle and
sincere, a word repeated *ad nauseam;* and he admits that
this particular love game was not worth the gloves he
pawned to pay for it. The young prostitute turns philosopher
and sentimentalist when she says, "It's always like that as
soon as the veil is lifted. They're all so ashamed of having
degraded themselves, and their hearts have more regret than
a heart can hold."

The "fertility rites" scene is followed almost immediately
by the death scene. When Kilroy, pestered by the Streetcleaners (Death), seeks help from Gutman, a beautiful nude
called Eva briefly appears on the balcony, a scene which
has symbolic implications or else Williams was clinging to
the pitch of the previous scene. Kilroy, for all his loneliness
and disappointments in love, is a man of courage—of Williams' kind. His action recalls the image in the early poem,

"Cried the Fox," in which the pursued animal—symbol of D. H. L.—cries to the pack to follow. In the same way Kilroy taunts the Streetcleaners to come and get him. These verbal hysterics are set out in solid capital letters and exclamation points. Kilroy accompanies his words with old-time boxer parries and faces what is, symbolically, the inevitable.

In a double scene—a Williams' favorite and an old technique—La Madrecita, with the body of Kilroy across her knees, speaks obituary praises at the same time as the medical students perform a post-mortem on Kilroy, "an unidentified vagrant." The Pietá begs the audience to remember him when he was at the peak of his career, this boy who speaks in a soft southern voice, and not when he was frightened and defeated. In somewhat involved metaphor she says of his admirers: "He stood as a planet among the moons of their longing," an image Williams had used before with reference to his broken Apollo. She makes an appeal to all failures, to all the deformed creatures to pray for one of their own whose heart was "as big as the head of a baby." And then, in one of the most incredible bits of fantasy, La Madrecita effects Kilroy's resurrection with a touch of flowers. After all this sentiment and theatrical legerdemain, Kilroy wakens; rubs his eyes; watches the medics remove the gold sphere—his solid gold heart; and hears them talk about "pathological lesions."

Kilroy grabs his precious golden heart and sets out on another noisy "rhubarb" chase with all the racket the stage can provide. Then comes the real shocker. The philosophical prostitute, Esmeralda, embraces all the failures and disillusioned in an extended burst of rhetoric, an incredibly articulate statement from the baby-faced mercenary whose virginity is periodically restored: "God bless all con men and hustlers and pitch-men who hawk their hearts on the street, all two-time losers who're likely to lose once more, the courtesan who made the mistake of love, the greatest of lovers crowned with the longest horns, the poet who wandered far from his heart's green country and possibly will and possibly won't be able to find his way back, look down with a smile tonight on the last cavaliers, the ones with the rusty armor and soiled white plumes, and visit with understanding and something that's almost tender those fading legends that come and go in this plaza like songs not clearly remembered, oh, sometime and somewhere, let there be something to mean the word *honor* again!" This is one of the fullest and most romantic prayers that Tennessee Williams has made for the defeated and the outcasts.

Poor old Kilroy, thinking he has found another true woman in Esmeralda, is soon disillusioned and discarded. His final comments about his experiences on Camino Real suggest that nothing really happened to him; he is still the cry baby, this time bitter over being cheated in love. Taking the advice of the old knight of dreams, Don Quixote, "Don't! Pity! Your! Self!"[7]—the typographical poetics are evidently meant to add profundity—Kilroy walks off, "mugging" to the audience, leering about his new friend, the romantic Good Samaritan. The play closes on a falsely optimistic note when the old knight, watching Casanova and Marguerite, speaks the symbolic line: "The violets in the mountains have broken the rocks!" As he speaks, the fountain begins squirting water, which would seem to be another last-minute gesture of hope —or a bit of attention to the scenery.

The idea upon which this play might have been built has considerable merit. Dante's *Inferno* rewritten in modern terms would provide a careful, imaginative dramatist with a ready-made frame in which to comment upon contemporary decadence. But Tennessee Williams, obsessed with sex and sentimentality, limited himself too narrowly. Unable to handle a large dramatic idea, he resorted to rhetoric and pantomime, and to such obvious symbols as the plane Fugitivo, the Streetcleaners, a dry fountain, and characters like A. Ratt. He also dragged out some hammy stage tricks. As Williams would have used screen devices to underline his points in *The Glass Menagerie,* in this play whenever a legendary character enters, a hunchback makes a somersault through a hoop ringed with bells; a bum leans out of a Skid-Row window to shout lines that are unnecessary; a gong is repeatedly used during the fiesta scene depicting the fertility rites; Kilroy at one point is supposed to go into a dance that reviews his biography—boxer, vagabond, and lover—a neat assignment for any actor.

The playwright has offered considerable explanation about his play, none of which is inclusive enough. He wrote from private theory rather than observation, and he gave universal significance to a very personal and special point of view. Having divorced himself from the life and people he can write about so effectively, he allowed himself to be dominated by theatrical devices. If there was any influence of Baudelaire and Rimbaud on the writing of this play—and there might have been some—the playwright sacrificed what he might have achieved in depth by copying only the mannerisms of these French writers. The play is a mixture of sentiment and sensationalism, of poetry and farce, of shrewd observation and vulgarity; and it has so wide a range of symbols that it should be a continuing delight for certain critics who do, however, stand the risk of being surprised about what their analysis may uncover.

Brooks Atkinson wrote as follows: " 'Camino Real' is a bold excursion into a theatre of lyric poetry that incantates fragments of life through the use of dialogue, pantomime, ballet, music, light and sound. If Mr. Williams' theme were not so abhorrent, everyone would probably appreciate the virtuosity of his craftsmanship." Mr. Atkinson continued that there was "no mistaking Mr. Williams' meaning. His world is going out with neither a bang nor a whimper but with a leer and a grimace of disgust. There is no health in it. With rare exceptions everyone succumbs to depravity. The Camino Real is a jail-yard of vice." The Puritans "had a way out and dreams of future glory. But Mr. Williams has nothing in reserve."[8] Harold Clurman wrote as follows: "Being essentially a youthful work, 'Camino Real' is immature. But like the youthful and immature work of most artists, 'Camino Real' is significant of its author's seed thoughts, impulses, and ambitions. Far from being obscure, the play reiterates its intention and meaning at every point. In fact, it is too nakedly clear to be a sound work of art." He continued by commenting upon the state of the American theater: "The sad fact of our theater is that a play like 'Camino Real' with all its faults ought to be produced, listened to, criticized with measure and affection, but that this is difficult when its production costs a fortune, when it is forced to become part of the grand machinery of investment, real estate, Broadway brokerage and competition for reputation. A play like 'Camino Real' should be produced—as it might be in France, for example—

with modest means in a small theater where it would be quietly seen, enjoyed and judged for what it is—a fallible minor work of a young artist of important talent."[9]

III *Orpheus Descending*

Tennessee Williams says of *Orpheus Descending*,[10] a revision of *Battle of Angels*, which was rewritten after fifteen years of theatrical experience: "On the surface it was and still is the tale of a wild-spirited boy who wanders into a conventional community of the South and creates the commotion of a fox in a chicken coop.

"But beneath the now familiar surface it is a play about unanswered questions that haunt the hearts of people and the difference between continuing to ask them, a difference represented by the four major protagonists of the play, and the acceptance of prescribed answers that are not answers at all, but expedient adaptations or surrender to a state of quandary."[11]

The theme of the poet in an unfriendly world is a recurrent one in Williams' plays. The last three stanzas of a poem, "Orpheus Descending,"[12] apostrophizes this special figure in rather flamboyant terms. Williams describes the unhappy life of the poet. He says to Orpheus that he must learn that some things, by their nature incomplete—an idea basic to the horror story, "Desire and the Black Masseur"—are to be sought for and abandoned; that it is in the nature of things that those who reach for the heights are destined to fall; that he, a fugitive and ashamed, must crawl within himself, for he is not the stars but the residue of victims torn by the avenging furies. The ambivalence of spirit and flesh within this character as described in the poem recall the symbolic figure of Alma Winemiller, the idealist turned prostitute, or the decadent aristocrat, Blanche Du Bois. Williams has given the classic myth his own interpretation and imposed it on the old play.

Orpheus is Val Xavier, the poet-itinerant-savior, who descends into the hell of a small southern town to rescue the dead Eurydice, or Lady (Myra of the old play), from Pluto, or Jabe Torrance, the cancer-doomed, flint-hearted husband who snatched her away from the romantic life she dreamed about. The particular corner of hell that Orpheus-Val Xavier enters is a grubby dry goods store with an adjacent confectionery which is done in shadowy poetic tones and which represents romantic memories of love and happiness. Preoccupied with the memory theme again, Williams makes this social parlor, refurbished during the play, represent the imitation of the Moon Lake Casino which Lady romantically associates with the rich boy who deserted her and with her father, called the Wop, who with his Casino was burned alive because he sold liquor to "niggers." And only in Williams' version of hell would there be the inevitable bedroom alcove, exotically curtained with an Oriental hanging in brilliant colors—a gold tree, scarlet fruit, tropical birds—obviously supposed to represent all that is not icy Puritanism.

The inhabitants of this hell are a motley assortment of commonplace townspeople, frowsy women, and silly and malicious gossips who savor recollections of "spooning" in the old Moon Lake Casino and reports of others' suffering. Their husbands—pot-bellied old boys who play with slot machines, guns, and bloodhounds—are remnants of the Mystic Crew—a kind of Ku Klux Klan which keeps foreigners, like the Wop, and "niggers" in their places. A ghoulish primitive, the Conjure Man, with his bird bones and blood-curdling Choctaw cry, seems to be Williams' own private symbol of pure freedom and death. But most important for Orpheus-Val Xavier are three women; for the play revolves around his relationship with them.

Val Xavier is a handsome southerner with an intimate, soft voice whose trademark of freedom, wild freedom, is still a snakeskin jacket instead of the job-holder's conventional blue business suit. He is now a man of thirty who is no longer sure that sex gives the answer to all questions. The guitar which he carries—that guitar for some critics is a phallic symbol—covered with names of famous singers, would also seem to be a symbol of his art and his purity. His art, he says, affords a purification after he has been contaminated by the world. Untainted in spite of his corrupt life "with the party"—is there a veiled reference here to homosexuality? —he belongs to neither of two classes, the buyers and the bought, but to those who are uncommitted and free. This man who admits that he has been penalized for vagrancy,

seems to want, at thirty, to exchange some of his wild freedom for security.

An old companion of his vagabond-entertainer days is
Carol Cutrere (Sandra Whiteside of the old play), who is
still the poor little rich girl but an older and even more
exotic one and more of an exhibitionist. She wears the exaggerated make-up of the theater. Asked why she makes such
a display of herself, she tells of her earlier humanitarian
ventures. She was at one time another kind of exhibitionist,
a religious fanatic and reformer who made speeches, wrote
protest letters about the brutal mistreatment of Negroes,
spent her inheritance to build clinics, and made a particular
exhibition of herself by dressing in burlap and walking bare-
foot to ask the governor to free a Negro taken with a white
whore. Arrested for vagrancy herself, she has made that her
career ever since. The early part of this biography hardly
fits the character, or any resemblance of the character, who
operates as Carol Cutrere, unless it is an extreme example
of the idealist who fell deep into the mud. There is also a
suggestion in this biography of a Williams attitude—a disin-
clination to take sides, to make judgments of good and evil,
to become committed.

Frustrated in the humanitarian ventures she reports upon,
she turns to sex—and with a terrible compulsion. She makes
her usual proposition to Val who refuses, saying that heavy
drinking and "shacking up" with strangers is for youngsters
and not a thirty-year old. These two exchange confidences
with an air *"of two lonely children,"* but the topic is the
same old line about sex, embroidered with tender words and
blunt biological facts.

Val, as in the former version, courts disaster when he seeks
to exchange his freedom for a job in the mercantile store and
becomes involved with the love-starved wife. It is his poetic
description of freedom and purity that seems to win her sympathy: "You know they's a kind of bird that don't have legs
so it can't light on nothing but has to stay all its life on its
wings in the sky? . . . You can't tell those birds from the
sky and that's why the hawks don't catch them, don't see
them up there in the high blue sky near the sun!" Robert
Brustein calls this bird a symbol of innocence that stays free
of the corrupting influences of the earth.[13] If Val's purity is

to be taken as a state of innocence before the corrupting experience of sex and if his commitment to the commercial world is another association with the dark forces, then Val Xavier is surely headed for trouble. For all the introduction of involved symbolism, the emphasis, however, is heavily placed on erotic scenes.

The relationship between Val and Lady affords Williams several opportunities to exemplify his familiar theories of human relationships. His touch theory is frequently illustrated: that love and understanding depend upon physical contact. Every character for whom Williams has any sympathy at all is lonesome. He has created a long, long procession of very lonely people. Val Xavier might be said to speak for them all: "Nobody ever gets to know *no body!* We're all of us sentenced to solitary confinement inside our own skins, for life! You understand me, Lady?—I'm tellin' you it's the truth, we got to face it, we're under a life-long sentence to solitary confinement inside our own lonely skins for as long as we live on this earth!" When Lady expresses the belief that the answer to loneliness is love, Val answers that it is a delusion that has fooled many people.

But he is soon taken in. When Lady suddenly sets up the sleeping arrangements in the little alcove and accuses him of robbing her cashbox, he makes a number of futile efforts to escape; and the mutual recriminations are ugly. Val's descriptions of Lady are nasty; he calls her an aging, unsatisfied woman who hired a stranger for a clerk by day but wanted him for a lover at night without paying extra. Invectives failing her, she strikes with her fists; but, when he turns to leave, she cries out in Tennessee Williams' double-sized, capital letters for him not to leave, that she needs him to go on living. Her uninhibited cries of passion are heightened by the appropriate mood music. Then Lady, a woman between thirty-five and forty-five, but described like a child in a trance, emotionally torn and hesitant, walks toward the alcove with the bedding in her arms. Encouraged by Val's whispered tenderness, she gathers strength to enter. He looks from his guitar to her—the old phallic guitar?—and the inevitable curtain suggests the bedroom scene.

Another aspect of the poetic spirit is represented by Vee Talbott, wife of an ignorant and brutal sheriff, who seeks release in her painting. A religious fanatic, she seems to work at her best in a frenzy, as when she painted the ascent of the Holy Ghost after a "vision." There is a curious, seemingly personal touch, in the playwright's account of the way in which she works: "I been painting all day, finished a picture in a ten-hour stretch, just stopped a few minutes fo' coffee and went back to it again while I had a clear vision. I think I got it this time. But I'm so exhausted I could drop in my tracks. There's nothing more exhausting than that kind of work on earth, it's not so much that it tires your body out, but it leaves you drained inside. Y'know what I mean? Inside? Like you was burned out by something? Well! Still!— You feel you've accomplished something when you're through with it, sometimes you feel—*elevated!*" She says of another painting, a Church of the Resurrection with a red steeple, "I just, just *felt* it that way! I paint a thing how I feel it instead of always the way it actually is. Appearances are misleading, nothing is what it looks like to the eyes. You got to have— *vision—to see!*"

These four main protagonists present interesting questions which should have been given fuller development. Unfortunately there are so many distractions and so much sensationalism that the stronger parts of the play are underdeveloped and obscured. Williams' inability to carry through a dramatic theme can be illustrated by the hysterical ending of the play—again, "something wild." Lady, as mercenary as her neighbors, corrupted obviously by her environment, for years a barren wife, ecstatically announces her pregnancy. The playwright gave this same final announcement to his heroines in *The Rose Tattoo* and in *Cat on a Hot Tin Roof.* Val Xavier, the life bringer, a symbol of wild and pure freedom, but trapped by love—the various sequences make this very hard to believe—wilts in reverence before this woman. But Jabe, the Pluto and the injured husband, in spite of severe hemorrhaging, described as a symbol of death as well as evil, is still able to hold a gun; he plugs Lady twice with a "hah!" and a curse; he threatens to burn her as he burned her father; his gleeful announcement tardily confirms Lady's suspicions.

Accompanied by a mob with blow torches, Sheriff Talbott —in drunken suspicion over the vagrant's attention to his wife, Vee, and also in response to Jabe's false charges of murder—drags Val away. There are terrible cries of anguish offstage. The Conjure Man returns shortly with the snake-skin jacket; Carol Cutrere drops from nowhere to deliver the final tribute to freedom: "Wild things leave skins behind them, they leave clean skins and teeth and white bones behind them, and these are tokens passed from one to another, so that the fugitive kind can always follow their kind. . . ." And then the cry of the tortured Val is repeated more terribly than before.

John Gassner, who called this play "one of the most chaotic contemporary works of genius," remarked that it is the violence rather than the meaning that remains uppermost. In a plot made up of a "multiplication of griefs, evils, and horrors," there are several levels of meaning; but "the snarled symbolism of the play" obscures both character and environment. "Myth is scrambled in the play when two legends about Orpheus become entangled in the symbolism of the work. The plot runs parallel to one legend of the bard's descent into the underworld; the other analogy is that of his being torn to pieces by the Bacchantes driven to frenzy by orgiastic religion." Translated in terms of this particular southern town and in those of a hero with so many different symbols blended together—"Val the poet, Val the idealized male pursued to his destruction by sex-hungry women, and Val the noble savage of Rousseauist romanticism" probably by way of D. H. Lawrence—the play attempts too much. The work is further complicated by Williams' presentation of two of his major themes conjointly: "the tragic isolation of the artist in the hell of modern society and the crucifixion of the pure male on the cross of sexuality." Though he considered the play a failure, Gassner recognized its value in relation to other contemporary attempts.[14]

Donald Justice said of the play:

This is a key work to the understanding of Williams. A revision of his first important play, *Battle of Angels,* it sketches in the crude outlines of virtually undisguised fantasy a conflict basic to his imagination, one which received its best-known treatment in the conflict between the "poetic" Blanche and the "real" Stanley in *Streetcar.* There, too, the "poetic" was destroyed by the "real"; but a certain ambivalence was developing. No longer was the conflict simply between good and bad; Stanley, in spite of everything, remained not altogether unsympathetic. Sexual energy in *Orpheus* had been associated almost exclusively with the "poetic," but in *Streetcar*, as the "real" takes over some of this energy, Williams' sympathy goes along with it and, evidently, ours as well. The better balance of forces makes for a better play.[15]

Henry Popkin gave some idea of the involved and confused pretensions and the garbled symbolism of the play when he described it in terms of the Christian references upon which it is built and the changes in those references from *Battle of Angels*. The last act has shifted from Good Friday to Holy Saturday; Myra, or Mary, has become Lady, or "Our Lady" a characteristic Williams' habit of imposing upon a universal religious figure his own fantasy—making the Mother of God a sex-starved, mercenary store keeper; Val becomes Orpheus and is associated with Christ, both of whom descend to hell, but Val-Orpheus is destroyed; Val's guitar, which is close enough to Orpheus' lyre, has a phallic significance, for the jealous, sexually unsuccessful townsmen approach Val with knives drawn as if to castrate him; Jabe, described as "like the very Prince of Darkness," destroys the lovers; a kind of symbolic resurrection seems to be implied by the shafts of light which play upon the scene; the final note of the play combines two familiar Williams themes—sexuality and religion—and a tribute to the snakeskin jacket is accompanied by a "religious chant."[16]

Tennessee Williams renamed this play *The Fugitive Kind*[17] for the movie version. In doing so he picked up a phrase used by decadent or aristocratic Sandra Whiteside of *Battle of Angels* as she describes herself and Val and tries to coax Val away from a commonplace life.

IV *Period of Adjustment*

Although *Period of Adjustment*[18] does, in fact, mark a change in mood from the themes of cannibalism, castration, and other forms of violence, it also concerns itself with the same frustrated men and with variations on southern womanhood that had been appearing in the plays of Tennessee Williams

for twenty years. Although this play was supposed to represent a comic and kindlier view of life, there is again an
ugly and unhealthy element that obtrudes. Harold Clurman,
among others, found the play not particularly funny: "In
fact what one finds is something disturbingly ambiguous, not
quite 'straight.' "[19]

The lives of four neurotics, each with his own special sex
problem, is revealed on a Christmas Eve—obviously a time
for love—in the living room of a "cute" little Spanish-type
suburban bungalow, one of many indistinguishable houses
along a certain block in Memphis. A low rumbling noise
and a falling picture evoke the explanation, loaded with
symbolic significance. This particular real estate development, called High Point, is built over a cavern and sinks
one or two inches every year. The stabilizing of one house
alone would be very expensive. The owners and dealers in
the area, who are the only ones aware of the condition, are
keeping it secret so that they can sell out without too great
loss. This kind of duplicity recalls Brick Pollitt's complaint
about mendacity, just as the television set and the sofa bed in
the little bungalow recall the setting of *Cat*. But if there is
an implied comment on moral standards symbolized by this
peculiar setting, Williams would seem to be suggesting that
his foursome are conventional Americans, all sick in the same
way. But a familiarity in the characters makes them seem
like variations of the old types.

Ralph Bates, boyish but thirty-five—Williams' heroes grow
older along with their creator—is described as having a gentle gravity, something like that of Rodin's "Thinker," and a
heart capable of love. He belongs to the tradition of the
poet-vagabond-philosopher which goes back to the Val
Xaviers and Hadrians and, even before that, to the hitch-
hiker who appeared in the early poems and short stories
and one-act plays: the character who had much to say about
love but whose best expression of it was glandular. Ralph
is married to the daughter of a diabetic old millionaire who
suffers from gallstones and is minus one kidney as well—the
overloaded biography again. Very acidly, this young man
with the loving heart, says that the old man has been cheat-
ing the undertaker.

This aging Kilroy, aware of the shadows of middle age at

thirty-five, is weary of his routine job and is worried about his passing youth. He sends a rude telegram of resignation to his father-in-law and also delivers his frank opinions. As is so often true with the Williams characters—Brick Pollitt and Carol Cutrere are other examples—there is little connection between the playwright's description of the character and the way he behaves. Ralph Bates acts like a spoiled middle-aged adolescent. Because of his independence, his wife Dorothea deserts him and takes the boy with her. He reports that his great contribution to family life was taking a buck-toothed bride out of the hands of a psychiatrist and making her think that she was attractive. He got one pay raise when she bore him a son, and since then he has been brooding over his wasted talent. Apparently his capacity for love has not paid very well.

For most of the first act this aging hero exchanges confidences with Isabel Haverstick, the wife of his wartime buddy, who has been temporarily abandoned to his hospitality. She is an attractive version of the garrulous southern belle: a protected, rather innocent child born of parents after twelve years of marriage. This daughter of an overprotective father talks and acts like a lost child; she is given to such profundities as quotations of her philosophy professor who said, "We are all born, live and die in the shadow of a giant question mark that refers to three questions: Where do we come from? Why? And where, oh, where are we going!" This very general statement that passes for philosophy keeps reappearing in the plays. The idea in slightly different words, but the same general questions, appeared first in one of the speeches of the Proprietor of the swank hotel in *Ten Blocks on Camino Real* written in 1948.

Many of the scenes which involve Williams' latest version of the refined little "baby doll" are, however, rather good comedy. For instance, there is at the beginning her long, drawn-out complaint for so little a thing as her blue zipper bag, a plea repeatedly ignored; there is another little-girl scene in which she tries to call her daddy to explain on the phone—the inevitable telephone scene—all about her marriage troubles; according to Williams, in a sweet and sentimental mood, the little girl meets life's sorrows for the first time. She dissolves in tears.

The wartime buddy, the "very good looking" George Haverstick, is a kind of frustrated Stan Kowalski. Famous for his yarns about women, he is in reality terrified before them. A twenty-four-hour husband, the day before his marriage he quit his job because the monotony got on his nerves; he takes his new bride on a circuit of visits to wartime buddies; and the honeymoon car is an antiquated Cadillac funeral limousine. He had met his wife in a veteran's hospital where he was under observation for a strange tremor; and since there was no physical cause, he was paid no physical disability. The tremor is later explained as "the shakes," a condition he suffers whenever he tries to make love to a girl.

Like poor old Kilroy, George has multiple troubles. Like his friend Ralph, he is a romantic with big, non-vulgarly commercial dreams. He tells his friend of his idea of moving to Texas where they can breed a herd of cattle—a symbolic noble breed not destined for the slaughter but for much less corrupt use on television commercials. Perhaps the extreme romanticism of the idea is supposed to be funny. He builds dreams of the way the two of them could turn their backs on a mendacious America and live an agrarian life that has dignity. Perhaps because Ralph has never had trouble "making out" with his girls, he answers this boyish pipe dream with a better one of his own. He wants to be the first man, the first Adam, to land on Mars and Venus where he can fertilize a new colony. It appears to be exciting to him to know that the idea is no longer impossible.

Dorothea, Ralph's unattractive wife whom he had married not for love but for the financial promise of her seemingly moribund father, was another patient of a psychiatrist; her trouble is like that of poor George, psychological frigidity. She would shiver violently every time she came within touching distance of a boy friend. Her father had to pay fifty dollars a session to discover that fact but it took Ralph Bates of the great loving heart only one night to effect a cure—a boast that might belong to all the Tennessee Williams boys of the oversized hearts.

The problem of the play, although it is titled *Period of Adjustment*, seems to be that of getting the married couples back into bed. Since it involves one wife who is a stranger and her husband who has been separated from his pal for some time, the playwright is provided with a ready-made opportunity to repeat his customary, extended, two-character scenes. The first act between bride Isabel and her host Ralph Bates gives each an opportunity to explain his or her own private marital problem and a good deal about his or her past. It culminates with the girl's hysterical account of her wedding night. And yet, in spite of a trumped-up theatrical situation, the dialogue is suggestive of the confusion and hysteria which took hold of little girl Isabel: "It isn't as if I'd given him to believe that I was *experienced!* I made it clear that I *wasn't.* He knows my background and we'd talked at great *length* about my—*inhibitions* which I know are—inhibitions, but—which an understanding husband wouldn't expect his bride to overcome at *once,* in a tourist cabin, after a *long—silent—ride!—*in a *funeral hack* in a *snowstorm* with the *heater not working* in a *shocked! condition!* —having just been told that—we were *both* unemployed and——"

The second act brings the wartime buddies together; and, after considerable "fripping" of the newlyweds, symbolizing the period of adjustment, undoubtedly, the men talk at length about their camp women and their dreams of agrarian life. Behind all this talk are the veiled references to George's difficulty. It is finally brought out into the open, and George's confession is made: "What I mean is, the point is—you *chose* your afflictions! Married into them. Mine I didn't choose! It just come on me, mysteriously: my shakes. You wouldn't even be interested in the awful implications of an affliction like mine." He holds up his shaking hand to prove his point. "S'pose it never lets up? This thing they can't treat or even find the cause of! S'pose I shake all my life like, like—dice in a crap shooter's fist?—Huh?—I mean at all moments of tension, all times of crisis, I shake! . . . Huh? And there's other aspects to it beside the career side. It could affect my love life. Huh? I could start shaking so hard when I started to make out with a girl that I couldn't do it. You know? Couldn't make the scene with her. . . ."[20] When Ralph states that the trouble is George's being "scared of impotence," the buddies begin checking experiences. And this is the general tenor of what Williams means by "serious comedy."

The third act opens with the kind of vulgar sex talk—decorated with Williams' tender words—which suggests that the playwright at forty-five was still writing in the idiom he used when he wrote in his late twenties the poem "The Angels of Fructification." It is also the kind of dialogue that prompted the late George Jean Nathan to call him the "genital-man" of the contemporary theater. Ralph's sage lecture about the art of love is interrupted, however, by the arrival of father and mother McGillicuddy, who are not only grotesque symbols of middle-class, commercial people but also carbon copies of the caricature which Williams has tagged the Moneybags. They have come to carry away daughter Dorothea's belongings; but, before they succeed, she relents and comes crawling back to her husband—with love. The play closes with no surprise whatsoever; each couple, correctly paired off, solves the problems of the marriage bed—and of life as well, apparently. As the curtain begins to fall, Dorothea, clad in a borrowed nightgown, is heard saying to her husband, "Careful, let me do it! It isn't mine!" Mr. Williams can be expected to keep his ear tuned to the box office to the last exclamation point!

Williams tried to give large significance to rather banal ideas, as, for instance, the notion that we must learn to get along together—preferably in bed. Howard Taubman observed that "Mr. Williams cannot—apparently does not wish to—leave the psychiatric atmosphere." To Taubman the characters are thin, one-sided; and their "temporary sexual incompatibilities" are repetitious "shadows of old portraits in the Williams gallery."[21] Most critics agreed that the playwright had evidenced his usual technical dexterity, his flare for dialogue, but that he had misspent his talents. Calling Williams "Broadway's laureate of sex writing," the critic in *Time* found the play more theater than truth, or too much "of Freud pinch-hitting for flesh and blood, of amusing little leitmotifs in place of incisive motivations."[22] Harold Clurman was more deeply disturbed by the cloudy and implied satire about nice, average Americans: "a great many American males are castrated by conformity, while others are sex-crazy to the point of ineffectuality, or sex-crazy because they are ineffectual"; the women are near-idiots because they are victims of either callous or overfond fathers. In Williams' failure to clarify his attitude toward his characters and toward his thesis, he is seriously at fault. "If the play is a piece of sexual-social satire on the average American, it is hardly very funny."²³

These plays involving the defeated charmers from Val Xavier in *Battle of Angels,* who is the same character in *Orpheus Descending,* through Kilroy and Brick Pollitt, to the two wartime buddies in *Period of Adjustment* represent a span of twenty years of playwrighting. Williams began by glamorizing the vagrant—the poetic rebel against social conformity who is so magnetically attractive that sex somehow gets mixed up with Life, Love, and Freedom. For twenty years the theme has not changed. The physical demands of women seem to get in the way of big ideas which are often brought in like afterthoughts—issues about racial tolerance, about human understanding, about Gestapo-like ruthlessness of Big Business. For twenty years the hero has retained the same kind of adolescent rebellious attitude, the same yearning for a kind of indefinite and irresponsible freedom, and the same talent for failure. But for Tennessee Williams such plays—and lack of development—seem to have been good business.

CHAPTER 6

The Degenerating Artist

I *Feet of Clay*

THREE STUDIES in deterioration—the short novel, *The Roman Spring of Mrs. Stone* (1950), and two plays, *Suddenly Last Summer* (1958) and *Sweet Bird of Youth* (1959)—seem to be attempts to evoke pity for artists who have become hopelessly lost. All three major characters have reason to suspect that their personal magnetism and attractiveness have hidden the fact that not one of them ever had real talent. All three madly cling to the last remnants of youth. The women desperately indulge in sex, hoping to delay old age; and the man continues illicit relationships with his kind. The women domineer over their men; they are possessive mothers or an insatiable mistress. For all of them life is a hollow existence, and they might warrant pity if the playwright were as interested in describing their condition as he is in portraying decadence. "Rainbow-tinted refuse," a phase applied to the work of Baudelaire, could be applicable to this phase of Tennessee Williams' writing.

Williams contrasts these vivid artist figures with innocuous commonplace people—sometimes with southerners who, like the artists, do not take a stand against evil. Other insights into southern "society" appear in the brutally cold-blooded evaluation of people according to their wealth and in the political corruption represented by the segregationists and youth groups. The predominant interest, however, lies in the sexual theme—and an increasingly morbid interest in the distorted variations upon this theme seems to have had an obsessive fascination for Williams during these later years.

II *The Roman Spring of Mrs. Stone*

The short novel *The Roman Spring of Mrs. Stone*,[1] which appeared in 1950, is a study of the disintegration of Mrs. Stone, a once prominent actress who finds herself a lonely, wealthy widow who is dependent upon the attentions of Paolo, an impoverished, beautiful young Italian gigolo. Mrs. Stone had chosen to retire in Rome where so much belonged to the past; there she joins the company offered by a certain Contessa, a "stately witch" who is excited by the memory of Mr. Stone's great fortune and who introduces her to three beautiful young men as companions for a "service" of a particularly intimate kind. The fourth, the boy Paolo, who is thirty years her junior, succeeds where others failed. This young adventurer, who cares for nothing but himself, is able to turn to his own advantage Mrs. Stone's unusual degree of loneliness—another of Williams' lonely people.

Mrs. Stone, who had retired from the stage at fifty because she no longer could play Juliet, had in her career-existence become a legend among her associates—not for what she was, a ruthless, self-centered woman, but as an image of devotion and kindness. Her twenty-five-year marriage to a wealthy businessman had been a companionship subordinate to her career. Their sexual relationship is a good illustration of the theory that Williams may have picked up from D. H. Lawrence. At the beginning their marriage almost collapsed because of her frigidity and apparent aversion and because of his timidity and awkwardness. They become illustrations of the old prototypes who are opposites of the natural sex mates—the aggressive, loveless woman and the businessman who can make money but not love. It is through their unsatisfactory sexual life that they find what both really wanted: she, a grown-up child that she could mother; he, a beautiful young mother whom he could adore.

As long as she is completely immersed in her career, the unsatisfactory nature of this arrangement was not apparent. The loneliness and barrenness of their life became obvious with her retirement when, against doctor's orders for her husband, they set out on a world tour. After her retirement and her husband's death, when she was no longer completely engrossed in her career, she also began to analyze herself and her actions. She did not admit to herself, however, that with the cessation of her career came a collapse of intellectual processes. Williams portrays the deterioration of this ruthlessly ambitious, mindless woman among the impoverished parasites in Rome who prey upon rich and lonely widows. He suggests the world of the streets: the shops, the luxury restaurants, expensive tailors, and the everlasting *letto* —the connubial bed.

When Paolo begged for an exorbitant sum, Mrs. Stone knew that she could pay him, dismiss him with dignity, and be alone. He was attractive to her sexually; and, although she was repelled by her feelings, she admitted to herself that her "longings" gave her a delightful sense of immediacy. Williams implies that she realized that she could indulge herself in intercourse without fear of pregnancy. The radiant Paolo of the beautiful body achieves his contrived and desired advantage; becomes her lover; and makes her believe, for the first time in her life, that she has found happiness. The continuing relationship is marked by her increased anxieties over the discrepancy in their ages, by their ugly quarrels, and by the incredibly rude insults of the youth. The affair culminates in a sordid evening when she sacrifices the last shred of her dignity and then loses him to a brash young Hollywood actress who is currently "between husbands."

In an early scene Williams introduces a woman journalist, another of his professional women who may be very successful in their careers but who would be most unsatisfactory in bed. This Meg Bishop has lost all traces of femininity from her ten-year association with important representatives of business and politics. It is she who bluntly discredits talent by calling it a kind of bluff and who tells Mrs. Stone that, as Juliet, she was like an imperial eagle who would tear her Romeo to pieces. About her love life she says that Mrs. Stone had married a fat little man that looked like "an Easter bunny" to avoid sexual intercourse; that she is now, because of her filthy millions, collecting about herself procuresses, effeminate dandies, and other shady characters; that her present life is escapism and is the topic of sniggering gossip in the world capitals—New York, London, and Paris.

It is also this Meg Bishop who compares the decay of the once proud city of Rome to the deterioration of the

woman before her. According to Williams, the woman journalist sees in Mrs. Stone the evil that is characteristic of
modern society, and so she becomes a symbol of all that is
corrupt in the world of "mendacity." The vignette of the
spiteful presswoman would seem to be an attempt on the
part of the writer to state a theme and to clarify a symbol
and to give universality to his story: Mrs. Stone epitomizes
the corruption of her time. This brief scene and these pointed
lines are quite typical of the way Williams, through a few
lines which sound like the writer's interruption of the narrative, tries to give a larger significance to the situation he
is describing. The scenes, however, with which he describes
corruption, are written with so much relish that they tell
more about the author's own thinking and interests than
about a degenerating society.

Mrs. Stone is frequently described as a vulture, a symbolic figure of rapaciousness. She is Tennessee Williams'
most unpleasant of aggressive women and his most obvious example of a character that might have been inspired by D. H.
Lawrence's theory of the loveless, dominant female. She seems
to be a "constructed" character—one built out of a theory
rather than created from observation and interpretation. The
vulture image applied to Mrs. Stone recalls the hawk—the de-
stroyer—in the legend which Val Xavier tells about the legless bird who never descends to earth. The novel has many
illustrations symbolizing her destructive nature. From a prissy,
ladylike girl she developed into a tomboy whose favorite
game was "King on the Mountain"; and in it she ferociously
beat off any competitors. In later years during her acting
career she substituted political tactics for kicking and scratching. For example, fifteen years before her retirement she had
obliterated the handsome, talented young actor who played
Orlando to her Rosalind and threatened to overshadow her;
she is described as a hawk swooping down on a defenseless,
small creature hidden in the grass.

The vulture symbol keeps reappearing. There was "a ra-
pacious bird" in the violet eyes of Mrs. Stone. When she
would visit her sick co-workers, there was something in her
look like the "hard eyes" associated with a bird. Warned by
the Contessa that Paolo is a little *marchetta,* a special kind
of male whore with his own special price, she laughed; the

sound of her voice was like that of a bird of prey. When she looked at a portrait of herself as Juliet, she noticed "something hawklike" in the expression of the eyes. In the final scene she rushes at the gossiping Contessa, and the gesture is compared to the violent attack of a large bird. This vulture image is in harmony with the portrait of a ruthless, ambitious woman. It does seem, however, despite a rapid deterioration, that so sharp a hawk would not be so blind to Paolo's shabby treatment or so completely unaware that, although he might not steal the jewels from the soap dish, he might readily murder her in bed. The portrait of Mrs. Stone is another illustration of the way that Williams has not taken time or thought to become acquainted with his characters. Again and again their biographies and their actions do not coincide.

In order to accentuate the degree of decay to which Mrs. Stone descends, Williams adds a character, a very handsome tramp who is so vulgar as to be almost ludicrous. The frequently recurring appearances of this obscene young man of such exceptional beauty raises some interesting questions about Tennessee Williams as an artist; for he obviously seems to be fiddling with the pornographic. The beautiful but ragged youth, stealthily, always alert, always on guard, pursues Mrs. Stone. He watches her balcony from the street below. One time, as she is standing there with a guest, he exposes himself. "As his hands came out of his pockets and converged in front of him, she realized that he was about to make water against the wall." At another time when Mrs. Stone was walking along the shops, she became aware that this same loiterer was following her, and she fled. Later she sees the reflection of this same figure in a shop window; when she heard the unmistakable sound of a man urinating, she fled. At another time her attention was again caught by the metallic tapping, and she saw the familiar figure. "Then with a barely noticeable gesture he divided the unbuttoned front of his coat by a couple of inches and Mrs. Stone's aghast look caught the flash of outrageous nudity which the slight motion exposed."

Early during her last evening with Paolo, when that adventurer's insults had forced her to leave him with his new girl, she is again arrested by the tapping. Distraught by what she has been going through, and aware that her millions are no longer a substitute for lost youth—as far as Paolo is concerned—she turns to the persistent interloper. Hysterically she tells him to look at her face, and she asks him why he follows her. Later when she overhears the Contessa's gossip she becomes aware how shamefully she has drifted. Then she asks one of her creator's pompous philosophical questions about the way in which time and life seem to drift. But at the end of this wretched evening when she is abandoned by Paolo, she again sees the obscene young man below her balcony. She wraps her keys in her white handkerchief and throws them down to him. The gesture gives her the line, arty and symbolic, and completely senseless: *"Look! I've stopped the drift!"* This is the incredible, final act of a character so frequently described as a hawk.

It is even more incredible that Tennessee Williams would have had the temerity to think that he was creating an acting role for Greta Garbo. This fact may be an illustration of how far he has moved from the world of reality and knowledge of people, and how deeply he has immersed himself in his own fantasies. The way in which he would universalize these dismal portraits is even more incredible. Only a very sick imagination could find a relation between the corruption of our time and a young tramp—an Italian vagabond?—who is everlastingly emptying his bladder.

The novel gives a dismal picture of Americans as well as Italians. Williams has indulged his contempt for women. There is the degenerating Mrs. Stone; the unfeminine, unpleasant Meg Bishop; and the greedy old Contessa, procuress for handsome Italian youths. There are also rich, insensitive American women on the periphery of this dubious society; all of them are ugly figures, most of them sex-driven. Williams' usual contempt for the businessman is heaped upon the "waxpaper king" Mr. Stone, a ridiculous plump little man with infantile eyes—not the look of childhood's innocence associated with the sexually fortunate—who may have made millions but could not make love.

Williams is able, however, to dramatize short scenes and to create a vivid impression. Paolo under the hands of the barber enjoys the hour as if it were a sexual experience; Williams compares the sensuality of the hour to "the jam of the gods"—whatever that may be. This is the scene in which Paolo confesses the progress of his affair with Mrs. Stone and mouths indecencies about her. There is another sharply drawn scene in which the Contessa, furious over being cheated by Paolo, warns Mrs. Stone. The tailor-shop scene in which the greedy gigolo dresses himself like a rich heir is excellent. There is a strong, final scene in which Mrs. Stone, angered by the Contessa's vicious slander, drives the woman from her living room. These are vivid, dramatic scenes which indicate that Williams can handle high-tensioned moments. *The Roman Spring of Mrs. Stone* also indicates that Tennessee Williams has considerable talent for satire—if he were willing to sublimate his preoccupation with sex. There seems hardly a character in this *novella* that is worth bothering about; and the continual meddling with sex either reflects an abnormal, sick view of life—or a determination to strike it rich.

III   *Suddenly Last Summer*

A curious, modern fable, *Suddenly Last Summer*[2] is set in a wealthy old woman's living room which looks out upon an exotic jungle garden in the Garden District of New Orleans. The setting, suggestive of one of Rousseau's jungle paintings, gives a surrealistic impression of another kind of hell—another appalling glimpse into Williams' own southern Gothic. The symbolism implied in the exotic flowers compared to human entrails dripping with blood and in the destructive sounds of jungle creatures—hissing serpents, shrieking birds, snarling beasts—gives another example of the way Williams imposes his personal interpretation on an art form, or a theory, or a myth.

Against this macabre setting the play, *Suddenly Last Summer*, lays bare the story of a southern aristocrat and her forty-year-old son as it is reported by Catharine Holly, a girl who never resisted telling the truth. An uneven play of four short scenes, the first and the last are variations of an interrupted monologue. The second and third are developed slightly as if written to extend the play or to provide a necessary blank space between the two sharply different accounts. The recital is heavily orchestrated with jungle sounds; there are harsh bird cries for the brutal phases, sweet bird songs for honest statements or tender sentiments.

The "well-groomed jungle" was as much a part of Sebastian Venable's well-designed life—exotic plants carefully tagged with Latin names and the Venus flytrap kept alive by fruitflies from Florida—as his life-work, poetry, became a ritual. After a nine-month gestation he delivered a poem, an annual poem for twenty-five summers, each exquisitely hand printed on an eighteenth-century press. Mrs. Venable says repeatedly that her son, Sebastian, was a poet, and then she makes the old familiar Williams distinction between the poet and man of business: "That's what I meant when I said his life was his work because the work of a poet is the life of a poet and—vice versa, the life of a poet is the work of a poet, I mean you can't separate them, I mean—well, for instance, a salesman's work is one thing and his life is another—or can be."[3] In reverent memory of her son she lifts the elegant gilt-edged volume with a gesture that suggests a religious rite.[4] She says that Sebastian's search for a clear image of God led the two of them to charter a boat for Encantades—the Enchanted Isles—to watch the hatching of the sea turtles and their desperate flight from the flesh-eating birds. This is a variation on the image of the legless bird and the marauding hawk as described by Val Xavier. "They were diving down on the hatched sea-turtles, turning them over to expose their soft undersides, tearing the undersides open and rending and eating their flesh."[5] Only the minutest number would escape. The mother explains that all good poets have to look harder for God than priests, who can rely on books and organizations. In another attempt to find God, the son almost became a Buddhist monk; but the mother, neglecting her dying husband, saved the boy for Shepheard's Hotel at Cairo and the Ritz at Paris.

Mrs. Venable describes herself and her son as a famous couple who were known as Sebastian and Violet. In their refusal to grow old, both mother and son developed a regimen of discipline and abstention; and they constructed each day as if it were a work of art—sculpture. She makes a great point of her son's purity; he was still chaste at forty. After his death she hysterically charges that her niece Catharine Holly is trying to destroy the legend of their beautiful association and her son's reputation. Mrs. Venable's money poses a threat to the girl; the older woman promises the psychiatrist, Dr. Cukro-wicz, to establish a Sebastian Venable Memorial Foundation for his special use if he will stop the girl's babbling about her knowledge of Sebastian's way of life. Mrs. Holly and her son, George, Catharine's mother and brother—two of Williams' southern grotesques—are nervous because the old woman is contesting Sebastian's will that should leave each of them fifty thousand.

Catharine Holly is the rarest specimen in the entire literary jungle of Tennessee Williams: she is a normal human being. A decent, intelligent girl, neither oversexed nor frustrated, a girl with a passion for truth-telling, she is indeed an extraordinary creature and one out of place in this particular coterie of grotesques. Surrounded by flat characters, a stupid greedy brother and a silly mother and a vicious old hag—her aunt Violet Venable, who is determined to have her intellectually castrated—but encouraged by the handsome young doctor who seems to be more interested in her story than in getting money for his hospital, she frankly recites one of Williams' more lurid stories.

The girl seems not to hate her Aunt Violet who has had her committed to a mental hospital because, according to the girl, hatred is compatible only with insanity. Williams gives to her exactly the same definition of love that he gave to the prostitute, Marguerite Gautier, who cynically told Jacques Casanova that it is only a matter of people's becoming accustomed to one another; and this repetition shows how the writer continually imposes himself upon his characters. Catharine says that Sebastian and she needed one another during that last summer of his death. She could offer him motherly love, the only kind he would accept. She could save him from himself: "Completing!—a sort of!—*image!*—he had of himself as a sort of!—*sacrifice* to a!—*terrible* sort of a——" The doctor finished the sentence with the word "God." On the other hand, he could offer her an escape from the memory of a near-rape by an expectant young father, a chance escort from a Mardi Gras ball.

The guilt sense which demands of Sebastian Venable such appalling retribution is the most horribly described illustration of a perverted Puritanism to be found in Williams;

the atonement theme is one of the obsessions that seems to have continually plagued Williams as it has a number of his characters.[6] Sebastian's problem was obscured as long as his mother served as a shield. When Mrs. Venable suffered a stroke and was replaced by Catharine, the girl soon discovered his sickness. Separated from his dominating mother he went to pieces; he no longer wrote; he substituted the apparently elegant youths who followed him with ragged urchins; his moral deterioration becomes even more obvious when he makes the girl wear a white lisle one-piece bathing suit which became transparent when wet—she was to serve as procuress, as his mother unconsciously did before her. Both the mother and the girl, neither of them shy as was Sebastian, attracted what he wanted. During this last summer he was soon followed by crowds of hungry boys who lived on the beach like scavengers.

On this last day of life, Sebastian, like all Williams' degenerates who wear white, was expensively and immaculately dressed. With Catharine he nervously ate a five o'clock lunch at a sea restaurant; the starved, naked children—some of them beyond childhood, many of whom Sebastian recognized from his sorties on the beach—watched them eat. They made noises with their mouths and stuffed their fists into their faces. Popping pills into his mouth, Sebastian told Catharine not to look at the beggars whom he sneeringly called the social disease of the country. Some of the children began their serenade, with tin cans strung together, tins flattened for cymbals, and stuffed paper bags. In her recital of the horrible last day Catharine makes a comment about Sebastian that characterizes the "moral paralysis" of so many of Williams' leading figures, and harkens back to the Judge in *Purification* who does not believe in any man's making a judgment about another, preferring that all men judge themselves. This may be a reaction on the part of the playwright against the Puritan strictures under which he grew up. Catharine's statement about Sebastian is this: "And thought nobody had any right to complain or interfere in any way whatsoever, and even though he knew that what was awful was awful, that what was wrong was wrong, and my Cousin Sebastian was certainly never sure that anything was wrong! —He thought it unfitting to ever take any action about anything whatsoever!—except to go on doing as something in him directed. . . ."

At the height of the insulting serenade, Sebastian, for once in his life, asserted himself; he ordered the waiters to beat away the little monsters. The poet threw a handful of paper money on the table, stalked out in a daze, and was soon pursued in the blazing white heat by the naked children. He screamed when they overcame him but when the waiters, the police, and others arrived, they found him flung against the white wall, as naked as his attackers. Catharine describes the scene: "Torn or cut parts of him away with their hands or knives or maybe those jagged tin cans they made music with, they had torn bits of him away and stuffed them into those gobbling fierce little empty black mouths of theirs." Then the final precious description of what is left of the body, done in images of red roses and white paper, recalls the detached and rhetorical description of the execution of the one-armed Apollo.[7] The Doctor reacts to Mrs. Venable's hysteria by saying, "I think we ought at least to consider the possibility that the girl's story could be true. . . ."[8]

As part of her confession Catharine Holly tells about the unpleasant experience she had at the Mardi Gras ball. It is a piece of dialogue that is brilliantly handled. It is told directly and explosively; it is rich in its satiric comment on southern "society." It is one of those patches of dialogue that justifies the frequent praise of Williams' feeling for natural speech and of his perception of character. She tells how her escort to the ball got so drunk that he could not stand; when she looked for a taxi to take her home, a stranger came to her help. He took her to a lover's rendezvous instead. Afterwards he said that all had better be forgotten because his wife was expecting a child. He took her home but in her anger she did not stay. She returned to the ball-room—unable to explain why, just as the mutilated Apollo was unable to explain why he struck the broker—she rushed on to the dance floor, found her abductor, and beat him for all she was worth. She became socially ostracized, began thinking of herself in the third person, and then Sebastian proposed the trip. It was for her like a return from dying. But even in the very plush hotels where she stayed, she felt that she was desperately running away from the "hot, ravenous mouth."

After this confession the Doctor gives Catharine an injection, a kind of truth serum, so that she will give the full, complete story about Sebastian. Her first reaction is to crush her mouth violently to his; clutching his body against hers, she tells him that she has been lonelier than death. Again we have the lonely character. Coming after the confession that she has made, this kind of action is out of character and is reminiscent of the sexy stage business Williams gave to Carol Cutrere when she was trying to get Val Xavier to go out into the woods with her. It is after the big kiss that Catharine tells the awful story of what happened at Cabeza de Lobo; she gives her account to the company of human birds assembled, the raucous jungle sounds giving way to occasional sweet bird calls and a white light of varying intensity playing upon her.

Williams has paced the recollection of the Sebastian Venable story to raise emotions rather than to encourage thought. His fascination with brutality—from birds preying on the baby turtles to the cannibalism at the end—suggests the extent to which he will go to create theatrical shocks. The cumulative effect of the story, concluding with the ghastly "poetic" description of cannibalistic children, tends to dissipate whatever significance Williams intended. After the girl's candid report, all the possible references or meanings in the earlier part of the play are overshadowed by the horror of the final picture. Robert Brustein calls this horror tale "a homosexual metaphor." The play represents another private and very sick view of the world.

Williams would give this grotesque piece of southern Gothic—a morbid extension of his own theory of guilt and retribution—a universal significance. He has Catharine—before her detailed confession—say, "I know it's a hideous story but it's a true story of our time and the world we live in and what did truly happen to Cousin Sebastian in Cabeza de Loco. . . ." Williams has carried his private symbolism to incredible extremes when he would make a decadent artist and aging homosexual, a sybarite who never took a stand for either right or wrong, whose sexual perversion extended to younger and younger boys, and who was finally devoured by these starving waifs—when he would make that particular figure in the particular situation described a symbol to represent all men of our times.

Brooks Atkinson wrote of *Suddenly Last Summer*: "A playwright cannot be charged with believing everything his characters do and say. They have a life of their own. But, as Mrs. Venable remarks about her dead son, Sebastian: 'A poet's life is his work and his work is his life.' And the frequency with which this joyless, nihilistic point of view turns up in Mr. Williams' plays ('Camino Real,' 'Cat on a Hot Tin Roof,' 'Orpheus Descending') suggests that it represents his experience and belief. It is not theatrical pose; it conveys his sense of reality." Mr. Atkinson admitted that the play is cleverly written. "Everything in the written play evokes in dramatic movements the central mood of evil, decadent luxury, cruelty, voracity, tropical degeneracy. The sensuousness of the phrasing and imagery (sunlight in Cabeza de Lobo 'looked as if a huge white bone had caught fire in the sky') and the immaculate, rose-perfumed description of Sebastian's corpse are evocative pieces of sheer writing. Believing in the validity of what he is saying, Mr. Williams has made an art out of malignance and maleficence, like Remy de Gourmont or Baudelaire."[9]

IV *Sweet Bird of Youth*

Tennessee Williams describes in *Sweet Bird of Youth*[10] the desperate efforts of an aging actress and an unsuccessful southern actor to cling to their hopes and their youth, and then confuses their plight with a racial theme and southern politics. With the exception of two minor figures, he has crowded his play with an assembly of sorry characters. In this psychiatric ward the artists have not retained any appearance of youthful innocence. There is neither the semblance of nor hope for decency among the other characters, who are either bigoted and vicious politicians or innocuous, average citizens. The playwright, in attempting to fuse these wildly disparate elements, imposed upon himself an impossible assignment.[11]

In scenes reminiscent of Mrs. Stone and Paolo, though more brutally described, aging actress Princess Kosmonopolis, shamed by the fiasco of a recent comeback, clings desperately to vestiges of youth with her last gigolo, Chance Wayne, a youngish, would-be actor whom she picked up in a Florida Cabana. For years he had tried to crash the theatrical world, and for years he had made surreptitious visits to Heavenly, Boss Finley's daughter, to whom he had bequeathed the venereal disease which necessitated a hysterectomy. Boss Finley, a Bible-quoting segregationist, threatens Chance Wayne with payment in kind if he returns. Out of ignorance, or the playwright's carelessness, Wayne has not heard of his mother's death, nor about the "whore's operation" on Heavenly. He returns; and, as if hypnotized, he remains to face the avengers.

The play opens in a hotel bedroom on an Easter Sunday morning with the sound of church bells and a choir singing the Allelulia [sic] Chorus.[12] The Princess seems to be emerging from a nightmare; and Chance Wayne, who is in bed beside her, lights the first cigarette of the day. Half-dazed, she cries for oxygen and a pill and stupidly asks about her bed-mate; when she wakes up she needs to identify her new lover so that she can make the proper adjustment. She and her present paramour have much in common. Both of them are minor talents who have never come anywhere near the top but have seen better days than the present. To both of them advancing age is comparable to the loss of their sexual organs. Both depend heavily on dope and liquor. In addition, Chance Wayne is a blackmailer. Chance says of himself, "I've had more chances than I could count on my fingers, and made the grade almost, but not quite, every time. Something always blocks me."[13] As he threatens the Princess with coercion, the decadent but still fiery actress appraises his career in terms that sound almost like the playwright's own confession: "You were well born, weren't you? Born of good Southern stock, in a genteel tradition, with just one advantage, a laurel wreath on your forehead, given too early, without enough effort to earn it."

The Princess casually meets his threats of blackmail with her own demands; she wants life, and on any terms, as a way to forget what she does not want to remember. Life to her is the same as love-making—a definition given by the young man in Williams' very early play, *The Case of the Crushed Petunias*, the work of a very young and a very inexperienced playwright. The Princess, desperate for sexual happiness and the illusion that they are innocent young lovers without shame, bids Chance to draw the curtains, turn on the radio —and prove himself. The big-double-bed scene comes earlier in the play than usual and the bed itself dominates the stage. The "between-acts" interlude has proven successful, obviously, because the Princess is signing traveler's checks like mad and talking about Hollywood contracts. This may be an attempt at comedy—with a rather dubious overtone.

Chance makes a long confession, speaking directly to the audience;[14] he tells about his youth in St. Cloud, and part of the speech might have been given to Kilroy: "I was a twelve-pound baby, normal and healthy, but with some kind of quantity 'X' in my blood, a wish or a need to be different." He also tells about his phenomenal love-making career among celebrities in the social register; his hysterical fear of losing his youth, of being killed in the war; and of his hope of flashing rolls of money to win his Heavenly. Though skeptical about his artistic talent, he has no doubts about his physical charm; he voices Williams' definition of love: "the biggest of all differences in this world is between the ones that had or have pleasure in love and those that haven't and hadn't any pleasure in love, but just watched it with envy, sick envy." He is philosopher one moment, an aging exhibitionist the next.

There is a complete change of subject with the second act. The first scene belongs primarily to Boss Finley; his son Tom; his daughter Heavenly; quite incidentally, to Scudder, her innocuous fiancé, a nice looking businessman of the Junior Chamber of Commerce type, a "gee," "golly," "gosh" boy; and to Heavenly's Aunt Nonnie. A pious-mouthed segregationist of the vilest sort, Boss Finley is a caricature of a southern politician—reminiscent of Huey Long. Currently promoting the career of his son, he admits that the clubs organized for Tom are only blinds for juvenile delinquents. Tom, a grotesque figure of degeneracy, is the eager agent of his father's revenge: the castration of Chance Wayne. In a curious but supercharged scene, reminiscent of the Brick-Big

Daddy clash in *Cat*, Boss Finley and his son Tom face each other like two stags after Tom has sarcastically referred to his father's expensive mistress, Miss Lucy.

The relationship between Boss Finley and his beautiful daughter is something else. In elaborate prose Williams describes in Freudian terms that the father feels toward his daughter something like the way he had felt toward the wife, when at the same age, he had desired her so intensely. The conversation of Boss Finley and Heavenly—and with the exception of a brief pantomime, her only scene in the whole play—is supposed to be accompanied by formal eighteenth-century music. In contrast to this aristocratic and refined overtone, the action of the scene exposes not only the girl's contempt for a father who drove away the poor boy she loved, but also her bitter reaction to the operation that made her a childless old woman. When she talks of entering a convent, the enraged father orders her to appear on the speaker's platform, dressed in white, not only to dissipate the ugly rumors of her corruption, but to save his political fortunes. Again long speeches—long, non-realistic dramatic readings—are directed to the audience. With all this surcharged emotionalism, there is no scene between Chance Wayne and this girl for whom he risks his manhood; and this omission is another instance of Williams' failure to develop the dramatic possibilities of his material.

The second scene of the second act is a hectic conglomeration of new characters and contrived situations. Buried in a nervous confusion of unrelated scenes is the ugly segregationist speech by Boss Finley which is "souped up" with lights and images on a video screen; he explains his support of white man's action in what has become a notorious case—a "nigger" had been picked at random and castrated to prove that "they" mean business about protecting white women. Boss Finley is interrupted by the Heckler, a shadowy character who seems to be a lone voice protesting racial brutality. Boss continues in pious tones to talk about his mission to save white man's blood from pollution. Speaking in terms of his sacred trust, and on the other hand, of his being the Negro's best friend, he mouths in bombastic terms his doctrine of blood pollution. The Heckler again interrupts his harangue with pointed questions about Heavenly. As

Boss Finley tells about the effigy of himself that was burned on the state university campus, the Heckler is dragged away and is thoroughly beaten. Chance makes no move to stop the brutality but Heavenly is sickened. The scene has the same savage quality which characterizes the torch slaying of Val Xavier in *Orpheus Descending* or the cannibalism reported in *Suddenly*.

A brief third act returns to the aging actress and Chance Wayne. When she is excited about the possibilities of her own return to Hollywood, she faces her companion with the brutal truth about himself: "Chance, you've gone past something you couldn't afford to go past; your time, your youth; you've passed it. It's all you had, and you've had it." The enemy, time, has eaten away his chances. The point is made that the laurel, with which he was honored as a young man, is now withered; he has nothing; he has returned to his home town and to the girl whom he diseased and who will not see him. The princess holds no delusions about herself and her chances for a new career; she sees both herself and Chance as monsters. The playwright, in explanatory prose, writes a plea for these doomed souls, both of whom face castration. It recalls the prayer for the derelicts and the disillusioned which Esmeralda gives at the end of *Camino Real*.

It is the universal significance which Williams gives to the final scene—his characteristic habit of making a wide application to a very personal or a very abnormal experience —that has aroused comment. The play closes as Tom Finley enters with three of his henchmen to carry out the much advertised mission of vengeance, and Chance gives a final speech that may make theatrical history: "I don't ask for your pity, but just for your understanding—not even that—no. Just for your recognition of me in you, and the enemy time, in us all."[15] Critic Harold Clurman asked: "What is it we are asked to recognize in ourselves? That we are corrupted by our appetite for the flesh and clamor of success? That we are driven to live debased existences by the constrictions and brutality which surround us? That the sound instincts of our youth are thus frustrated and turned to gall? And that we have an inordinate fear of age, for the passing of time makes us old before we mature?"[16]

Marya Mannes wrote of *Sweet Bird:* "It is the nature of the excitement that disturbs me deeply: a violence of corruption and decay in which all natural appetites are diverted—and perverted—toward destruction, and in which a poet's imagination must feed on carrion." She felt "blank amazement at the final curtain, in which the about-to-be-castrated Chance, alone on the stage, beseeches the audience with tears in his eyes not to judge him but to understand him, for he is in each of us, and our innocence is lost with his. To which I was tempted to shout, as Liza did in *Pygmalion,* if not in *My Fair Lady,* 'Not bloody likely!' "[17]

Henry Popkin commented on the inextricably involved Christian and mythological symbolism in the play, and the simpler symbolism of the trait names, as for instance, Chance Wayne: chances waning. The action takes place on Easter Sunday and all the main characters hope for resurrection, wish for a rebirth in their own way—Chance Wayne, Heavenly, The Princess (her original name was Ariadne, the princess who led Theseus out of the labyrinth), and Boss Finley. Mr. Popkin noted that Boss Finley is most directly identified with Christ; this racist talks of being inspired by the Voice of God to carry on his drive against race pollution and of his being crucified, that is, burned in effigy on the university campus on Good Friday.[18] For all the Christian symbolism, there is in Williams very little respect for religion. In this, as in previous plays in which religious figures appear, there is an overtone of exhibitionism and contempt, a tendency to overstate a personal attitude that is very much like a sophomore's discovery of atheism.

Robert Brustein called the play "a private neurotic fantasy" about time and castration. Heavenly lost her sexual organs by a hysterectomy; a Negro, seized at random, was castrated as part of Boss Finley's program; the aging Boss Finley has been called impotent by his expensive mistress; the Princess, because of her advancing years, sees the end of her acting career, age being a form of castration; Chance Wayne, as the final curtain goes down, faces revenge-castration at the hands of Tom Finley and his delinquents. Mr. Brustein advanced the very interesting idea that the play is a confused symbolic statement—partly Christian, partly pagan—about innocence and corruption; that "the sweet bird of youth" is an echo of that legendary bird described by Val Xavier in *Orpheus Descending;* that the bird is a symbol of childhood innocence and that the force of corruption is experience—sexual experience. What makes the whole play a "nebulous nightmare," according to Mr. Brustein, is the way in which Williams confuses frankly sexual images with Calvinist notions of guilt. He said that the dramatist had imposed an involved literary screen to cover up a sexual theme.[19]

When the play opened, all seven of the daily New York newspaper critics praised it highly; but a few murmured grudging reservations. "Whatever its shortcomings, *Bird* opened with the sweet smell of commercial success in its beak. The advanced ticket sale reached $390,000 and the screen rights were sold to MGM for a sliding-scale sum that may reach $400,000."[20] The critic in *Time* found the play extremely artificial: "*Sweet Bird of Youth* is very close to parody, but the wonder is that Williams should be so inept at imitating himself. The sex violence, the perfumed decay, the hacking domestic quarrels, the dirge of fear and self-pity, the characters who dangle in neurotic limbo—all are present—but only like so many dramatic dead cats on a cold tin roof." He pointed out a number of parallels to *Cat:* the dominating woman, the childless wife in the one, the fading movie queen in the other; a homosexual athlete in one, a virile male but an impotent actor in another; Big Daddy repeated in Boss Finley, for the first "psychologically emasculated his son" and the second threatens "physical castration."[21]

When Williams described the violent story from Herodotus that he adapted as a youngster, he ventured the opinion that it set a pattern for much of his subsequent writing. His Val Xavier is stripped and hanged in *Battle of Angels;* and he is murdered by blow torches or perhaps torn apart by dogs in *Orpheus Descending*—either method is morbidly vicious. His Byron in *Camino Real* describes with relish the burning, bursting body of Shelley. A big black man in "The Black Masseur" devours his small white client, a ceremony given religious significance; and in *Suddenly Last Summer* starved Italian youngsters hack chunks out of the effete poet and stuff their greedy mouths. The girl in this play came near to facing mental castration, and the heroine in *Sweet Bird* has undergone a hysterectomy before the play opens. As the last curtain goes down, the avengers close in on the hero to deprive him of his sexual organs.

What all this brutality signifies is a study in itself. In his article, "Prelude to Comedy," Williams insists that an artist uses the material of his own life; perhaps that may be so. Perhaps these later plays are for him a kind of catharsis after undergoing psychotherapy. But it is the tendency to give personal experience a universal significance that worries a number of critics, many of whom have been liberally quoted in this chapter.

Sweet Bird of Youth was the last play Tennessee Williams wrote before he turned to what he called "serious comedy" in *Period of Adjustment* (1960). These last plays do not add significantly to the stature of a playwright whose work began so hopefully in the short plays and short stories of his earlier years. There is in the later work the hysterical note of a writer who has spent his slight store of material and is forced to repeat himself again and again. The interest in sex that marked some of his early work has become his main preoccupation, so that the whole range of human experience is narrowly limited to this one phase of life. With the exception of a few shadowy characters—who are more like personifications—the leading figures are corrupt or degenerate; and nothing is achieved through knowing them. The repetition of characters and scenes suggests that the creative springs which promised so much have dried up. And yet, in spite of the dearth of material, Williams' technical skill has become more sure and more frightening. He has found out that he can hypnotize an audience—or some parts of it.

CHAPTER 7

The Literary World of Tennessee Williams

I *Themes*

THERE WAS REAL PROMISE in the early short stories and in the short plays of Tennessee Williams that he would add to the understanding of the South: genteel women who had outlived a tradition in which charm was their greatest asset; old maids of both sexes who had been warped by a life-denying southern Puritanism; men and women of an old tradition of honor who found themselves competing with a cheap *ersatz* culture; the lonely individual who found himself out of place in a vulgar materialistic society; the recurring elements of the vigilantes who tortured and killed not only the Negro but the foreigner; childish men and women of arrested development who might be respected citizens but whose concerns never went beyond the immediate and the physical. He described misfits and failures, but he described them with sympathy and honesty. These men and women do not belong to the South alone; they have a universality that makes them a part of all people everywhere.

After his first two major theatrical successes, Williams expressed an artistic theory that might give a clue to all that he has written: "Every artist has a basic premise pervading his whole life, and that premise can provide the impulse to everything he creates. For me the dominating premise has been the need for understanding and tenderness and fortitude among individuals trapped by circumstance."[1] All of his plays have been concerned, to some degree, with little people in a mechanistic society; but his urge to reach a large audience has forced him to obscure this basic theme by overemphasizing other and sometimes rather dubious subjects or by grossly exaggerating character and scene. With the years and with experience he has become as much of a theatrical magician as a dramatist. A later statement also gives a clue to his playwrighting. Walter Winchell reported in July, 1960, that Williams admitted becoming more and more interested in making money as he got older; he said that acquiring money did something for the ego.

Williams concerned himself with a number of variations on the theme of "individuals trapped by circumstance," and any one of them warrants the attention of a man of his talent. A frequently recurring theme relates to the decadence of southern aristocracy: Carol Cutrere, the hysterical exhibitionist (Cassandra Whiteside in *Battle of Angels*) in *Orpheus Descending* and *Fugitive Kind,* who is a wild, drunken, speed-crazy, sex-starved, one-time heiress; Amanda Wingfield who is reduced to nagging poverty; Blanche, who at times is another Carol Cutrere; Big Daddy, the last of the large southern plantation operators and his heavily drinking son, Brick, who is cowed by so much vitality; Mrs. Venable and Sebastian who are sterile relics of an older aristocracy.

Repeatedly Williams has contrasted the poet and the average man; and to the poet he has given a nobler sense of values and a compassion for humanity. The poet is always the romantic who rebels against conventions and who demands for himself a wild freedom which is incompatible with an urban society. He is a character who feels, but often more deeply, evidently, then he can articulate. He often "plays it cool," for he erupts only in suppressed monosyllables. Williams follows the literary convention of the romantics—or an idea he took from D. H. Lawrence—which assumes that the poet is the great lover whose path to freedom is crowded with sex-starved women. Williams also reflects another literary convention: that the creative artist is the last relic of a decadent culture and that the corruption in genius expresses itself in art forms, an idea basic to the characterization of Sebastian Venable. On the other hand, there seems to be an autobiographical basis for the characterization of Tom Wingfield in *The Glass Menagerie,* a highly sensitive young man seeking adventures so that he can write. These poets are lonely people, and all of them might repeat Val Xavier's words: "Nobody gets to know *no body!* We're all of us sentenced to solitary confinement inside our own skins for life!"

The most obviously trapped individuals are the delicate and unconventional characters: the southern gentlewomen like Laura Wingfield who cannot adjust to contemporary society; or others like a Blanche Du Bois or an Alma Winemiller, torn between natural instincts and ideals imposed by a Puritan culture; or derelicts like hard-luck Kilroy, stranded and helpless in a ruthless, business society—none of them prepared for survival in a highly competitive world—are of special interest to the playwright. Because of Williams' sympathy, however, he so overworks the circumstances of their misfortunes that he becomes nearly sentimental. Moreover, these sensitive people refuse to face the truth about themselves, a habit which prevents their making a reasonable adjustment. This self-blinding also afflicts the not-so-delicate Big Daddy and his son Brick until their mutual truth-telling tears away the protective covering. The same resistance to reality motivates the vicious Mrs. Venable in her attempt to destroy her niece.

Williams frequently touches upon religious themes; but, like his literary idol, D. H. Lawrence, he seems to have no deep religious convictions. Christianity, as represented by Episcopalianism, is a constant target for his contempt. His ministers are grotesque or silly. He associates southern Puritanism with old maidishness to be found in both sexes; it is the opposition, time and again, to a fully realized sexual experience. This is illustrated in the early short story, "The Important Thing," or the play, *Summer and Smoke.* On the other hand, there is a strong Calvinist tinge in the themes of guilt and atonement that appear in the short plays, *Auto-Da-Fé* and *The Purification;* in the short story, "Desire and the Black Masseur; and in the later plays, *Suddenly Last Summer* and *Sweet Bird of Youth.* Guilt in all of these works is expressed in sexual terms alone; it would seem that the quality of innocence which Williams gives to so many of his adult children belongs to the period before the corruption of sexual experience. In the short story, "Desire and the Black Masseur," Williams toys with the idea that the sins of the world represent an incompleteness to be atoned for in suffering and that violence is a kind of compensation for what has been left unformed. This story—a compound of homosexuality, cannibalism, ideas of personal sacrifice, and the Easter myth—exemplifies also the way that Williams can overload an art story. He returned to the same basic material in *Suddenly Last Summer*.

There is frequently an ambiguous suggestion that equates spiritual purity with sexual or other excesses: the "broken Apollo" of the story "One Arm" keeps a radiance in spite of his sordid history. Brick Pollitt radiates spiritual beauty despite his dipsomania. Williams also has a strange way of giving his created characters a symbolic religious meaning. Val Xavier appears to the mad artist Vee Talbott—and the mad people are favored by Williams—as Christ on the Cross. The racial bigot Boss Finley calls himself inspired by the Voice of God and sees himself as crucified for his campaign against blood pollution. The idea of phallic worship and the celebration of the Easter season are tied in with guilt complexes in the early story, "Desire and the Black Masseur," and in the later play, *Sweet Bird of Youth*.

Whatever philosophic pattern underlies these curious expressions is not very readily apparent. Critics have failed to discover significant meaning in the very confused and involved symbolism with which Williams expresses himself. There seems to be little good or decency in the world—if the scenes, the characters, and their statements are to be credited. The gloomy scenes of *Camino Real* and the southern town in the *Battle of Angels* series represent a modern hell. Maggie the Cat and Big Daddy find very little in people that is admirable. Sebastian would find God, not through humanitarian, selfless, disinterested love, but in the horrible destruction of baby sea turtles desperately rushing to safety.

These curious expressions may be another indication of the playwright's immaturity—like the adolescent and rather sophomoric acceptance of the tenets of atheism; or they may be another manifestation of his romanticism which expresses itself in rebellion against the status quo. They may be, in part, an expression of the conflict within himself, the same conflict which torments an Alma Winemiller.

From the very early short play, *Ten Blocks on Camino Real*, to his sortie into "serious comedy," *Period of Adjustment*,

Tennessee Williams has had a character repeatedly ask the Big Question. It is expressed more or less in the same way: Where did I come from? Why am I here? Where am I going? Are all the cosmic fireworks just for this? Williams never gets beyond these large and safe philosophic and rather meaningless generalities which he gives to his characters as if he had discovered something really profound. In much the same way he at times expresses his criticism of world conditions by using a word like "mendacity"—as he does in *Cat*— a word which Brick never particularizes, or which Big Daddy equates with symbols like church or clubs, or with his unsatisfying intercourse with an unloved, unattractive wife.

It is to Brick Pollitt that Williams applies the phrase, "moral paralysis," a condition which he considers basic to that character's personal tragedy. It is curious that so many of his characters, both protagonists and background figures, have this same weakness. The Judge in *The Purification* prefers not to judge the actions of men but would have the guilty judge themselves. Oliver Winemiller in "One Arm" accepted his new life among the New York homosexuals without self-appraisal. Little Lucio in *The Strangest Kind of Romance* sees God as like himself, unable to do anything about injustice. The hangers-on in *Baby Doll* and *Sweet Bird of Youth* passively allow ugliness to express itself in very ugly ways. Sandra Whiteside in *Battle of Angels* seems to exemplify the folly of taking a stand. Sebastian Venable, who never took a stand on anything, asserted himself only when he was made physically uncomfortable. These are only some of the characters whose moral fiber is flimsy, and who escape their various moral responsibilities in liquor, sexuality, homosexuality, or dope. The persistence of this characteristic, like the persistence of loneliness, raises questions about the way in which Williams creates his characters. There are many fiberless and very many lonely people in the world—but there do seem to be a few of the strong, the sane, the principled, the adjusted.

The almost neurotic recurrence of the loneliness theme would seem to suggest that the writer is again imposing upon his characters his own personal state of mind. From the early Val Xavier, who talks of peoples' being imprisoned inside their skins and not ever getting to know anyone, to

Mrs. Stone's very special kind of loneliness which makes her a special target for the procuresses and gigolos in Rome, to Catharine Holly whose loneliness makes her interrupt a most graphic chapter in her personal biography to wrap herself around the Doctor in an amorous kiss—just to mention a few examples—it seems that all the protagonists in all the poems, in all the short stories, and in all the plays sing the same old refrain—"nobody knows how lonesome I am"—a song accompanied by appropriate off-stage mood music like mournful locomotive whistles, or bird calls. In twenty years of playwrighting Williams has created more lonely people than the sociologists have found in all the lonely crowds.

Williams has worked with a number of interesting themes; but the favorite—and the one that obscures most of the others —is the idea of sex as the symbol of freedom, sex as the great liberator, sex as the only valid manifestation of religion and of love, sex as the only synonym for life. He may have begun with an interest in another theme; but after the success of *The Glass Menagerie,* and as if he were trying to maintain his popular appeal, he blurs an interesting theme with scene after scene which does little more than add sexual excitement. For a man of so much talent, it is a pity that, as his critics have so often lamented, he should be suffering from sex on the brain.

II *Women Characters*

Williams first achieved recognition for his delineation of southern gentlewomen: Amanda Wingfield and her daughter Laura, Blanche Du Bois, and Alma Winemiller. These dramatic figures had been anticipated or developed from characters in short stories and in one-act plays: *Portrait of a Madonna;* "Portrait of a Girl in Glass"; and, to some extent, the mother and daughter in "Three Players of a Summer Game." They all seem to reflect a Victorian culture in the South which required that a lady be charming but not a breadwinner. They live in a world of their own imagination and are unable to cope with a highly competitive, commercial society. Their dreams center on men who were never there; and, with the exception of the fragile Laura, their training in Puritan renunciation has made them hysterical about sex. This conflict between celibate idealism and instinct, according to Williams, drives these refined young ladies to prostitution. On the other hand, the idea of Puritan virtue as a protective shield is exemplified in young John Buchanan's attitude to Alma and in the fate of the girls in "The Important Thing" and "The Night of the Iguana."

Another type of Southerner is the aggressive, domineering mother character—an insensitive figure. In *Auto-Da-Fé* appears an early version of the mother; obsessed by notions of cleanliness and propriety, she contrasts to the son who is aware of the social and spiritual corruptions around him. Amanda Wingfield is at times the southern gentlewoman; at others she is a heckling, scolding mother who drives her son from his home. Mrs. Venable, fighting against age so that she can travel with her son, has for years curbed his attempted escapes to freedom. Big Mama, apparently cursed by a lack of sex appeal, takes over the estate from her dying husband as if she had long been the head of the family.

There are a number of sexually aggressive women who dominate their men, a type which may have been derived from similar women in D. H. Lawrence. Mrs. Stone, not a Southerner, but a ruthless career woman, makes of her husband a pathetically dependent boy; Cassandra Whiteside in *Battle of Angels* and later Carol Cutrere in *Orpheus Descending*, a sex-starved aristocrat, are continually "on the prowl" for men; Estelle Hohengarten, a grim rum-runner, seduces the husband of Serafina in *The Rose Tattoo;* Margaret, Brick's wife in both the short story "Three Players in a Summer's Game" and in the play *Cat on a Hot Tin Roof,* grows in power as Brick disintegrates; Dorothea, the multi-millionnaire's daughter in *Period of Adjustment,* is described as both psychologically frigid and aggressive, but without sex appeal; the Princess Kosmonopolis in *Sweet Bird of Youth,* like Mrs. Stone, seems to be sexually insatiable. There are a number of landlady cats "yowling" for sex on their various back fences, women who seem not to be restricted to the South: the heavy aggressive landlady in "The Malediction" and *The Strangest Kind of Romance;* Olga Kedrova, the tireless brothel-keeper, in "The Mattress by the Tomato Patch."

Another type of girl is again characterized almost entirely by her attitude toward sex: she does not worry about her promiscuity. Most of these girls are Williams' heroines, but he often describes them with a mixture of the absurd and the precious. Taken alone, Margaret the Cat belongs to this group; she is a liberated, "cussing," little scrapper who would not hesitate to go to bed with a man to test his virility. Giggling teen-ager, Nellie, in *Summer and Smoke*, Stella in *Streetcar*, and Rosa in *The Rose Tattoo* are all portrayed as normal American girls; they are blessed, however, with Williams' special literary sex appeal. Closely allied to them, though a bit addle-pated, is the would-be comedy character, Baby Doll, who appears in *Twenty-Seven Wagons Full of Cotton* and later in *Baby Doll*.

Williams describes Blanche Du Bois as a refined gentlewoman, but he gives her the biography of a prostitute. In two short plays, *Hello from Bertha* and *The Lady of Larkspur Lotion*, he portrays the physical and mental decay of two aging whores without romancing about it. In *This Property is Condemned* he describes a juvenile delinquent in her sister's cast-off clothes—a child innocent, ignorant, and fighting alone. It is a straightforward study. On the other hand, Williams sometimes spices up a scene with a flashy prostitute to whom he proceeds to give rather weighty lines as in the cases of Esmeralda in *Camino Real*, Rosa Gonzales in *Summer and Smoke*, or some of the girls of easy virtue in *The Rose Tattoo*.

Williams has a theory that women of the social service professions are mechanical and stiff, or starchy like their uniforms: examples are the woman accompanying the institution doctor in *Streetcar*, the spinsterish teacher in *The Rose Tattoo*, the nurses in *The Battle of Angels* series and in *Suddenly Last Summer*. Some attention should be given to Williams' commonplace, average woman who is a gossip, who often is seemingly as heavy in the head as in the buttocks and who forms the hopeless contrast to the heroines. These females represent the dull-witted, conventional type of housewife: the townswomen in the *Battle of Angels* series; the man-crazy women in *The Rose Tattoo*; Mrs. Bassett, the interfering neighbor in *Summer and Smoke*; the commonplace bystanders in *Sweet Bird*; and Mrs. Holly, Catharine's mercenary mother, in *Suddenly Last Summer*.

III *Male Characters*

Hadrian in *You Touched Me!*, an adaptation from a D. H. Lawrence character, became a prototype of all of Williams' sexually attractive young men. Described as a good-looking, virile youth and used as a symbol of Pan and of an uninhibited love life, this young man is also prone to philosophic outbursts. Variations on this type continue for twenty years; the only differences rest upon degrees of virility. As late as 1956 Williams was describing his hero, Val Xavier in *Orpheus Descending*, as a "wild spirited boy" who was stirring up a "commotion in a chicken coop"—words that go back to Hadrian's conflict with Emmie, the virtuous housekeeper who took after the fox in the chicken coop. Another type of character that harks back to the early poems and short stories is Moony of the one-act, *Moony's Kid Don't Cry;* a handsome young itinerant, he rejects a conventional job as too dull to endure and takes to the road. This free lancer, combined with the virile youth in Val Xavier of the *Battle of Angels* series, becomes a kind of lover-Christ symbol, a poet-dreamer representing the epitome of freedom, a vagabond with a book about to be written, and a man able to resist permanent employment much better than he can resist women. He is something of an adolescent who apparently believes that the answers to the great imponderables are achieved through sexual intercourse. And yet, it is because of his random defense of a Negro, in one play, that he is destroyed by an ugly southern mob. This same character appears several years older and many versions later in *Orpheus Descending* and *The Fugitive Kind;* cynical about solutions of love, still resisting permanent residence and employment, he is trapped by a woman whose child he fathered.

Williams becomes ecstatically lyrical over the radiant male, Stanley Kowalski, in *Streetcar* whose primitive vitality excuses his crudeness and brutality. John Buchanan in *Summer and Smoke* is almost a trial sketch for Stan, a youth whose drinking and wenching leave him as physically pure as a Greek god. Alvaro-Eat-a-Horse in *The Rose Tattoo* is a comic version of the radiant male, ready to seduce the daughter of the willing widow. Vacarro in *Twenty-Seven Wagons* is a revenge-rapist but in *Baby Doll* he is not only gifted with radiant sexual energy but such beautiful virtues as compassion, a sense of justice, a sense of humor, and a preference for plain drinking water.

Tennessee Williams began as a poet, and the poet is a character in a number of the early stories. His first major achievement, Tom Wingfield, a somewhat autobiographical poet-vagabond in *The Glass Menagerie,* is repeated with variations. Tom is a frustrated young man, a sensitive and patient dreamer trapped in an unimaginative business world and in an unpleasant home. Kilroy, the average American and the perpetual GI in *Camino Real,* is this same dreamer-itinerant pursuing answers to the eternal questions. A feckless variation, Brick in *Cat,* a completely passive individual softened by alcohol, but apparently as good-looking as a Greek god, is illogically described as a tragic figure. Ralph Bates, the forty-seven-year old hero of *Period of Adjustment,* who prefers the freedom of the itinerant to the dullness of an office job, is the latest variation of the poet-dreamer-itinerant-lover.

In contrast to these primitive or poetic males are the frequently only sketched-in satiric figures of businessmen. Williams has not only continued the American literary tradition that traduces the man who makes money, but has again taken his cue from Lawrence. Jabe Torrance, in *The Battle of Angels* series, is not only an ugly storekeeper but the leader of the vigilantes who burned alive the Wop, his wife's father. Harper, in the one-act *The Last of the Solid Gold Watches,* is an impudent "whelp" in contrast to the admirable old-timer. The middle-aged tourist husband in *Lord Byron's Love Letter* gets an adolescent thrill out of a marching band. The husband of Mrs. Stone represents Williams' idea that it takes no brains to make money. The salesman who appears briefly in *The Rose Tattoo* is a gross caricature of swindler and practical joker. Inept, flabby, and bigoted, Archie, husband of Baby Doll, is the unsuccessful money man. Gooper in *Cat* wracks his brain to cheat his brother-in-law out of the plantation. Gutman, a kind of master of ceremonies in the sixteen blocks of *Camino Real,* is a hard-headed, hotel proprietor catering to rich clients.

Among other male characters are the dynamic older men: Big Daddy in *Cat* not only has drive and vitality but some kind of moral standard; a shorter version of this same type is the old drummer, Mr. Charlie Cotton, in *Last of the Solid Gold Watches;* Captain Rockley in *You Touched Me!* has the same zest for living and his anecdote about the porpoise with sex appeal seems to anticipate Big Daddy and his elephant story; and a similarity between Big Daddy and Boss Finley in *Sweet Bird* has been noted, although the latter is the rankest of segregationists. Almost a parody of evil, the racists, ignorant and brutal, but often in positions of power, appear briefly as pot-bellied avengers in the *Battle of Angels* series.

There are a few innocuous good boys, but they are without poetic insight or business acumen: Jim O'Connor, Laura's dream hero; Roger Doremus, the mama's boy and friend of Alma Winemiller; or Scudder, the rather simple Chamber-of-Commerce youth who courts Heavenly Finley. Other male characters include the gigolos, Paolo and Chance Wayne, and the ministers who, like the businessmen, are satirically presented. Episcopalian rectors are made either grotesque or silly: the Reverend Tutwiler in "The Yellow Bird" preaches to dreary lengths about Puritan negations; the Reverend Tooker in *Battle of Angels* is referred to as an indifferent minister; the ineffectual Reverend Guilford Melton in *You Touched Me!* becomes a fit mate for the housekeeper; the Reverend Winemiller in *Summer and Smoke* appears as a conventional old maid; the Reverend Tooker in *Cat* continually treks to the bathroom but leaves the family abruptly at the time of crisis.

A survey of the character types which reappear continually gives proof to the playwright's complaint that it was difficult for him to find new subjects to write about.

IV *Dramatic Development*

In the production notes for *The Glass Menagerie,* Tennessee Williams expressed his theory of dramatic writing:

> Expressionism and all other unconventional techniques in drama have only one valid aim, and that is a closer approach to truth. When a play employs unconventional techniques, it is not, or certainly shouldn't be, trying to escape its responsibility of dealing with reality, or interpreting experience, but

is actually or should be attempting to find a closer approach, a more penetrating and vivid expression of things as they are. . . . Everyone should know nowadays the unimportance of the photographic in art: that truth, life, or reality is an organic thing which the poetic imagination can represent or suggest, in essence, only through transformation, through changing into other forms than those which were merely present in appearance.[2]

In "Something wild . . . ," the introduction to *Twenty-Seven Wagons Full of Cotton* (1945) he said, "In my opinion art is a kind of anarchy, and the theater is a province of art." In this same preface Williams expressed admiration for director Willard Holland of the St. Louis Little Theater group, The Mummers (operating between 1935-40): "Holland's work never failed to deliver, and when I say deliver I mean a sock!" He says of Holland's theater, "It was like a definition of what I think theater is. Something wild, something exciting, something that you are not used to. Offbeat is the word."[3] What Williams liked particularly about this small theater was its principle of delivering, somewhere between the opening and the closing curtain, a good hard punch—a kind of a knock-out blow, evidently.

These two statements, taken together, may explain why Williams has never concerned himself with the organic development of drama but rather with highly charged dramatic scenes that will deliver a good shock. Again and again there are individual scenes of power, indicative of real dramatic genius—often highly emotional scenes that reveal a talent for achieving what is theatrically effective. These scenes are Tennessee Williams at his best. As typical of the wide range of good scenes the following might be mentioned: the delicately renewed acquaintance between Laura Wingfield and her dream hero, Jim O'Connor; the violently erotic clash between Blanche Du Bois and Stan, who carries her off to the bedroom; the comedy courtship scene between Serafina and the newly arrived truckdriver; the comedy scene when Baby Doll tries to protect her virtue; the dramatic truth-telling scene in which Catharine Holly reports the last summer of Sebastian Venable; part of the Brick-Big Daddy interview in which each man peals off a protective covering and is left exposed.

Although Williams can write theatrically good scenes—he has been called "a vivid and exciting *scene* wright"—he has not yet been able to meet a dramatic problem head on, to build a play as a unified work of art. His rejection of the realistic mode has apparently freed him from responsibility of making logical relationships between disparate themes in one play. Unable, apparently, to develop fully one theme, he scatters his energy among several. The grotesque hell in the *Battle of Angels* series exposes tormentors and tormented, characters born partly from literary prototype, partly of the playwright's observation, but created more from his personal prejudices. *You Touched Me!* goes off into several direction at once. In *Cat* Williams was concerned with homosexuality, the inheritance of considerable property, and the ticklish and strained areas of family relationships and difficulties in communication. In *Sweet Bird* he mixed up lurid scenes between an aging actress and her current gigolo with those involving a grotesque villain of segregation. *The Rose Tattoo* begins on a serious, almost tragic note, with the inconsolable widow, and soon descends into farce and eroticism. This habit of multiplying discordant elements in a play is paralleled by the way he sometimes overloads a characterization, or the biography of a character. This tendency of including too much of everything coincides with his idea that theater should provide a shock. Williams often is more concerned with what is theatrical than with truth.

The fact that he does not meet a dramatic problem may account for the episodic quality of his plays. He will present a clash between two people in one scene or one act and then repeat the pattern in the following scene with different characters. For instance, Act I of *Cat* is almost a Maggie monologue, with an occasional assent or disagreement from Brick; Act II is given almost entirely to Big Daddy, with Brick still rattling his glass and contributing a few words. *The Glass Menagerie* and *Camino Real* are entirely episodic. The first scene of *Suddenly Last Summer* presents Mrs. Venable's concept of her son and his death, and the last gives another view of the same situation as reported by Catharine Holly.

This habit of thinking in episodes may explain why certain scenes have not been motivated or anticipated. There are a number of omissions in *Summer and Smoke* which make the sequences illogical: the death of the old doctor and the abrupt change in character of the leading figures. In much the same way, Williams brings about a sudden maturity in Baby Doll, for which there has been no preparation. The final act of Mrs. Stone, her acceptance of the lewd vagrant, seems to have been devised to shock the readers. The abrupt changes of mood in *Sweet Bird* seem to have been contrived for contrasts, not from character. Sometimes important scenes at the climax have not been written. There is no scene in *Summer and Smoke*—and the play demands it—which represents the exchange of position of John the doctor and Alma the gentlewoman. The clash between Stan and Blanche in *Streetcar*, if the play represents two principles in contemporary society, is evaded in the shrilly dramatized rape scene, which is effective theater but hardly justified in the play. There is no scene between Chance Wayne and Heavenly; but Williams, like an operator afraid of what his marionettes might do, brings in other characters and a segregation theme. And again, in *Cat*, the most important scene—the father-son search for understanding—reaches a climax and blows up into explanatory prose. Williams launches into a discussion about homosexuality and the taboo surrounding it, and "mystery" of character, among other things. This digression suggests that the playwright himself felt a certain incompleteness—or else it gave him an opportunity to play a game with his readers. The episodic construction easiest for Williams can be illustrated by variations on the memory technique, tried out in an early one-act, *The Long Goodbye;* this technique is used in *The Glass Menagerie* and in a number of later plays. The story of Blanche Du Bois is unfolded in a series of more and more shocking revelations of the depths to which she has fallen. It is like peeling off layers of a past, the self-exposure of a nymphomaniac who pretends to be a lady. Something of the same pattern is used in *The Rose Tattoo* as Serafina's delusions of love are scaled away. It is perhaps the shift from revelation of her once happy love to a comic courtship that partially dissipates the effectiveness of this play. Val Xavier's recollection of his erotic adventures from his early boyhood is a large part of his characterization. The two important scenes in *Suddenly* are only the two different accounts of remembered scenes and experiences, and the dramatic excitement of Catharine's deliberate, piece-meal telling provides the tension of the last scene. Early attempts at this technique of delayed, bit-by-bit confession are found in the one-act, *The Dark Room,* and also in the recounting of Captain Rockley's past in *You Touched Me!*

To heighten the dramatic impact, Williams often plays one scene against another. For instance, in *You Touched Me!,* there is considerable double-playing in the living room and in the excitement and raids in the chicken house. In *Streetcar* all during Stan's report about Blanche's dubious career, she is singing sentimental moon songs in the bathroom. Near the close of *Camino Real* two scenes are played at the same time: during the operation in which Kilroy's big golden heart is taken from his body, the Piéta figure holds the vagabond across her knees, a scene evidently meant to equate Kilroy with Jesus—and all humanity. In the third act of *Cat,* while Big Daddy cries with pain offstage, the caterwauling family is "stopped cold" by Maggie's announcement of her pregnancy.

In his "Note of Explanation" to the Broadway version of Act III of *Cat,* Williams wrote, "Some day when time permits I would like to write a piece about the influence, its dangers and its values, of a powerful and highly imaginative director upon the development of a play, before and during production."[4] In the "Foreword" to *Camino Real* he described how he and Elia Kazan had worked together. This cooperation is not a new situation, for the late George Jean Nathan described it in connection with his review of *You Touched Me!* Many a play has become successful because of a discerning director or, just as possibly, been ruined by the wrong one. It is to be hoped that Williams will write fully about his own experience, an account which could be expected to throw light on the American professional theater. His own successes—to give a few important examples—have been closely linked with the brilliant directing of such men as Eddie Dowling, *The Glass Menagerie;* Elia Kazan, *Streetcar, Camino Real,* and *Cat;* Harold Clurman, *Orpheus Descending;* and José Quintero, *Summer and Smoke,* in the off-Broadway production.

V *Devices and Decorative Elements*

Many a critic has twitted Tennessee Williams for his excessive use of theatrical tricks. He has resorted to all kinds of symbols—some of them effective, some not. In the "Foreword" to *Camino Real* he expresses his opinion about the effectiveness: ". . . symbols, when used respectfully, are the purest language of plays. Sometimes it would take page after tedious page of exposition to put across an idea that can be said with an object or a gesture on the lighted stage."[5]

The little glass ornaments belong to Laura; the snakeskin jacket seems to be an imaginative mark of freedom for Val Xavier; but the rooster in the hen-house is not a happy parallel for young Hadrian, the pilot. The trunk full of faded dresses and letters placed in the center of the stage represent not only Blanche but her intrusion. The fountain and the anatomy chart in *Summer and Smoke* are rather amateurishly obvious. Vacarro's whip in *Twenty-Seven Wagons* is in keeping with his good-neighbor policy. *The Rose Tattoo* is cluttered with roses, goat cries, and such properly selected symbols on dressmaker dummies. In *Camino Real* the Streetcleaners, A. Ratt, and the plane called Fugitivo are symbols not worthy of a writer who thinks of himself as a poet. In *Cat* the big double bed and the monstrous television console are obvious enough. The jungle with its hideous cries and sweet bird songs provides a highly emotive background for *Suddenly.* And perhaps the small-town mercantile store and the confectionery decorated to represent the Moon Lake Casino save many words needed to explain two attitudes toward life in *Battle of Angels* series; but they do seem rather contrived.

A number of characters are symbols, flat characterizations rather than people: the female busybodies from Mrs. Bassett in *Summer and Smoke* to the man-chasing women in *The Rose Tattoo;* Catharine Holly's mother and her brother, who fear the girl's honesty, become symbols of stupid greed; Alma means soul, an appropriate characterization of the earlier appearance of the heroine in *Summer and Smoke;* and John Buchanan is a symbol of the flesh. Cukrowicz is said to mean sugar, a term that does not exactly fit the doctor in *Suddenly;* and the Conjure Man in the *Battle of Angels* series may be a symbol of freedom or he may be some kind of involved Freudian sex-death symbol—it is hard to say.

But when Mrs. Stone is made to be a symbol of the corruption of our time, or poor Kilroy is every little struggling man in contemporary society, or the experiences of Chance Wayne are to be taken as symbolic of contemporary man, then the symbolism is so far-fetched that it belongs to the private world of Tennessee Williams. Or when the playwright imposes upon the figures born of his own sprightly imagination and his own peculiar sex-obsessions the figures of Christ and of Mary his Mother—as when he tries to bring together Val Xavier and Christ, or the love-starved, middle-aged wife Myra, and then Lady, and the Virgin Mary—then he has, indeed, overstepped himself. The sexual symbols in the later plays have become more involved and obscure. It can be said with justice that Williams has created a happy hunting ground for the rather special collectors of phallic symbols.

Tennessee Williams' spectacular success is often due to his ability to project a poetic idea in terms of vivid color and sound; and of this capacity innumerable examples have already been cited. Williams works hard to achieve the right emotional color, the suggestive design; and for this effect he seems often to have turned to painting: the vivid color in the scene of the poker game in *Streetcar* is likened to a Van Gogh picture; the setting for *Summer and Smoke* should resemble the nonrealistic design of a de Chirico; the blue sky in *The Rose Tattoo* is found in the Italian paintings of the Renaissance. Much is made of jungle noises in the mad scenes toward the end of *Streetcar* and in many scenes in *Suddenly,* where the setting is reminiscent of a Rousseau jungle. In *Sweet Bird* the gracious dignity of Heavenly Finley is conveyed by Mozartian music; the "Blue Piano" in *Streetcar* underscores the sexual theme, and in *Suddenly,* jungle cries and bird songs suggest the conflict.

In support of the expressionist technique Williams makes a number of bold experiments. Characters step out of a scene and talk at great length to the audience; they recite great blocks of exposition, often interesting and good talk, but a bit artificial. The women in *Battle of Angels* gossip about their love affairs in the old Moon Lake Casino; Tom Wingfield comments—at times superfluously—about the various scenes in *The Glass Menagerie;* Kilroy appeals directly to the audience for pity in *Camino Real;* Brick in *Cat* confides directly and at length; Chance Wayne digresses interminably in *Sweet Bird.*

Some of the worst scenes in all of the plays are those in which necessary exposition is conveyed by telephone: the decadent aristocrat in the *Battle of Angels* series yells her crudities over it; Blanche makes her useless calls to her dream hero; Alvaro discloses by telephone to Serafina that her husband was not faithful; Gutman on the Plaza uses the phone—to represent the big executive perhaps. There is also much silly long-distance phoning in *Cat;* the Hollywood contract business in *Sweet Bird* is, of course, by telephone; and the financial predicament of the Meighans in *Baby Doll* is communicated in the same fashion.

The need for "something wild" and chaotic seems to have been answered in a number of nonrealistic scenes—some of them only slightly motivated. Williams achieves tension when he has his main character almost frozen in a difficult situation; he acts as if he were hypnotized. Williams early worked out this type of tension in his treatment of Miss Jelkes, who is unable to leave the men in "The Night of the Iguana." Val Xavier, Kilroy, and Chance Wayne are all characters of circumstance, each of them seemingly unable to cope with his predicament. This may be part of Williams' technique for evoking pity, but it gives his heroes an artificial inertia. Each of these plays concludes in violence: *Auto-Da-Fé, Twenty-Seven Wagons, Battle of Angels* and its successors, *Suddenly Last Summer* and *Sweet Bird.* Another method of achieving "something wild" is apparent in the chase scenes: the everlasting goat chasing in *The Rose Tattoo,* the wild scampering all over the theater in *Camino Real,* the incredible and sometimes amusing pursuit in *Baby Doll.*

VI   *The Dialogue of Tennessee Williams*

If Eugene O'Neill had been able to write dialogue as natural and idiomatic as that to be found in some part of every play of Tennessee Williams, his stature as an American dramatist would have been secure. The greatest contribution of Williams, the mid-century playwright, is his handling of speech. Scene after scene, no matter how different in mood and subject—no matter how artificially projected in action —does, somehow, convey the impression of idiomatic language. Critics have noted from the beginning that Williams has been clever in the way he combines cliché and original speech. A stylized soliloquy given directly to the audience may serve as awkward exposition; but the talk, sometimes, is naturally handled. Through words Tennessee Williams has repeatedly been able to arouse emotional excitement, to increase suspense, and to enhance the understanding of character and emotion.

But it is a pity that Williams has not been able to strike out of his plays those rhetorical lines that are loud, artificial, and pompous. They are similar to the often pretentious pronouncements about art, artists, and the theater that he gives to the newspapers, pronouncements that have very little connection with the plays themselves. Just before the opening of *Summer and Smoke* Tennessee Williams wrote:

> God knows pretention has been known to pay off in some branches of the arts. Inflated reputations and eclectic styles have cast an aura of gravity over much that is essentially vacuous in painting, obscurity has disguised sterility in a good deal of verse.
>
> But the theatre, which is called the charlatan of the arts, is paradoxically the one in which the charlatan is most easily detected. He must say intelligibly what he has to say and unless it is well worth saying he does not have a Chinaman's chance of surviving. Even cheap entertainment is honest. It is all honest that does what it professes to do, and there is too much hot light and too many penetrating eyes set upon the stage for the willful obscurantist to pull his tricks.[6]

Perhaps he wrote this too early in his career, or perhaps he cannot distinguish what is good from what is weak. Joseph Wood Krutch in his review of *The Glass Menagerie* observed that "a hard, substantial core of shrewd observation and deft, economical characterization" was "enveloped in a fuzzy haze of pretentious, sentimental, pseudo-poetic verbiage." Krutch was concerned—and the years have proved him correct— that these defects resulting from self-indulgence might increase; and he urged the playwright to strike out any line he especially liked.[7]

VII *The Literary Position of Tennessee Williams*

Tennessee Williams expressed his early theatrical credo in a preface to *Battle of Angels* in March, 1944: "I have never for a moment doubted that there are people—millions!—to say things to . . . We come to each other, gradually, but with love. It is the short reach of my arms that hinders, not the length and multiplicity of theirs. With love and honesty, the embrace is inevitable."[8] This expression of sweetness and love was reflected in his early plays. John Gassner wrote: "Most noteworthy in these one-acters are evidences of a rare compassion for life's misfits and a general ability to transcend crude reality. . . . Williams is particularly affective in his treatment of battered characters who try to retain shreds of their former respectability."[9]

But Williams' pity for the delicate gave way to a kind of morbid preoccupation with disease. His craftsmanship became more insidiously clever and effective, but his view of life sickened. Respect for his theatrical talents is coupled with outspoken criticism of his use of them. Speaking of *Suddenly Last Summer*, Gassner wrote: "It matters little whether the gruesome details of the poet's death are literally true. The play emanates from the author's mind, and what really matters is the sensational expression of his most nihilistic mood. But no matter how much he is obsessed with morbid pessimism, Williams is not destroyed as an artist; he presses the nettle of neurosis to his bosom and it brings him honor through creative achievement."[10]

Apropos the same play, Tom F. Driver evaluated Williams' writing career as follows:

> Tennessee Williams is now at a point in his career where a very important choice must be made. Either he must push further with the kind of poetic exploration of basic questions of existence that he dealt with in *The Glass Menagerie*, *Streetcar*, *Camino Real*, and *Cat on a Hot Tin Roof*; or else he must settle for the kind of shock material he has given us recently, material better suited to the more lurid pages of *Esquire* than to the serious stage. To judge from the last season's *Orpheus Descending* and from *Suddenly Last Summer*, he is making the easier choice, the one that demands less in terms of observation and intellect while it feeds more on pri-

vate phantasmagoria. In this way it will not be difficult for him to lose the high stature in our theater which his early plays so deservedly earned for him. He is still master at effect. A play of his is still an exhilarating event. But he once was more, and no doubt could be so again.

Louis Kronenberger, apropos *Sweet Bird*, commented upon the development of the playwright:

Since, in his own work, Mr. Williams goes on repeating himself, critics can hardly do otherwise. And the sense of repetition can only increase their dissatisfaction, only strengthen their indictment. Whether a world of loathing and disgust, of sex violence and race violence, of lurid and bestial revenges, constitutes Mr. Williams' personal reaction to life or simply his philosophic vision of it, it has come to seem compulsive in him rather than convincing in his people. And with a growing loss of perspective of all feeling for contrasts, of all power of control, even his enraged symbols lose their force, have ceased really to be symbols and become mere props, have passed even beyond props into parodies.[12]

Reviewing the work of Tennessee Williams at the revival of *The Glass Menagerie* eleven years after its opening, Brooks Atkinson asserted:

To see it again is to realize how much he has changed. There is a streak of savagery in his work now. The humor is bitter. The ugliness is shocking. He has come a long way since 1945—growing in mastery of the theatre, developing power, widening in scope. He has also renounced the tenderness that makes "The Glass Menagerie" such a delicate and moving play.

Probably he was closer to the characters of "The Glass Menagerie" than he has been to those of his later plays. . . . There must be overtones of his own life in this tale of a dingy alley, shrouded down in poverty and despair. It is a perfect blend of humor and pathos, making a kind of sad poetry that is lovely, touching and a little grotesque. Mr. Williams has never improved on the daintiness and the shy allusiveness of the prose writing in this introductory play.[13]

At thirty-one Tennessee Williams became the best-known American dramatist of the decade; by the time he was forty-one, he had won five major awards. This concrete record of success attests to the very solid position he has achieved in the current American theater in spite of the contradictory appraisals of his work. It is bromidic to say that it does not take the critics' acclaim to make a play a hit, or that hokum and sentiment, that shock and pathos have a perennial appeal, or that a very ordinary play can be a success. It is obvious that Williams has been able to reach not only the public which has supported him royally but also a number of critics whose votes count in naming awards. Equally discerning critics have deplored the cheap sensationalism and the ugly innuendoes that creep into the plays; they have also become concerned about the malign influence of this clever playwright on both theater and public taste.

There can be no doubt that Williams has made his special contribution to the cast of southern characters, many of whom carry his special mark. There are a few who seem to have been allowed lives of their own, as, for example, Laura Wingfield and her mother Amanda; Mr. Charlie Cotton, the shoe salesman of the solid gold watches; one or two of the pitiful aging prostitutes like Bertha; or the juvenile delinquent in *This Property is Condemned;* or the old ladies in *Lord Byron's Love Letter.* These are all characters from the earlier work. Catharine Holly might be added to the list.

But there has always been so much of the personal and very intimate in his writing that his work would seem to afford material for some future biographer. To even the most casual observer there appear parallels in the personal story and the literary work, and the repeated use of the same material under various guises, sometimes contrived and sometimes not, makes of the increased acquaintance with the writing of Tennessee Williams a kind of study in parallels and repetitions and variations—a kind of detective study to discover how very much has been written on very slight experience.

It is not the physical experience, however, that is of real importance. Almost from the beginning Tennessee Williams has characterized most of his people according to his own prejudices, his own or borrowed theories, and his own neuroses. He has again and again played variations on the conflict between flesh and spirit, the Cavalier and the Puritan, and the natural man and the overcivilized modern, an idea that he seems to have adopted from Lawrence. He develops this conflict in two different characters, in Alma and John of *Summer and Smoke;* or the ambivalence in the character of Blanche Du Bois he had illustrated in a number of short stories and was to use again in the plays. Or, he has played a number of variations on his theory of childhood innocence and corruption from experience, as illustrated by Val Xavier and Chance Wayne. Or, from a Puritan background he inherited a grim philosophy of guilt and atonement and made use of the concept in several horror scenes—as in "Desire and the Black Masseur" and in *Suddenly Last Summer.* Or, out of his own apparent shyness he has made loneliness a dominant characteristic of most of his characters, as has been illustrated many times over. Or, his own definition of love, limited entirely to sexual terms, or love as a kind of dull habit without enthusiasm or devotion, he has imposed on a number of characters.

He confessed that "an atmosphere of hysteria and violence" which characterized his first published story has been the keynote of all subsequent work. There is a cruel strain continually reappearing—from the vicious attacks of the chow on the trapped kittens described in "Portrait of a Girl in Glass" to the gruesome scene of cannibalism described with graphic detail in *Suddenly.* There is the morbid preoccupation with castration, suggested by the drawn knives of the angry townsmen crowding the dingy dry goods store as they make their way toward Val Xavier, and even more graphically by the avengers crashing the final scene in *Sweet Bird of Youth.* Williams has a way of romanticizing horror as, for instance, in the detached rhetorical description of the execution of Oliver Winemiller in "One Arm," or the horrible description of the burning of Shelley's body in Block Eight of *Camino Real,* or in the picture of the starved little cannibals who gorge on the body of Sebastian Venable.

Along with this aspect of cruelty is the ever-appearing strain of tenderness, the references to intimacy, the appeals to sentimentality. Throughout the work there is a pervading softness. There are frequent expressions of sentimental pity for the failures, the maladjusted, for the weak. The phrase, "charm of the defeated," keeps on reappearing, as for instance with reference to the killer-homosexual in "One Arm" and to the seeming homosexual, Brick Pollitt, to name only two. The derelict and the fugitive continually receive the playwright's blessing—perhaps from his heart, as he himself nervously skips, by his own confession, from one city to another, one part of the world to another, the discontented vagabond. Esmeralda gives a special prayer for the disillusioned romantics, and Maggie apostrophizes the beautiful and weak people. And yet, the itinerants, all the Val Xaviers and the Kilroys, whose lives would seem to call for a little toughness and maturity, for some reason seem to be soft gentlemen. There is a special pity for those whose youth is passing, for the worst enemy of them all is time. These various sentiments of softness are diffused through all the work of Tennessee Williams.

A third pervading quality—in addition to his predilection for violence and for softness—is Williams' everlasting preoccupation with sex. The late George Jean Nathan hoped that the playwright would grow up enough to discover that it was not his own innovation. Since human relationships achieve harmony in Williams' plays only through sexual intercourse, the word live has had only one definition. In play after play he has capitalized on the excitement leading up to the seduction scene, played every possible trick he could think of to arouse erotic interest. The "anticipatory scene" is frequently lengthened out of proportion to others in the play, or it is raised to such climactic pitch that it obliterates other aspects of theme, character, or dramatic development. This preoccupation with the erotic has been fully described in the rape scene in *Streetcar* and in *Twenty-Seven Wagons Full of Cotton,* and in the scenes leading to the big double bed in *The Roman Spring of Mrs. Stone, Camino Real,* the *Battle of Angels* series, *Baby Doll, Sweet Bird,* and in the latest play, *Period of Adjustment.* The cheapness of many of these scenes and the dramatist's preoccupation with finding new ways of describing with greatest possible particularity an ordinary fact of life, raise some questions about his integrity as a dramatist. If it is true, as often said, that America is as sex obsessed as a medieval monastery, Tennessee Williams has, indeed, been a very smart businessman.

As the sex authority of the contemporary stage or as the romantic rebel who sought to face up to the remaining taboos in the contemporary theater, Tennessee Williams has not only portrayed graphically the beautiful animal, Stanley Kowalski, whose sexual life is almost deified, but he has dealt with a number of deviations from normal sexual expressions—homosexuality in *Cat,* pederasty in *Suddenly,* fornication and implied pederasty in *Streetcar,* fornication and its health consequences in *Sweet Bird,* incest in *The Purification,* masochism in *Twenty-Seven Wagons Full of Cotton,* lesbianism intimated in *Something Unspoken;* and we cite only a few examples.

Considering the topics that he has dealt with, it is ludicrous that he should everlastingly give to his very special portrayals a universal significance. Critics have repeatedly objected to his habit of giving wide reference to his very special characters and his very special situations. Mrs. Stone's incredible plunge into corruption—expressed in dirty sexual terms—is made to represent the decay of western civilization. The horror tale about a homosexual in *Suddenly* is intended to be a "true" story of our time. The drug-addicted, blackmailing, venereal-diseased, and self-pitying Chance Wayne asks the audience to see themselves in him. The shady real estate development and the four sexual psychopaths in *Period of Adjustment* apparently were intended to represent the lives and characters of average Americans.

This habit of universalizing his small portraits has been characteristic of Williams from the beginning. Little lost Lucio in *The Strangest Kind of Romance* sees God as helpless as himself against the factory world and its injustices. Tom Wingfield shakes a little rattle as the church bell strikes an early hour, the universal little man making his comment in the universe. Jim O'Connor fulsomely talks of love changing the world as his comfortable little romance has changed his life. Amorous Alvaro Mangiacavallo, about to go to bed with Serafina, embraces the audience with the cheery encouragement that it is the time of roses for everybody. Kilroy in his "rhubarb" chase all over theater aisles, boxes, and balconies would seem to symbolize all men's rebellion against loss of dignity or impending death.

Much has been written about the sensitivity, the allusiveness, the "special quality" of characterization, about the hidden contradictions and motivations within the characters of Tennessee Williams. Critical comment has also raised questions about the ambiguity with which the playwright handles character and situation.

Williams has long made a practice of suggesting more than he describes or states, of seeming to hold back something, of being unwilling to meet his readers and audience openly. In the very early poems, as we have illustrated, he would set off a line, often a confused or a pompous metaphor, as if to give it special meaning. The question has been raised whether this wasn't a trick to cover up the lack of thought or an image uncompleted. He cunningly speaks of the "mystery" of life and of character, and of wanting to leave his audiences "wondering." The word "mysterious" keeps reappearing in the plays and the comments about theater, but the application very often appears to be deliberate obscurity. Williams vaguely refers to the "basic desire" of Little Anthony Burns, the little homosexual who is devoured by the Negro; at the end of the story there is a "mysterious" analogy between the gory meal and the religious crucifixion orgy taking place in a nearby church. For some incredible reason, when the desperately thirsty peasant in *Camino Real* is shot for trying to drink at the fountain, the castenets rattle "mysteriously." In Williams' explanation of the violence in the writing of the "Southern Gothic" school, he talks of the special horror—not of cancer nor the atom bomb—but something "mysterious" upon which he and his coterie have a special corner. As already noted, Williams defended himself from attacks of being deliberately obscure about Brick Pollitt's homosexuality by talking about the "mystery" of character. He himself has written so much about this quality of mystery that in some quarters his explanations have been taken seriously. Other critics see in all this talk of mystery, as in the involved and confused symbolism, a disguise to cover up a reluctance to state his case clearly—or an inability to handle the problem he has introduced.

It is this amazing complex of character and motive, of talent and technique, of an extremely limited and special portrayal of life—it is this complex that has made Tennessee Williams one of the best-known literary figures of the middle twentieth century. It is ironic that the playwright who could never describe a businessman except in terms of contempt and that the artist who has made so many pronouncements about art and freedom should have cooperated so whole-heartedly with the investors in the entertainment industry for mutual profit. It is this artist who had Brick Pollitt drink his way through *Cat* because of his disgust with the "men-dacity" in the world about him.

Although Tennessee Williams seems to be writing about the South or contemporary society, he is more often writing about himself:

> I don't pretend to write about a world that has become increasingly violent. I may write about troubled people, but I write from my own tensions. For me, this is a form of therapy. It may be that audiences release their own tensions as a result. I certainly hope so. But in any case, I don't choose my themes or my characters with melodramatic thunder aforethought.
>
> Frankly, there must be some limitations in me as a drama-tist. I can't handle people in routine situations. . . . If these people are excessively melodramatic . . . well, a play must concentrate the events of a lifetime in the short span of a three-act play. Of necessity, these events must be more violent than life.[14]

Tennessee Williams has become a name; and, for the general public as well as for many among the professionals, he is the greatest poet-dramatist to have appeared on the American scene since Eugene O'Neill. Through his unabashed use of the stage and modern techniques, he has opened immense new possibilities. He has demonstrated again the dramatic excitement inherent in the use of old theatrical devices. Even though his plays may fall apart upon analysis, in his best work something of importance remains—an insight into character and motivation, an understanding of the lack of communication between people, an awareness of the appalling emptiness and cruelty in the hearts of many well-fed Americans, and the very difficult position of the little people. Tennessee Williams has an instinctive sense of theater and with his increased technical skill he may yet become a significant literary figure. As for his picture of life to date, some critics have been kind; some have ridiculed the pretentions or deplored the ugly view of America that he presents. Others are frankly worried that, at a time when American spiritual and cultural values seem to be at stake, so much money and attention should be spent on an art which is, at times, not only sick but frankly venal. It is to be expected that the artistic position of this writer will be more accurately assessed in the years ahead; but even then his position in mid-twentieth-century American life is certain to be of increasing interest to the sociologist and the psychologist.

Notes and References

Chapter Two

1. *Five Young American Poets* (3rd series; New York, 1944). Most of the poems in this early collection, some of them revised, were included in *In the Winter of Cities* (New York, 1956).

2. Dudley Fitts, "Talking in Verse," *New York Times Book Review* (July 8, 1956).

3. John Woods, "Tennessee Williams as a Poet," *Poetry*, XC (July, 1957), 256-58.

4. *One Arm and Other Stories* (New York, 1948, 1954).

5. In "Frivolous Preface," *Five Young American Poets*, Williams said that it was a friend of his, another young poet, Clark Mills, who introduced him to Hart Crane, Rimbaud, and Rilke. In the "Serious Preface" to the same volume he made the comment that he rated Hart Crane above Eliot and as equal to Keats, Shakespeare, and Whitman. He said that there was nothing to argue about; his evaluation derived from a very personal feeling.

6. A play called *The Night of the Iguana* was produced at Festival of Two Worlds, at Spoleto, Italy, summer, 1959. The characters have been considerably changed and the new emphasis is worth noting. There are three corrupt figures: a handsome, alcoholic tour guide; a lesbian and vengeful female tourist; an oversexed female hotel owner. There are two romantics: a "ninety-seven-year-young" poet and his granddaughter who is a painter. Of the original story the captive iguana remains. For an amusing insight into Tennessee Williams' nervous and piecemeal methods of composition, as represented by this work, see Henry Hewes, "Broadway Postscript," *Saturday Review* XLII (August 1, 1959), 30.

7. *American Blues: Five Short Plays* (New York, 1948). Publisher's note, page 3: Mr. Williams did not want this early experimental play included in the collection.

8. Cypress Hill is the name given to the ghoulish southern lover's lane in the Mississippi setting in *Battle of Angels* and *Orpheus Descending*.

9. *Twenty-Seven Wagons Full of Cotton and Other One Act Plays* (New York, 1946, 1953).

10. Tennessee Williams confessed: "My longer plays emerge out of earlier one-acters or short stories I may have written years

before. I work over them again and again." "Talk with the Playwright," *Newsweek* LIII (March 23, 1959), 75.

11. *Twenty-Seven Wagons Full of Cotton*, 1944, was produced in New York in May, 1955, as one of a three-part performance, *All in One*.

12. "THE THEATRE: New Show in Manhattan," *Time* LXV (May 2, 1955), 78 (Courtesy TIME; copyright TIME Inc., 1955).

13. *Battle of Angels* was published in *Pharos*, Nos. 1 and 2, Murray, Utah, 1945; by New Directions, 1945, and with *Orpheus Descending*, 1958.

14. Henry Popkin suggested the involved symbolism when, noting that the play ends on Good Friday, he says Myra is a variant of Mary, and Sandra, the mythological figure, Cassandra. [Henry Popkin, "The Plays of Tennessee Williams," *The Tulane Drama Review* IV (Spring, 1960), 60.] Williams added his own confusion by imposing on these biblical and mythological figures his own personal theories: a love-starved, middle-aged woman as the mother of Christ, and a sex-mad decadent as the virginal girl who refused Apollo's advances and was cursed.

15. The poem, "Cried the Fox," dedicated to D. H. Lawrence, which appeared in *Five Young American Poets*, relates the image of a fox chased by hounds to the poet hounded by conventional society.

16. The third title for this play seems to be taken from this line, *The Fugitive Kind*. It is a movie script based on the fifth revision of the play titled *Orpheus Descending*.

17. These are almost exactly the same lines that Williams used in a poem, "The Legend" (New Mexico, 1940), about an oversexed girl and the boy she caught.

18. For an account of this early fiasco, see Tennessee Williams' introduction, "The Past, the Present and the Perhaps," to *Orpheus Descending* printed with *Battle of Angels*, 1958; and John Gassner, *Theatre at the Crossroads* (New York, 1960), p. 78.

19. *I Rise in Flame, Cried the Phoenix* was published by New Directions, 1951, in two limited editions, autographed. Ten of the hand-printed copies were on Umbria paper, specially bound, and priced at $50; three hundred copies on American handmade paper, were boxed, and priced at $15. An inexpensive acting edition was also published, 1951, by Dramatists Play Service.

20. *You Touched Me!* (New York, 1947). Produced in Cleveland and Pasadena before *The Glass Menagerie*.

21. D. H. Lawrence, "You Touched Me," *The Complete Short Stories* (London, 1955), II, 394 ff. In the Lawrence story, Matilda and Emmie are sisters, worn out caring for their dying father, but with comfortable prospects until the return of Hadrian, the

adopted charity boy. It is Matilda's mistaken touch that wakens
their feeling for one another, he at twenty-one, she at thirty-two.
He proposes the marriage idea to the old father who immediately
changes his will so that the property goes to the girls only if she
marries Hadrian. The story is an unromantic study about sexual
attraction and conventions, and it is also a blunt account of the
economic basis for marriage.

22. The Hadrian-Matilda character types Williams had developed slightly in the short play, *The Case of the Crushed
Petunias.*

23. Other examples of scenes played simultaneously: in Act I,
during Emmie's scene with the Reverend Melton, the Captain
scuffles with Phoebe; during the minister's tenor solo, the Captain
rhapsodizes at considerable length about the alluring female
attractions of the porpoise; in the scene in which the minister
and spinster compare their celibate ideas about matrimony, Hadrian
stands at the side, "looking on with an air of Pan-like secrecy."

24. Joseph Wood Krutch, "Drama," *The Nation,* CLXI (October
6, 1945), 349-50.

Chapter Three

1. *The Glass Menagerie,* Williams' seventh long play—successfully tried out in Chicago—opened in New York City, March 31,
1945, with Laurette Taylor, Eddie Dowling, Julie Haydon, and
Anthony Ross. Two weeks later the play won the New York
Drama Critics Circle Award on the first ballot, the first time in
the group's ten-year history. It was revived, November 21, 1956,
at New York City Center with Helen Hayes, James Daly, Lois
Smith, and Lonny Chapman.

2. Stark Young, "The Glass Menagerie," *The New Republic,*
CXII (April 16, 1945), 505. Young, who came from the same
locality as Tennessee Williams, praised the speech as fresh, living,
abundant, and free of stale theatrical diction: "Behind the Southern
speech in the mother's part is the echo of great literature, or at
least respect for it."

3. In his own "Preface" in *Five Young American Poets,* Williams
confessed that during the years he was employed in the shoe
factory he had a habit of hiding in the men's toilet and working
out rhyme schemes. When he was discovered, he was fired. One
might draw the conclusion, from his plays, that he has been
deeply angered at the business world ever since. For an apparently
autobiographical description of Williams' relationship to his older
sister, see "The Paper Lantern," a poem in *New Directions in
Prose and Poetry,* Number Nine (New York, 1946).

4. The late George Jean Nathan reviewed *You Touched Me!* in

The Theatre Book of the Year, 1944-1945 (New York, 1945), pp. 89-90; he wrote that the drunk scene had been rewritten four times under Dowling's supervision; that many of Amanda's and Tom's lines were rephrased and improved by the actors who played the roles.

5. There is a detailed description of Laura's room in the story, "Portrait of a Girl in Glass."

6. Euphemia Van Rensselaer Wyatt, "The Drama," *Catholic World*, CLXI (May, 1945), 166: "The only flaw in the sequence of his [Tom Wingfield's] memories is how he could recall the long scenes between his sister and the Gentleman Caller unless he and his mother had been eavesdropping."

7. John Gassner, *Theatre at the Crossroads* (New York, 1960), p. 84: The stage directions "may strike us as redundant and rather precious; the young playwright was straining for effect, perhaps without realizing how well he had succeeded in making his simple tale hauntingly self-sufficient." The late George Jean Nathan, *op. cit.* (1945-1946), p. 90, noted that there were thirty-nine different interruptions of screen pictures. Another observation on the original production was recorded in *Time*, XLV (April 9, (1945), 88: "A mood that should flow delicately out of the play itself is artificially sprayed over it. Narrators, soft lights, and atmospheric music, however, are a lazy man's theatrical devices" (Courtesy TIME; copyright TIME Inc., 1945).

8. Joseph Wood Krutch, "Drama," *The Nation*, CLX (April 14, 1945), 425.

9. *A Streetcar Named Desire* opened in New York, December 17, 1949, for 855 performances. After a two-and-one-half-year tour across country, the play returned to New York City Center, May 23, 1950, and returned again in February 15, 1956, with Tallulah Bankhead as Blanche du Bois. See *New York Times* (March 4, 1956 and March 11, 1956), for the controversy between the playwright and the actress over the performance. The play was produced off-Broadway, March 3, 1955. The first European performance at Manchester, England, September 27, 1949, was followed by the opening in London's West End, October 12, 1949, and by a major theatrical controversy. For a discussion of the role of the British Arts Council, tax-free production of *Streetcar*, questions of morality and the differences between British and American tastes, see Brooks Atkinson, "Overseas Tornado," *New York Times* (December 11, 1949). For British reactions see T. C. Worsley, "The Arts and Entertainment," *The New Statesman*, XXXVIII (December 17, 1949), 723-24, and J. C. Trewin, "The World of the Theatre," *The Illustrated London News*, CCXV (November 5, 1949), 712. The play, adapted by Jean Cocteau,

opened in Paris, October 17, 1949, and became a large box-office success. For pictures of the Paris production, with emphasis on the jungle motifs, see *Life* XXVII (December 19, 1949), 66. The play was performed in Stockholm, Rome, in Mexico City in 1949; banned in Namur, France; and raised a minor storm when production rights were refused in Madrid, December, 1949.

10. Harry Taylor, "The Dilemma of Tennessee Williams," *Masses and Mainstream,* I (April, 1948), 53-54, questioned whether there could be a real opposition between the delicate, deranged Blanche and the primitive Stanley Kowalski.

11. Tennessee Williams, "On the Streetcar Named Success," *New York Times* (November 30, 1947).

12. The relationship between Stella and Stan recalls a D. H. Lawrence theme, that the source of a new life rests in the "togetherness between a man and a woman." Stella would seem to epitomize the Lawrence ideal of a soft, yielding woman.

13. Williams made use of the technique of piecemeal confession in a number of short plays, as for example, *The Dark Room* and *The Purification;* he was to use it often in the later plays.

14. On the personal significance of this line to the playwright, see Tennessee Williams, "Prelude to a Comedy," *New York Times* (November 6, 1960).

15. Mary McCarthy, "Streetcar Called Success," *Sights and Spectacles, 1937-1956* (New York, 1956), p. 133 ff. Her forthright appraisal so enraged Gore Vidal—see "Love, Love, Love," *Partisan Review,* XXVI (Fall, 1959), 619—that he admitted that for years he could not read her drama reviews. This is only one example of the emotional evaluations that have contributed to the controversial position of the playwright.

16. Roger Asselineau, "Tennessee Williams La Nostalgie de la Pureté," *Études Anglaises,* X (October-December, 1957), 434.

17. Williams anticipated this scene in the one-act, *Portrait of a Madonna* and in the early poem, the revised version of which appears as "The Beanstalk Country," in *In the Winter of Cities,* p. 25.

18. Brooks Atkinson, " 'Streetcar' Tragedy," *New York Times* (December 14, 1947).

19. Joseph Wood Krutch, "Drama," *The Nation,* CLXV (December 20, 1947), 686.

20. *Summer and Smoke*, first produced in Dallas, summer, 1947, with Margo Jones, director, opened in New York City, October 6, 1948, for 100 performances. See controversial letters in *New York Times* (January 16 and 30, 1949), on the comparative success of "poetic" drama and extravaganzas. The play was

revived off-Broadway at the end of the 1951-1952 season, a production which opened up the real possibilities of the small theater. For an appreciative discussion of this José Quintero production for the "Circle in the Square," see John Gassner, *Theatre at the Crossroads,* pp. 218-23. The "La Jolla [California] Playhouse," October 29, 1950, took the play on a fourteen-week tour of western cities. It opened in Paris, October 17, 1953, in the illustrious "Théâtre de l'Oeuvre" with an elaborate setting; in Boston, December 25, 1949.

21. The lover's rejection of a childhood sweetheart because she could offer only the spiritual life of a nun rather than physical passion is comparable to a scene in D. H. Lawrence's *Sons and Lovers.* This early play recalls another aspect of Lawrence as found in *The Plumed Serpent,* where the opposites—intellect and passion, reason and instinct—are played against each other. The conflict between these opposites within one character Williams was to dramatize often. Alma Tutwiler in the short story, "The Yellow Bird," is a more robust and passionate convert to passion, and with more determination rejects the restrictions of Episcopalian refinement. Of course, she may only be the same character in a more advanced state of degeneracy.

22. Brooks Atkinson, "Summer and Smoke," *New York Times* (October 7, 1948).

23. Harold Clurman, "THEATRE: Man with a Problem," *The New Republic,* CXIX (October 25, 1948), 25-26.

24. Joseph Wood Krutch, "Drama," *The Nation,* CLXVII (October 23, 1948), 473-74.

Chapter Four

1. *The Rose Tattoo* opened in New York City, February 3, 1951, for 306 performances; opened in Boston, December 3, 1951; played the 1952-1953 season in Paris.

2. Harold Clurman, "THEATRE: Tennessee Williams' Rose," *The New Republic,* CXXIV (February 19, 1951), 22.

3. Henry Popkin, *op. cit.,* p. 53.

4. John Mason Brown, "Saying it with Flowers," *Saturday Review,* XXXIV (March 10, 1951), 23, called particular attention to this poorly handled scene.

5. The persistence with which Williams clings to the ideas and imagery of innocents and innocence is obvious from the many quotations given; but it is worth a study in itself. See Robert Brustein, "Williams' Nebulous Nightmare," *The Hudson Review,* XII (Summer, 1959), 255-60. A good discussion of innocence and corruption, and, symbolic characters used repeatedly.

6. Williams wrote some of his most pretentious rhetoric in "The Timeless World of a Play," the foreword to *The Rose Tattoo*. After several paragraphs about the "emotional rush of time" and "a world outside of time," he said: "The great and only possible dignity of man lies in his power deliberately to choose certain moral values by which to live as steadfastly as if he, too, like a character in a play, were immured against the corrupting rush of time. Snatching the eternal out of the desperately fleeting is the great magic trick of human existence." See the late George Jean Nathan, "The Rose Tattoo," *The Theatre Book of the Year, 1950-1951* (New York, 1951), p. 210, on this "pseudolearned treatise" which "seeks to justify his alley-cat stuff and indeed make it a cosmic epic." Nathan called it not only "metaphysical twaddle" but also "rank dramatic presumption."

7. John Mason Brown, *op. cit.*, pp. 23-24, deplored the wasted talent and wasted material, the overloading of intuitive characterization with pretentious writing and emotionalism. The late Wolcott Gibbs, "The Brighter Side of Tennessee," *The New Yorker*, XXVI (February 10, 1951), 54, suspected that there was much less in the play than all the histrionics might lead one to think, although he found a number of scenes rather fine. Harold Clurman, *op. cit.*, questioned the playwright's ambiguity in handling character, a trait also characteristic of *Streetcar* and *Summer and Smoke*. F. W. Dupee, "Theater Chronicle," *Partisan Review*, XVIII (March-June, 1951), 333-34, felt the play disintegrated because it rests on the outworn myth that the primitives are better sexed than most Americans. The critic in *Time*, "New Play in Manhattan," *Time* LVII (February 12, 1951), 53-54, deplored the excesses in romanticism and in sensationalism. Henry Popkin, *op. cit.*, p. 59, makes several additions to phallic symbols.

8. *Cat on a Hot Tin Roof* opened in New York City, March 24, 1955 for 694 performances; it closed November 17, 1956; it won for the playwright his second Pulitzer Prize and his third New York Critics Circle Award. The screen rights were purchased for Grace Kelly in 1955. The play was performed in the famous "Théâtre Antoine," Paris, in the 1956-1957 season; and in Lisbon, Portugal, October 23, 1959, in spite of bitter criticism.

9. *Three Players of a Summer Game and Other Stories* (London, 1960). The title story, told in a curious medley of beautiful prose and affected passages, portrays the deterioration of a young aristocrat because of some mysterious disgust, his brief affair with a southern widow, and his passive return to a dominating wife. Although some of the scenes are clumsy or overwritten, the characterizations are good. The strong wife and weak husband re-

lationship recalls the same situation in D. H. Lawrence, *Women in Love*.

10. Blanche Du Bois, like Maggie, also charged her husband with homosexuality and her marriage was also destroyed.

11. Williams plays with the idea of lesbianism in *Something Unspoken*, a title that becomes part of the explanation of the Brick–Big Daddy conversation; again the handling of the topic is evasive, deliberately so.

12. Marya Mannes, "The Morbid Magic of Tennessee Williams," *The Reporter*, XII (May 19, 1955), 41, apropos *Cat* and five of the previous plays, wrote: "He *has* caught the true quality of experience, it *is* cloudy and fiercely charged, and the human beings *are* live and in crisis. I would except only one word, and that is 'common.' The crises of Williams are never common. They are the creation of a very strange and very special imagination, potent enough and poetic enough to impose itself on an audience and hold it in a common trance." The effect of this theatrical magic Marya Mannes described not as illumination and catharsis but as "emotional exhaustion." "It is a shock treatment, administered by an artist of great talent and painful sensibility who illumines fragments but never the whole. He illumines, if you will, that present sickness, which *is* fragmentation."

13. Williams, in the "Preface" to the Broadway version of the third act, commented upon the influence of the director upon the work of the playwright. See *New York Times* (April 7, 1955) for the deletion of the elephant story.

14. Brooks Atkinson, "Williams' 'Tin Roof,'" *New York Times* (April 3, 1955).

15. "New Play in Manhattan," *Time* LXV (April 4, 1955), 98 (Courtesy TIME; copyright TIME Inc., 1955).

16. Eric Bentley, "Theatre," *The New Republic*, CXXXII (April 11, 1955), 28.

17. Walter Kerr, "Cat on a Hot Tin Roof," *New York Herald Tribune* (March 25, 1955). Tennessee Williams answered the charge that he was deliberately obscure in "Critic Says 'Evasion,' Writer Says 'Mystery,'" *New York Herald Tribune*, April 17, 1955.

18. Arthur B. Waters, "TENNESSEE WILLIAMS: ten years later," *Theatre Arts* XXXIX (July, 1955), 73.

19. Robert Hatch, "Theater," *The Nation*, CLXXX (April 9, 1955), 314.

20. *Baby Doll* opened in New York City, December 18, 1956, and precipitated a censorship fight. The National League of Decency (Roman Catholic) objected: "The subject matter of this film is morally repellent both in theme and treatment. It dwells almost without variation or relief upon carnal suggestiveness in

action, dialogue and costuming." Elia Kazan, who made the film partly in Benoit, Mississippi, said he was trying to get in the film what he felt in the South. "Not the way things should be, not the way they will some day be, but the way they appeared to me there and then. I wasn't trying to be moral or immoral, only truthful." "New Kazan Movie Put on Blacklist," *New York Times* (November 28, 1956).

Chapter Five

1. *Camino Real* opened in New York City, March 19, 1953, for sixty performances. The number of impassioned letters reprinted in the *New York Times* (April 5 and May 3, 1953), suggests the controversy aroused by the play. It was revived in San Francisco during the 1955-1956 season; produced at Bocum's Festival of American Drama in West Germany, March 1955; and successfully staged in London, April 8, 1957.

2. This line, according to the playwright who quotes himself, is one of the key speeches of the play, the other being one at the end: "The violets in the mountains have broken the rocks." The author explains the meaning of the play as follows: "Life is an unanswered question, but let's still believe in the dignity and importance of the question." Tennessee Williams, "Reflections on a Revival of a Controversial Fantasy," *New York Times* (May 15, 1960).

3. Of "Three Poems" included in *New Directions in Prose and Poetry*, Number Nine, 1946 (New York, 1946), one entitled "Camino Real" is a series of bedroom vignettes written in broken prose and particularly, foreign phrases and capital letters. The short version, *Ten Blocks on Camino Real* (1948), seems to have been inspired by a sojourn in Mexico which he described as "an elemental country where you can quickly forget the false dignities and conceits imposed by success, a country where vagrants as innocent children curl up to sleep on the pavements and human voices, especially when the language is not familiar to the ear, are soft as birds." Tennessee Williams, "On a Streetcar Named Success," *New York Times* (November 29, 1947). An interesting observation was made by Brooks Atkinson, "Camino Real," *New York Times* (March 29, 1953); he wrote that Williams "first thought of the play when he was sick in a desolate corner of Mexico, without friends and with an uneasy feeling that he might never escape. But the sickness still permeates the play that derives from that experience."

4. Foreword to *Camino Real*, reprinted from *New York Times* (March 15, 1953).

5. Williams, *op. cit., New York Times* (May 15, 1960).

6. This is another favorite line of the playwright. Euphemia Van Rensselaer Wyatt, "The Drama," *Catholic World,* CLXXVII (May, 1953), 148, wrote: "The urge toward symbolism apparent in *The Rose Tattoo* has overwhelmed Tennessee Williams bringing with it an upward swerve in his philosophy even if it is steeped in ugliness. 'Camino Real' is not so much a play as a modern masque, a feverish dream." John Gassner, *Theatre at the Crossroads,* p. 83, commented on Williams' use of symbols: "He grew fond of the poetry of French symbolism and decadence, apparently liked Hart Crane especially, and early developed a penchant for using symbols, large and small."

7. As in the early poems where topography takes the place of poetry, so in the plays punctuation and capital letters seem to be a substitute for dramatic development.

8. Atkinson, *op. cit.*

9. Harold Clurman, "Theater," *The Nation,* CLXXVI (April 4, 1953), 293-94. Variations of the phrase, "phantasmagoria of decadence," with reference to *Camino Real,* or the same idea, have been used by a number of critics. J. C. Trewin, "The World of the Theater," *The Illustrated London News,* CCXXX (April 27, 1957), 702, found the play deliberately obscure but highly atmospheric; Thespis, "Plays and Films," *English,* XI (Summer, 1957), 186, thought the play poorly coordinated but exciting theater; Theophilus Lewis, "Theatre," *America,* LXXXIX (April 4, 1953), 25, had fun contriving his own complicated metaphors to explain Williams' view of life; and the critic for *Newsweek* wryly observed that some very bright first-night patrons knew exactly what Williams was talking about: "New Play," *Newsweek,* XLI (March 30, 1953), 63; John Mason Brown, "Seeing Things (The Living Dead)," *Saturday Review,* XXXVI (April 18, 1953), 28, was depressed by the sickness represented in the play.

10. *Orpheus Descending,* the fifth rewriting of *Battle of Angels,* opened in New York for sixty-eight performances. It was produced in Paris, February 16, 1959; in London, May 15, 1959; and by the Grammercy Arts Theatre, New York, October 5, 1959, a successful off-Broadway performance two-and-one-half years after its Broadway opening, twenty years after the Boston fiasco of *Battle of Angels.*

11. Tennessee Williams, "The Past, the Present, and the Perhaps," "Preface" to *Orpheus Descending.*

12. Tennessee Williams, *In the Winter of Cities* (New York, 1956), p. 28.

13. Robert Brustein, "Williams' Nebulous Nightmare," *The Hudson Review,* XII (Summer, 1959), 257.

14. John Gassner, *Theatre at the Crossroads,* pp. 223-25.

15. Donald Justice, "The Unhappy Fate of the 'Poetic'," *Poetry,* XCIII (March, 1959), 402.

16. Popkin, *op. cit.,* pp. 60-61.

17. *The Fugitive Kind,* billed as an original screen play, seems to be only a filmed version of *Orpheus Descending,* with minor adaptations. When it opened in New York, December 8, 1959, Tennessee Williams was "booed" at the preview; he "turned and booed them back," saying that they "looked like the juvenile kind," and not the sort of audience to view a $2,000,000 movie. Arthur Gelb, "Williams Booed at Film Preview," *New York Times* (December 8, 1959).

18. *Period of Adjustment* opened in New York City November 10, 1960, and closed March 4, 1961. Published by New Directions (1960).

19. Harold Clurman, "Theatre," *The Nation,* CXCI (December 3, 1960), 443-44.

20. "Rubio y Morena," a short story published in *New Directions in Prose and Poetry,* Number Eleven, 1949 (New York, 1949) describes the "psychic impotence" of a writer, Kamrowski, until he is initiated by a whore, a large, simple-minded Mexican girl in a third-class hotel; the story begins with a clinical account of the writer's sex problem. See Stanley Edgar Hyman, "Some Trends in the Novel," *College English,* XX (October, 1958), 2, on the disguises of love theme—writing of homosexual love in heterosexual imagery—which he calls "Albertine strategy" from the Marcel Proust characterization. Proust metamorphosed a boy, with whom the male protagonist was involved, into a girl. Hyman cites the story, "Rubio y Morena," as an example, the mannish Mexican girl Amada being the disguised figure. He also sees the "Albertine strategy," underlying *The Roman Spring of Mrs. Stone.*

21. Howard Taubman, "Hospital Ward," *New York Times* (November 20, 1960).

22. "THE THEATER: New Play on Broadway," *Time* LXXVI (November 21, 1960), 75 (Courtesy TIME; copyright TIME Inc., 1960).

23. Clurman, *op. cit.,* pp. 443-44.

Chapter Six

1. *The Roman Spring of Mrs. Stone* (New York, 1950). This short novel, along with *The Rose Tattoo,* a product of his first sojourn in Italy, is his only attempt at longer fiction. It reflects an increasing tendency toward precious writing and an interest

in vulgarity and decadence for itself—a characteristic that became prominent in his work of the 1950's. Williams explained how he came to write the novel: "The one time I wrote a novel ("The Roman Spring of Mrs. Stone") was just to organize material for a film for Greta Garbo. It started out with that intention but she obviously wasn't interested in making it." Quoted by W. J. Weatherby, "Lonely in uptown New York," *Manchester Guardian Weekly* (Air Edition, July 23, 1959), p. 14. In 1960 the Italian government barred Vivien Leigh and Company from making a film of the novel in Rome.

After the disappointing reception of *Orpheus Descending*, the playwright asked for an off-Broadway production of *Suddenly Last Summer*. It was produced January 7, 1958, at the miniature New York Playhouse with the one-act, *Something Unspoken*, under the title, *Garden District*. *Something Unspoken* describes an overbearing southern aristocratic woman, another hawklike female, conniving unsuccessfully to become regent of the Daughters of the Confederacy. It also touches upon the strange, undefined relationship with her companion of fifteen years, a fragile widow, delicate but tough-minded, who resembles an older Laura Wingfield. Much is made of "something unspoken," in this fifteen-year association that recalls the murky, not quite candid—on the part of the playwright—father-son groping for truth in *Cat on a Hot Tin Roof*.

3. Brooks Atkinson commented on the autobiographical quality of this line: "And the frequency with which this joyless, nihilistic point of view turns up in Mr. Williams' plays ("Camino Real," "Cat on a Hot Tin Roof," "Orpheus Descending,") suggests that it represents his experience and belief. It is not a theatrical pose; it conveys his sense of reality." Brooks Atkinson, "Garden District," *New York Times* (January 19, 1958).

4. Favored treatment has been given Tennessee Williams by his publishers: *One Arm and Other Stories*, limited edition (1948), $7.50; *The Roman Spring of Mrs. Stone*, limited autographed edition (1950), $7.50; *Hard Candy*, a special boxed edition (1954), $8.50; *I Rise from the Flame, Cried the Phoenix*, limited edition (1951), $15.00. *Hard Candy*, a collection of stories—some of them extremely well written—about homosexuals, weakly sexed men, adolescents awakening to sex, landladies of insatiable lust, continues the emphasis represented by the plays of the 1950's.

5. See Henry Hewes, "Broadway Postscript," *Saturday Review*, XLI (January 25, 1958), 26, on what appear to be autobiographical details in the play; also for the relationship between the subject matter and the playwright's own experience undergoing psychoanalysis.

6. Williams worked on the themes of homosexualism and cannibalism in the macabre short story "Desire and the Black Masseur"; but he gave them cosmic significance by adding ideas of guilt and retribution. A key line in the story reads as follows: "By surprise is man's desire discovered, and once discovered, the only need is to surrender."

7. A study of the final scene in *Battle of Angels* and of that in *Suddenly Last Summer* indicates the degree of technical sophistication that Williams had developed, even though both scenes were written for their shock effect.

8. Tom F. Driver, "Accelerando," *The Christian Century*, LXXV (January 29, 1958), 136, called this conclusion "the most 'neurotic curtain'" he has ever seen. "It reveals that the play as a whole is too nervous to make a dramatic statement and must settle for a sensual wallop." Elizabeth Hardwick, "Theater Chronicle," *Partisan Review*, XXV (Spring, 1958), 283-84, wrote of the specious quality of the play. She reported that, at the conclusion of the girl's story, she and the audience felt that they had been hearing a confession of lies.

9. Atkinson, *op. cit.*

10. *Sweet Bird of Youth*, Williams' ninth play since *The Glass Menagerie*, was first produced at Coral Gables, Florida, 1956; opened in New York City, March 10, 1959, for ninety-five performances.

11. Henry Hewes, "Tennessee's Easter Message," *Saturday Review*, XLVI (March 28, 1959), 26, noted that there had been eight versions of the play. In an interview reported in "Talk with the Playwright," *Newsweek* LIII (March 23, 1959), 75. Tennessee Williams admitted that "'Sweet Bird' is the toughest one I've ever done. . . . It's required a lot of rewriting, addition of fresh material. . . . It deals with (among other things) venereal disease and an ovariotomy—off stage of course—which have to be treated in a delicate kind of way." The playwright further describes his own tensions and the advice from his analyst. He later confessed to W. J. Weatherby, *op. cit.*, as follows: "'Sweet Bird' was in the works too long. The whole second act was particularly hard for me. I was deeply interested in the two main characters, but the other characters did not have the same interest for me, and it was awfully hard for me to write the second act, which was largely about the social background of the story. Sometimes I wish I had made it a shorter play and not tried to deal with so much. I was already tired when I came to the rehearsals and I was in no condition to do all the rewriting I had to do, and I was inundated with notes suggesting the changes— from somebody other than the director. I felt castrated."

12. The equating of phallic worship and the resurrection might derive from Williams' reading of D. H. Lawrence. Kenneth Tynan, "Ireland and Points West," *The New Yorker* XXXV (March 21, 1959), 90, raised questions about the Easter timing; he asked why castration is equated with resurrection.

13. Tennessee Williams, "Williams' Wells of Violence," *New York Times* (March 8, 1959), reprinted as the foreword to *Sweet Bird of Youth*, admitted to a friend asking if he hadn't felt "blocked as a writer," that he had. "Oh, yes, I've always been blocked as a writer but my desire to write has been so strong that it has always broken down and gone past it."

14. Critics have continually objected to the lengthy passages spoken directly to the audience as too artificial, as not in keeping with the more natural development of a scene.

15. *Sweet Bird of Youth* was based on an unproduced one-act, *The Enemy: Time.*

16. Harold Clurman, "Theatre," *The Nation,* CLXXXVIII (March 28, 1959), 281-82.

17. Marya Mannes, "Sour Bird, Sweet Raisin," *The Reporter,* XX (April 16, 1959), 34.

18. Popkin, *op. cit.,* pp. 59-61.

19. Brustein, *op. cit.,* pp. 256-60.

20. Sam Zolotov, "Williams' Drama Attracts Throng," *New York Times* (March 12, 1959).

21. "THE THEATER: New Plays on Broadway," *Time* LXXIII (March 23, 1959), 58. (Courtesy TIME; copyright TIME Inc., 1959).

Chapter Seven

1. Lincoln Barnett, "Tennessee Williams," *Life* XXIV (February 16, 1948), 113.

2. Tennessee Williams, production notes for *The Glass Menagerie,* p. ix.

3. Tennessee Williams, "Something Wild . . ." Introduction to *Twenty-Seven Wagons Full of Cotton,* pp. vii-x.

4. Tennessee Williams, "Note of Explanation," *Cat on a Hot Tin Roof,* p. 151.

5. Tennessee Williams, Foreword to *Camino Real,* p. ix-x.

6. Tennessee Williams, "Questions without Answers," *New York Times* (October 3, 1948).

7. Joseph Wood Krutch, "Drama," *The Nation,* CLX (April 14, 1945), 424.

8. Gassner, *op. cit.,* p. 77.

9. *Ibid.,* pp. 80-81.

10. *Ibid.,* p. 227.

11. Tom F. Driver, "Drama," *The Christian Century*, LXXV (January 29, 1958), 136. (Courtesy of the author.)

12. Louis Kronenberger, "The Season on Broadway," *The Best Plays of 1958-1959* (New York, 1959), p. 14.

13. Brooks Atkinson, "Theatre: Early Williams," *New York Times* (November 22, 1956).

14. "THE PLAYWRIGHT: Man Named Tennessee," *Newsweek* XLIX (April 1, 1957), 81. See also Tennessee Williams, "A Writer's Quest for a Parnassus," *New York Times Magazine* (August 13, 1950), on writing as a violent activity and need for change of residence to maintain supercharged effort; Tennessee Williams, "The Writing is Honest," *New York Times* (March 16, 1958), a preface to William Inge's *The Dark at the Top of the Stairs*, asserting that honest writing cannot be separated from writer, that writing is a reflection of his essential nature; for one of the fullest expressions of thesis that the source of a man's work is his life, see Tennessee Williams, "Prelude to a Comedy," *New York Times* (November 6, 1960).

Selected Bibliography

PRIMARY SOURCES

A. *Works*

"The Summer Belvedere" in *Five Young American Poets* (Third Series) New York: New Directions, 1944.

Battle of Angels; with a note on the play by Margaret Webster and an account of its production in the city of Boston by the author. Pharos, nos. 1-2, Murray, Utah, 1945; New York: New Directions, 1945.

The Glass Menagerie, New York: Random House, 1945; acting edition, New York: Dramatists Play Service, 1948; with an introduction by the author, London: Lehmann, 1948; "New Classics Series," New York: New Directions, 1949.

Twenty-Seven Wagons Full of Cotton and Other One-Act Plays, New York: New Directions, 1946; "Falcon Press Book," London: The Grey Walls Press, 1947; "Modern Readers Series"; (new edition) New York: New Directions, 1949; London: Lehmann, 1949; London: Secker and Warburg, 1949; (third edition) New York: New Directions, 1953.

You Touched Me! (with David Windham; suggested by a short story by D. H. Lawrence). New York: Samuel French, 1947.

A Streetcar Named Desire, New York: New Directions, 1947; London: Lehmann, 1949; acting edition, New York: Dramatists Play Service, 1953.

One Arm and Other Stories, limited edition, New York: New Directions, 1948; trade edition, 1954.

Summer and Smoke, New York: New Directions, 1948; acting edition, New York: Dramatists Play Service, 1950; London: Lehmann, 1952; London: Secker and Warburg, 1952.

American Blues; Five Short Plays, acting edition, New York: Dramatists Play Service, 1948.

The Roman Spring of Mrs. Stone, limited autographed edition, New York: New Directions, 1950; trade edition, New Directions, 1950; London: Lehmann, 1950; (new edition) London: Secker and Warburg, 1957.

The Rose Tattoo, New York: New Directions, 1951; London: Secker and Warburg, 1955.

I Rise in Flame, Cried the Phoenix, two special limited editions, New York: New Directions, 1951; (acting edition) New York: Dramatists Play Service, 1951.

Selected Bibliography

Camino Real, New York: New Directions, 1953; London: Secker and Warburg, 1958.

Hard Candy (limited edition), New York: New Directions, 1954; (new edition) New Directions, 1959.

Cat on a Hot Tin Roof, New York: New Directions, 1955; London: Secker and Warburg, 1956.

Four Plays (*The Glass Menagerie, A Streetcar Named Desire, Summer and Smoke, Camino Real*), London: Secker and Warburg, 1956.

In the Winter of Cities; poems. New York: New Directions, 1956.

Baby Doll; the script for the film incorporating the two one-act plays which suggested it: *Twenty-Seven Wagons Full of Cotton* and *The Long Stay Cut Short;* or, *The Unsatisfactory Supper,* New York: New Directions, 1956; London: Secker and Warburg, 1957.

Orpheus Descending, London: Secker and Warburg, 1958; same with *Battle of Angels,* New York: New Directions, 1958.

The Fugitive Kind, "A Signet Book," New York: The New American Library, 1958.

Suddenly Last Summer, New York: New Directions, 1958.

Garden District (*Something Unspoken* and *Suddenly Last Summer*), London: Secker and Warburg, 1959.

Sweet Bird of Youth, New York: New Directions, 1959.

Period of Adjustment, New York: New Directions, 1960.

B. *Articles by Tennessee Williams or reports of interviews in which he has been quoted—listed chronologically.*

WILLIAMS, TENNESSEE. Two Prefaces, "Frivolous Version" and "Serious Version," to "The Summer Belvedere," his poems in *Five Young American Poets,* 1944. Early poems written from experiences during itinerant years. Poets the most destructible element in American society. Appreciation of Hart Crane.

————. Production notes to *The Glass Menagerie,* 1945. Expressionism better than realism as a technique for communicating the truth. Use of screen device, music, and lighting as production means for conveying mood of the play.

————. "Something Wild . . ." Foreword to *Twenty-Seven Wagons Full of Cotton,* 1946. Definitions of art and of theater. Tribute to the Mummers of St. Louis (1935-40) and their director, Willard Holland. Need for more community theaters.

————. "On the Streetcar Named Success," *New York Times* (November 30, 1947). On the frightening impact of sudden popularity. Escape to Mexico and work on a play called *The Poker Night* which later became *A Streetcar Named Desire.*

LEWIS, R. C. "A Playwright Named Tennessee," *New York Times* (December 7, 1947). Interview. On the changes made in *The Glass Menagerie* at the suggestion of Eddie Dowling. Lewis's observation on the personality of Williams.

WILLIAMS, TENNESSEE. "Questions without Answers," *New York Times* (October 3, 1948). Difficulties of a popular playwright beset by a curious public. Observations on pretensions in the theater, on his own unintentional obscurity.

————. Introduction to *Reflections in a Golden Eye* by Carson McCullers, New Directions edition, 1950. Author of novel attacked as one of Southern Gothic school. The artists and the insane easily hurt and lonely. Southern writer's concern with perversion and horror. His intuitive sense of the incommunicable mystery which inspires dread. Gothic writer's use of grotesque and violent symbols for purposes of concentration.

————. "The Timeless World of a Play," Foreword to *The Rose Tattoo*, reprinted from the *New York Times* (January 14, 1951). On the pressures of time which deprive human beings of dignity. Plea for sympathy and understanding of the little people. A play as a means of catching the fleeting, significant moments. Universal disguise of real feelings.

————. "A Writer's Quest for a Parnassus," *New York Times Magazine* (August 13, 1950). Romantic's need for change of pace and of place to enable him to keep writing.

————. Foreword to *Camino Real*, reprinted from the *New York Times* (March 15, 1953). Play represents the writer's idea of present time and world. People represent basic attitudes. Sense of freedom in play and desire to give audience same feeling. Comments on the influence of Elia Kazan on the play. Belief that the play is clearly stated. Observations on the use of symbols in the play.

————. "Foreword . . . And Afterword," *Theatre Arts*, XXXVIII (August, 1954), 34-35. Preface to the text of *Camino Real*. "Foreword" reprinted from the *New York Times* (March 15, 1953). "Afterword" takes issue with critics who insist that playwrights think, and makes some broad generalizations about art.

HEWES, HENRY. "Tennessee Williams—Last of our Solid Gold Bohemians," *Saturday Review*, XXXVI (March 28, 1953), 25-26. Interview. The meaning of *Camino Real*, the use of symbols, comments on honor and the romantic in contemporary society, on the problems of interpreting a play to prospective backers.

WILLIAMS, TENNESSEE. "Note of Explanation," Foreword to the Broadway version of Act III of *Cat*. Some observations on the director's influence on a play. Elia Kazan's suggestions for changes in the last act.

WATERS, ARTHUR B. "TENNESSEE WILLIAMS: ten years later," *Theatre Arts*, XXXIX (July, 1955), 72. Interview. Brick not homosexual. Williams' affection for Blanche and Maggie, for all of his plays except *You Touched Me!*

WILLIAMS, TENNESSEE. "Critic Says 'Evasion,' Writer Says 'Mystery,'" *New York Herald Tribune* (April 17, 1955).

———. "Person — To — Person," Foreword to *Cat on a Hot Tin Roof* (1955). The very lonely and personal nature of writing and the intense need among all people for communication.

———. "THE PLAYWRIGHT: Man Named Tennessee," *Newsweek*, XLIX (April 1, 1957), 81. Interview. Observations on pessimism and violence in the plays, on the strain of creative activity.

———. "The Past, Present, and Perhaps," Foreword to *Orpheus Descending* (1958), reprinted from the *New York Times* (March 17, 1957). Reminiscences of Boston production of *Battle of Angels*. Personal interest in play and revisions leading to *Orpheus Descending*. Details of own itinerant life before first writing fellowship.

———. "The Writing is Honest," *New York Times* (March 16, 1958). Preface to the text of William Inge's *The Dark at the Top of the Stairs*.

SHANLEY, JOHN P. "Tennessee Williams on Television," *New York Times* (April 13, 1958). Interview. On censorship in America and abroad.

WILLIAMS, TENNESSEE. Foreword to *Sweet Bird of Youth*, reprinted from the *New York Times* (March 8, 1959). Comments on first writing, violence of first story. Surprise over amount of violence accepted by audiences and critics. Underwent psychoanalysis to find help in writing. Discussion of the word "hate" and its significance. On a writer's expressing his own strength and weaknesses in his work. Observations on guilt.

———. "Talk with the Playwright," *Newsweek*, LIII (March 23, 1959), 75-76. Interview. On problems encountered writing *Sweet Bird*. Comments on writing habits.

WEATHERBY, W. J. "Lonely in Uptown New York," *Manchester Guardian Weekly* (Air Edition, July 23, 1959). Interview. Candid reporting on personal life and literary concerns. On writing for actresses. Observations on writing *Sweet Bird*.

WILLIAMS, TENNESSEE. "Reflections on a Revival of a Controversial Fantasy," *New York Times* (May 15, 1960). On important lines and thematic idea of *Camino Real*.

GELB, ARTHUR. "Williams and Kazan and the Big Walkout," *New York Times* (May 1, 1960). Interview. Comments about the end of a fabulously successful partnership.

WILLIAMS, TENNESSEE. "Tennessee Williams presents his POV," *New York Times* (June 12, 1960). Material not from sewers but "the main stream of life." Recent excursions in drama into ugly, hidden facets of human behavior "a very healthy extension." Belief that every human experience and behavior material for dramatist, if "presented with honest intention and taste." Small belief in essential dignity or decency of man. General interest in stage characters who share universal "shames and fears." Believes "essential ambiguity of man" needs to be described.

————. "Prelude to a Comedy," *New York Times* (November 6, 1960). On writing for a living. Difficulties of being a public figure. Source of a man's work in his life. Tribute to Proust's *The Remembrance of Things Past*.

SECONDARY SOURCES

A. *Of biographical and literary interest. (Many foreign secondary sources exist but are not listed.)*

BARNETT, LINCOLN. "Tennessee Williams." *Life*, XXIV (February 16, 1948), 113. Good biographical account up to the production and assured success of *Streetcar*.

GASSNER, JOHN. "Tennessee Williams: Dramatist of Frustration." *College English*, X (October, 1948), 1-7. Good discussion of early life and first works.

MOOR, PAUL. "A Mississippian Named Tennessee." *Harper's*, CXCVII (July, 1948), 63-71. Interesting biographical details and observations of early years.

RICE, ROBERT. "A Man Named Tennessee." *New York Post* (April 21-25, April 27-May 4, 1958). Some good reporting on the life and work of the dramatist.

WEATHERBY, W. J. "Lonely in Uptown New York." *Manchester Guardian Weekly* (Air Edition, July 23, 1959). Candid reporting on personal life and literary concerns of the playwright.

B. *Critical evaluations of individual plays and pictures of New York productions.* (Listed alphabetically by play title.)

Baby Doll (Film)

HEWES, HENRY. "The Boundaries of Tennessee." *Saturday Review* XXXIX (December 29, 1956), 23-24. Tribute to Williams as a poet, and a series of answers to various charges against him.

KNIGHT, ARTHUR. "The Williams-Kazan Axis." *Saturday Review* XXXIX (December 29, 1956), 22-23. Summary of motion picture code. Williams' peculiar sexual obsessions and violence and Kazan's genius for inventing scenes to project Williams' ideas.

PRYOR, THOMAS M. "How to Police the Movies is Under Pressure Again." *New York Times* (December 23, 1956). Catholic censorship of film passed by Motion Picture Association of America. A review of censorship codes.

SCOTT, NATHAN A., JR. "MOVIES: The Baby Doll Furor." *The Christian Century,* LXXIV (January 23, 1957), 110-12. Vehemence of irrelevant critical objections. Not a pornographic film but a comic grotesque. Dubious kind of laughter evoked.

Camino Real

ATKINSON, BROOKS. "Camino Real." *New York Times* (March 29, 1953). Playwright's illness during early writing reflected. Horrible meaning of life too clear. Craftsmanship interesting at beginning, soft and generalized later. Symbolism at end is of Williams' own private variety.

BENTLEY, ERIC. "Essays of Elia." *The New Republic,* CXXVIII (March 30, 1953), 30-31. Genuine element in Williams—his realism, his portraiture, his expressive dialogue. *Camino* only a scenario for a production.

CLURMAN, HAROLD. "Theater." *The Nation,* CLXXVI (April 4, 1953), 293-94. Much self-revelation in play, concepts in line with "the mystique of romanticism," parts too boldly presented, parts deliberately obscured.

HAYES, RICHARD. "The Stage." *Commonweal,* LVIII (April 17, 1953), 51-52. Desperate theatrical tricks imposed on slight material. Play a reflection of a sensibility becoming deliquescent.

MILLER, JORDAN Y. (ed.). *American Dramatic Literature.* New York: McGraw-Hill, 1961, pp. 139-41. An unusually explicit analysis of *Camino Real* as an example of expressionism.

NATHAN, GEORGE JEAN. "George Jean Nathan's Monthly Critical

Review," *Theatre Arts,* XXXVII (June, 1953), 88. A stew of every theatrical mannerism from Kaiser, Cocteau, Wedekind, Strindberg, Stein, Sartre, and Schönberg. Williams best when not borrowing other people's philosophies but writing simply from feeling.

Cat on a Hot Tin Roof

ATKINSON, BROOKS. "Williams' 'Tin Roof'." *New York Times* (April 3, 1955). Work of a mature artist. Williams not interested in story but in unconscious motivations, lack of communication among people. A thoroughly subjective play yet crystal clear.

BENTLEY, ERIC. "Theatre." *The New Republic,* CXXXII (April 11, 1955), 28-29. An incomplete play, material ambiguously handled. Mixture of sensitive dialogue, pungent humor, and uninhibited rhetoric. Controversial nature of Williams illustrated by answers to Bentley's review. *The New Republic,* CXXXII (April 25, 1955), 23; Bentley says that writer's responsibility is not to be vague and equivocal.

GIBBS, WOLCOTT. "Something to Remember Us By." *The New Yorker,* XXXI (April 2, 1955), 68. Play about emotions beyond common experience, treated as a parody of a highly successful commercial play with much philosophical window dressing.

HATCH, ROBERT. "Theater." *The Nation,* CLXXX (April 9, 1955), 314-15. Comments on symbolism of the consulting room, on the unpleasantness of characters, on Williams' capacity for laying bare human weaknesses.

————. "THE THEATRE: New Play in Manhattan." *Time,* LXV (April 4, 1955), 98. Considerable talent marred by intemperate feelings. Play scatters because writer did not decide on main issue. Sense for theater destroyed by reliance on noisy contrivances.

————. "Cat on a Hot Tin Roof." *Life,* XXXVIII (April 18, 1955), 137-42, Barbara Bel Geddes as Maggie, Ben Gazzara as Brick, Burl Ives as Big Daddy, in pictures of the New York production.

————. "Cat on a Hot Tin Roof." *Theatre Arts,* XXXIX (June, 1955), 18 and (July, 1955), 74-77. Pictures of the New York production.

The Fugitive Kind (Film)

CROWTHER, BOSLEY. "Screen: Fugitive Kind." *New York Times* (April 15, 1960). Two brave, lonely people in William's usual sordid world and moral corruption. Tribute to acting of Anna Magnani and Marlon Brando.

————. "Williams' Fugitives." *New York Times* (April 24, 1960). In spite of violence and bloody faces the most credible and poetic work of Williams since *Streetcar*.

NASON, RICHARD. " 'Fugitive' is Shot," *New York Times* (July 5, 1959). This screen version of *Orpheus Descending*, set in a seedy Mississippi town, filmed in Milton, New York, about eighty miles north of Manhattan. Interesting description of one morning's work: problems of assembling cast, town, and suitable weather, etc.

The Glass Menagerie

ATKINSON, BROOKS. "Theatre: Early Williams." *New York Times* (November 22, 1956). Appreciation of delicacy, perfect blend of humor and pathos, allusiveness, as contrasted to savagery of later plays.

GILDER, ROSAMOND. "Spring Laurels." *Theatre Arts*, XXIX (June, 1945), 325-27. Comparison between Williams' play and Saroyan's *My Heart is in the Highlands*.

KRUTCH, JOSEPH WOOD. "Drama." *The Nation*, CLX (April 14, 1945), 424-25. Extraordinary talent for characterization but glaring weaknesses. Some unhappy attempts at poetry could easily be struck out.

NATHAN, GEORGE JEAN. "You Touched Me!" *The Theatre Book of the Year 1945-1946*. New York: Knopf, 1946. Extended discussion of directors who have saved plays. Revisions made in Williams' play by Eddie Dowling, the director, and actors.

YOUNG, STARK. "The Glass Menagerie." *The New Republic*, CXII (April 16, 1945), 505-6. Glowing tribute to the acting of Laurette Taylor as Amanda Wingfield, to the southern speech of Williams.

————. "THE THEATER: New Play in Manhattan." *Time*, XLV (April 9, 1945), 86-88. Appraises the delicacy of material and treatment but deplores the artificial theatrical elements imposed upon it. Tribute to Laurette Taylor.

————. "SPEAKING OF PICTURES . . . Laurette Taylor Does Season's Best Acting." *Life*, XVIII (June 11, 1945), 12-13, excellent series of shots of Miss Taylor at the phone.

————. *Theatre Arts*, XXIX (May, 1945), the four actors of the original production; *Theatre Arts*, XXIX (June, 1945), 327, Laurette Taylor as Amanda; *Theatre Arts*, XXIX (October, 1945), 554, Julie Haydon and Laurette Taylor.

Orpheus Descending

ATKINSON, BROOKS. "Virtuoso Theatre." *New York Times* (March 31, 1957). Anything of Williams superior to dead-level of ordinary plays. Original title, "Something Wild in the Country." Some beautiful writing, genuine poetry, and real humor in spite of violence and melodrama. First two acts worth attention.

DRIVER, TOM F. "Drama." *The Christian Century*, LXXIV (April 10, 1957), 455-56. The old themes treated with theatrical shock and occasional humor. A "preachy" play with nothing to say.

MR. HARPER. "Morpheus Descending." *Harper's Magazine*, CCXIV (May, 1957), 76-77. An allegory in melodrama and farce. Williams' too obvious display of his intentions. Amusement over his sensual Italians.

HATCH, ROBERT. "Theatre." *The Nation*, CLXXXIV (April 6, 1957), 301-2. Social protest in ugly, vicious terms, reflecting playwright's loathing of southern bullies.

HAYES, RICHARD. "THE STAGE: The Tragic Pretension." *Commonweal*, LXVI (April 26, 1957), 94-97. The nature of tragedy and the lack of it in Williams' play.

MARSHALL, MARGARET. "Theatre: Orpheus in Dixie." *The New Republic*, CXXXVI (April 8, 1957), 21. Two plays in one, a morality and a drama of social protest; Williams' lost chance in not focusing play on Lady Torrance.

————. "THE THEATER: New Play, Old Play," *Time*, LXIX (April 1, 1957), 61. Includes all the best qualities of Williams but fails because of poor structure, theatricalism, and the usual obsessions.

Period of Adjustment

BRUSTEIN, ROBERT. "Disputed Authorship." *The New Republic*, CXLIII (November 28, 1960), 38-39. Usable autobiographical material exhausted. Author's peddling of love, sex, and understanding with Freudian tinge.

CLURMAN, HAROLD. "Theatre." *The Nation*, CXCI (December 3, 1960), 443-44. Disturbed by implications in a seemingly unpretentious, intentionally comic play.

HEWES, HENRY. "Snowflakes in Tennessee." *Saturday Review*, XLIII (November 26, 1960), 28. Enthusiasm with reservations.

TAUBMAN, HOWARD. "Hospital Ward." *New York Times* (November 20, 1960). Writer's inability to get away from psychiatric concerns.

Selected Bibliography

————. "THE THEATRE: New Play on Broadway." *Time*, LXXVI (November 21, 1960), 75. Some well-written scenes, some superficial; little organic development and too much sex.

The Rose Tattoo

ATKINSON, BROOKS. "Tattooing." *New York Times* (June 3, 1951). Report of second view. Elimination of lewd episode and other small changes for ordinary amenities. Objective, imaginative delineation of sensuous, admirable woman. Tragedy and robust humor. Freedom of style brought to theater by lyric dramatist.

BEYER, WILLIAM H. "The State of the Theatre: Hits and Misses." *School and Society*, LXXIII (March 24, 1951), 181-83. Enthusiastic, uncritical summary.

BROWN, JOHN MASON. "Saying it with Flowers." *Saturday Review*, XXXIV (March 10, 1951), 22-24. Comments on effect of Italy on Williams as reflected in *The Roman Spring of Mrs. Stone* and *The Rose Tattoo*.

CLURMAN, HAROLD. "THEATRE: Tennessee Williams' Rose," *The New Republic*, CXXIV (February 19, 1951), 22. Strength of play in personal observation and sensibility; weaknesses from imposition of author's desires upon characters.

DUPEE, F. W. "Theatre Chronicle." *Partisan Review*, XVIII (March-June, 1951), 333-34. Play disintegrates because written on outworn theory of uninhibited sex and fulfillment.

GIBBS, WOLCOTT. "The Brighter Side of Tennessee." *The New Yorker*, XXVI (February 10, 1951), 54. Interest not in plot nor character but in vividness of certain scenes.

MARSHALL, MARGARET. "Drama." *The Nation*, CLXXII (February 17, 1951), 161-62. Good first act followed by cheap and vulgar farce, a play written from "many levels of thought and feeling."

NATHAN, GEORGE JEAN. "The Rose Tattoo." *The Theatre Book of the Year 1950-1951*. New York: Knopf, 1951. Comments on pretentious "Preface." Play a "peep-show," a "sexually luxuriant" plot flavored with "mystical gravy." Sensational, sex melodrama.

————. "THE THEATER: New Play in Manhattan." *Time*, LVII (February 12, 1951), 53-54. Though in different vein, the same sensational extremes.

————. "The Rose Tattoo." *Life*, XXX (February 26, 1951), 80-84. Pictures of New York production. Maureen Stapleton as Serafina, Eli Wallach as Alvaro, Phyllis Love as Rosa, Don Murray as Jack Hunter.

A Streetcar Named Desire

ATKINSON, BROOKS. " 'Streetcar' Tragedy." *New York Times* (December 14, 1947). Appreciation of characterization of Blanche, a distinct individual, not to be repeated. Implication that she belongs to the theater.

GIBBS, WOLCOTT. "Lower Depths, Southern Style." *The New Yorker*, XXIII (December 13, 1947), 50-54. Tribute to Williams that Blanche story credible; characterizations and scenes too abruptly handled; deplores embroidery and stage effects.

KRUTCH, JOSEPH WOOD. "Drama." *The Nation*, CLXV (December 20, 1947), 686-87. Considerable advance in skill. Material distressing, mood and atmosphere morbid. Williams an extremely subjective playwright.

McCARTHY, MARY. "Streetcar Called Success." *Sights and Spectacles 1937-1956*. New York: Farrar, Straus, Cudahy, 1956, pp. 132 ff. Excessive overloading of both scene and character. Patent commercialism of the play.

NATHAN, GEORGE JEAN. "A Streetcar Named Desire." *The Theatre Book of the Year 1947-1948*. New York: Knopf, 1948, pp. 163-66. On the difference between the unpleasant, the disgusting, and the enlightening. Play a "theatrical shocker." Of Williams' writing: "sometimes sounds altogether too much like a little boy proudly making a muscle." Substitutes magic of lights for magic of poetry.

SHAW, IRWIN. "THEATER: Masterpiece." *The New Republic*, CXVII (December 22, 1947), 34-35. Enthusiastic review of play as parable of beauty shipwrecked on rocks of vulgarity.

————. "A Streetcar Named Desire." *Life*, XXIII (December 15, 1947), 101-4. Portrait of Williams and pictures of New York production: Jessica Tandy as Blanche Du Bois, Marlon Brando as Stanley Kowalski, Kim Hunter as Stella, Karl Malden as Mitch.

————. "Paris 'Streetcar'." *Life*, XXVII (December 19, 1949), 66. Sordid elements exaggerated.

————. "A Streetcar Named Desire." *Theatre Arts*, XXXII (February, 1948), 35. Picture of the final tableau.

Suddenly Last Summer

ATKINSON, BROOKS. "Garden District." *New York Times* (January 19, 1958). Perfectly contrived study of corruption, repugnant material musically expressed.

CLURMAN, HAROLD. "Theatre." *The Nation*, CLXXXVI (January 25, 1958), 86-87. Clever horror story. Variation on old themes, characters, and images but "the product of a general concept and shrewd theatre technique rather than of living experience."

DRIVER, TOM F. "Drama." *The Christian Century,* LXXV (January 29, 1958), 136-37. Preoccupation with emotional shock material which obscures the comment about human relationships. Williams, as master of effect, at crucial point in his career.

HARDWICK, ELIZABETH. "Theater Chronicle." *Partisan Review,* XXV (Spring, 1958), 283-84. Repetition of familiar characters and a yarn beyond credibility.

HAYES, RICHARD. "The Stage." *The Commonweal,* LXVIII (May 29, 1958), 232-33. Diabolically clever treatment of a private vision given out as a fable of universal significance.

HEWES, HENRY. "BROADWAY POSTSCRIPT: 'Sanity Observed'." *Saturday Review,* XLI (January 25, 1958), 26. Possible relationship between revelation in play and writer's experiences under psychoanalysis.

——. "THE THEATER: Two by Two." *Time,* LXXI (January 20, 1958), 42. Williams a master at weaving spells, theatrical but not enlightening.

Summer and Smoke

BROWN, JOHN MASON. "Seeing Things." *Saturday Review,* XXXI (October 30, 1948), 31-33. Oversimplified handling of conflict in symbols, yet high moments in play; written by a man of great sensitivity.

CLURMAN, HAROLD. "THEATRE: Man with a Problem." *The New Republic,* CXIX (October 25, 1948), 25-26. Theme overplayed at expense of characterization. Play clouded with theories. Puritan obsession in need of new and interesting twist.

GABRIEL, GILBERT W. "Playgoing." *Theatre Arts,* XXXIII (January, 1949), 10-11. Portrait. Margaret Phillips as Alma Winemiller and Tod Andrews as John Buchanan.

KRUTCH, JOSEPH WOOD. "Drama." *The Nation,* CLXVII (October 23, 1948), 474-84. Author's sympathy not with healthy characters but with gentlewomen of too little resistance. Allegorical quality of play.

NATHAN, GEORGE JEAN. "Summer and Smoke." *The Theatre Book of the Year 1948-1949.* New York: Knopf, 1949, pp. 114-21. Sex obsessions, fancy figures of speech covering misty thinking. Playwright's weaknesses: debatable delineation of character, adolescent point of view, honest beginnings ending in "theatrical fabrication."

PHELAN, KAPPO. "The Stage and Screen." *The Commonweal,*
XLIX (October 29, 1948), 68-69. Dubious whether this, the
third version of Williams' One Woman, analyzed in Freudian
terms, belongs in America before 1916. Excessive symbolism.

————. "THE THEATER: New Play in Manhattan," *Time,* LII
(October 18, 1948), 82-83. Material underwritten, depend-
ence on vague poetry and vivid stagecraft.

Sweet Bird of Youth

ATKINSON, BROOKS. "Theatre: Portraits of Corruption." *New York
Times* (March 11, 1959). In this study of degenerate ele-
gance and evil, pity for the damned.

CLURMAN, HAROLD. "Theatre." *The Nation,* CLXXXVIII (March
28, 1959), 281-83. A study in Williams' self-revelation told in
melodramatic scenes. Oversimplification and distortion in
characterization, "more ugliness than lyricism."

HEWES, HENRY. "Tennessee's Easter Message." *Saturday Review,*
XLII (March 28, 1959), 26. Repetition of old material with
clinical touch as if a confession from writer. Curious intrusion
of Easter message, incompletely assimilated.

MANNES, MARYA. "Theater." *The Reporter,* XXVI (April 16, 1959),
34. Disturbing nature of excitement elicited by such violence,
corruption, and decay.

TYNAN, KENNETH. "Ireland and Points West." *The New Yorker,*
XXXV (March 21, 1959), 90-92. Little relevance to observed
reality. Curious for revelation of playwright's character.

————. "Lovers in Quest of Youth." *Life,* XLVI (April 20,
1959), 71-73. Portrait of Geraldine Page as the Princess and
Paul Newman as Chance Wayne.

You Touched Me!

GILDER, ROSAMOND. "Poetry, Passion and Politics—Broadway in
Review." *Theatre Arts,* XXIX (November, 1945), 618-21.
Summary of characters and plot.

KRUTCH, JOSEPH WOOD. "Drama." *The Nation,* CLXI (October 6,
1945), 349-50. As production second to *The Glass Menagerie,*
suffered from overenthusiastic reviews of first. Work of an
emotionally and technically immature playwright.

WYATT, EUPHEMIA VAN RENSSELAER. "The Drama." *Catholic
World,* CLXII (November, 1945), 166-67. An amusing summary of the many facets, symbols, and stage tricks which
crowd the play.

YOUNG, STARK. "At the Booth." *The New Republic,* CXIII (October 8, 1945), 469. Reacts against violent criticisms of the

play. An entertaining and civilized play needing to be re-written.

————. "You Touched Me!" *Theatre Arts,* XXIX (December, 1945), 680. Small picture with double scene and full cast. Montgomery Clift as Hadrian, Marianne Stewart as Matilda, Catherine Willard as Emmie, Edmund Gwenn as Captain Rockley, and Norah Howard as Phoebe.

C. *Critical evaluations of several plays.*

ASSELINEAU, ROGER. "Tennessee Williams ou La Nostalgie de la Pureté." *Études Anglaises,* X (October-December, 1957), 431-43. Relates traumatic experience of early poverty in St. Louis and ambivalence of own personality—part Puritan and part Cavalier—to his writing; also discusses Williams' treatment of moral problems.

BOYLE, ROBERT. "Williams and Myopia." *America,* CIV (November 19, 1960), 263-65. Answer to H. G. Gardiner, "Is Williams' Vision Myopia?" *America,* CIII (July 30, 1960), 495-96. Belief that Williams' characters make "ultimate moral choice," that his work is a reflection of man's drive to perfection.

BRUSTEIN, ROBERT. "Why American Plays are not Literature." *Writing in America.* New Jersey: Rutgers, 1960. On commercial influences which militate against good dramatic writing.

————. "Williams' Nebulous Nightmare." *The Hudson Review,* XII (Summer, 1959), 255-60. Comments on cartoon quality of characters, nightmarish element in later plays, and on the involved metaphors and symbols used by Williams in his sexual obsession.

DONY, NADINE. "Tennessee Williams: A Selected Bibliography." *Modern Drama,* I (December, 1958), 181-91.

DOWNER, ALAN. *Recent American Drama,* No. 7, University of Minnesota Pamphlets on American Writers (1961), pp. 28-33. A guarded appraisal of this "gothic writer" whose work is like an antique map bounded by Cancer, the human mob, mutilation, and mendacity.

DRIVER, TOM F. "Accelerando," *The Christian Century,* LXXV (January 29, 1958), 136-37. Relates *Suddenly Last Summer* to the previous plays as an indication of Williams' development.

FALK, SIGNI. "The Profitable World of Tennessee Williams." *Modern Drama,* I (1958), 172-80.

FITCH, ROBERT E. "La Mystique de la Merde," *The New Republic,* CXXXV (September 3, 1956), 17-18. Concern about obsession with sex and obscenity in the hands of a skilled literary artist.

GARDINER, HAROLD C. "Is Williams' Vision Myopia?" *America,* CIII (July 30, 1960), 495-96. Reply to Mannes-Williams argument about the state of modern theater, *New York Times Magazine* (May 29 and June 12, 1960). Attacks Williams' artistic philosophy: that he has nothing to do with the "war between the spirit and the flesh"; that characters are not ambiguous, that only ambiguity revolves around sex and violence; that he portrays man in terms of "shames and fears," mostly sexual.

GASSNER, JOHN. *The Theatre in Our Times: A Survey of the Men, Materials and Movements in the Modern Theatre.* New York: Crown, 1954. A study in the contrast between "poetic realism" and symbolism in the earlier plays.

————. *Theatre at the Crossroads.* New York: Holt, Rinehart, and Winston, 1960. Discussion of early one-acts in relation to later plays, of the increasing technical skill but dangerous symbolic involvement; an appreciative description of the José Quintero production of *Summer and Smoke,* concern about complex mythical and symbolic overloading in *Orpheus Descending,* about the satanic view of the world in *Suddenly Last Summer* and *Sweet Bird of Youth,* and about Williams' peculiar sense of the comic.

HIGHET, GILBERT. "A Memorandum." *Horizon,* I (May, 1959), 54-55. A witty and amusing series of recommendations in the style of Seneca about increasing the sex and horror interest. A clever exposé.

JONES, ROBERT EMMET. "Tennessee Williams' Early Heroines." *Modern Drama,* II (December, 1959), 211-19. Thesis that Alma Winemiller, Cassandra Whiteside, Blanche Du Bois, and Amanda Wingfield are the same character at different stages.

JUSTICE, DONALD. "The Unhappy Fate of the 'Poetic'," *Poetry,* XCIII (March, 1959), 402-3. *Orpheus Descending,* a portrayal of Williams' concept of the poet in American society, a key work to the understanding of the playwright.

KRUTCH, JOSEPH WOOD. "Why the O'Neill Star is Rising." *New York Times Magazine* (March 19, 1961). Modern concept of tragedy as illustrated by O'Neill, Miller, and Williams. The last a gifted dramatist whose characters not involved in a "tragic predicament" but an "unsavory mess."

LUMLEY, FREDERICK. *Trends in 20th Century Drama: A Survey since Ibsen and Shaw.* New Jersey: Essential Books, 1956. Feeling in plays of debased tragedy. Exciting idea in *Camino Real* but no characterization. *Cat on a Hot Tin Roof* most cruel, most sensual.

Selected Bibliography

MANNES, MARYA. "Plea for Fair Ladies." *New York Times Magazine* (May 29, 1960). On the depravity and violence in the current theater. Answered by the playwright, "Tennessee Williams Presents his POV," *New York Times Magazine* (June 12, 1960).

POPKIN, HENRY. "The Plays of Tennessee Williams." *The Tulane Drama Review*, IV (Spring, 1960), 45-64. Comment on archetypal patterns, the "very cool" Adonis and the Gargoyle, a nervous older woman; on Williams' Bohemian doctrine, his sensationalism, and his "spiritual geography"; on his nostalgic treatment of the past, on truth and self-deception; on the symbolism and taboos in the plays.

TAYLOR, HARRY. "The Dilemma of Tennessee Williams." *Masses and Mainstream*, I (April, 1948), 51-55. Comments on writer using autobiographical material, sees Williams as still "the traumatized youngster."

TYNAN, KENNETH. "American Blues: The Plays of Arthur Miller and Tennessee Williams." *Encounter*, II [England] (May, 1954), 13-19. On the difference in temperament, artistic credos, and methods of working represented by the two dramatists.

VOWLES, RICHARD B. "Tennessee Williams and Strindberg." *Modern Drama*, I (December, 1958), 166-71. Suggests affinity between the two rather than influence of Swedish dramatist on the American.

Index